'All of life is here – birth, death, struggles with illness, hard work, lots of laughter. It will make you smile gently to yourself, laugh out loud, shed a quiet tear and feel angry at the changes happening in our countryside'

NFU *Countryside Magazine*

'A riveting read ... a warning to newcomers about the dangers of upsetting village hierarchies and sensibilities'

*Country Life*

Aged 34, Ian Walthew unexpectedly ended his media career as a worldwide marketing director of the *International Herald Tribune* after nearly a decade living and working abroad. He is now a full-time writer.

For more information please visit: www.ianwalthew.com.

# A PLACE IN
# MY COUNTRY

*In Search of the Rural Dream*

## IAN WALTHEW

PHOENIX

*For Belinda*
*Millicent, Bede and Edgar*

In memory of:
JW
BW
CK
PG

A PHOENIX PAPERBACK
First published in Great Britain in 2007
by Weidenfeld & Nicolson
This paperback edition published in 2008
by Phoenix,
an imprint of Orion Books Ltd,
Orion House, 5 Upper Saint Martin's Lane,
London, WC2H 9EA

An Hachette Livre UK company

1 3 5 7 9 10 8 6 4 2

A CIP catalogue record for this book
is available from the British Library.

ISBN 978-0-7538-2388-0

Typeset by Deltatype Ltd, Birkenhead, Merseyside

Printed and bound in Great Britain by Clays Ltd, St Ives plc

The Orion Publishing Group's policy is to use papers that
are natural, renewable and recyclable products and made
from wood grown in sustainable forests. The logging and
manufacturing processes are expected to conform to the
environmental regulations of the country of origin.

www.orionbooks.co.uk

# AUTHOR'S NOTE

This is a story of two journeys, my own, but within a much larger one, that of the English countryside. It is but a brief moment in time in one tiny patch of Albion, a country I am proud to be from. I have tried to be as truthful and accurate as my understanding at the time and my memory allow, given that I never set out to write this book when I moved there. I have changed all names, many geographical indicators and some minor incidental details (as well as excluding many experiences and conversations at the request of some of those who appear within this story), to afford at least a degree of privacy in a process which I am fully aware is deeply intrusive. On very few occasions I have merged an incident, or a conversation or two, for reasons of brevity or discretion. My apologies for any unintended misrepresentations or offence in trying to paint one small corner of that very much larger, ever-changing picture that is the English countryside.

I am neither an academic nor a journalist, so this book was never intended to provide either a complete or an entirely balanced view of even a few hundred acres of England. Indeed, in my decision to buy what was once the home of an agricultural labourer, I was no neutral observer; in fact I was a participant in some of the problems that I describe. Nor am I an expert on farming or modern estate management; nor do I offer any real solutions to the problems facing the lives of country people.

There are many voices I did not hear, many people I did not meet, and many things I have learnt since; there is yet more I am still to understand.

Mostly, though, I hope I will take the reader to a world that, for all its mutability, is nonetheless how I like to think of England: regions of breathless beauty, full of devilment, humour and rich untold histories.

# PROLOGUE

Dawn on the first day of the new millennium and I wake up in the sand, taut, cold and hung-over.

My first thought of the twenty-first century is so strong that it speaks itself to an empty beach and a moping, disinterested Pacific swell: 'I have never felt further away from being the man I want to be.'

Despite the timing, this isn't millennial angst. I have no acute sense of foreboding, no heightened expectation for the future, not even regret for past sins. It is my here and now that is utterly screwed.

'Why don't you draw a strategy tree?'

Spare me.

'Yes, that's a very good idea.'

'People like to know how contextually their objectives fit into the larger picture.'

This is the new century I have returned to from my holiday in Australia; a conference room in Paris, watching my colleagues listen to energetic and deluded presentations. There is an impostor present, one who has no faith in himself, nor in the enterprise, his stomach permanently knotted in anxiety. I shouldn't be here. Am I a part of this, firing people in one place while we hire in another; talking with one side of our mouths about the needs demanded by the past to those we 'let go', and with the other, about the hopes offered by the future to those we 'take on'?

I look out of the window and see nothing but our vacant reflections in the dark glass. On the dusk flight from London to Paris on my first day back in England, the sky to the east had been clear, but to the west, thick clouds came in from the Atlantic. I had fantasised about the plane crashing into the sea.

In the meeting room the mood is gloomy. Owners are unhappy and plans are not working, targets will not be reached. We sound despondent and disappointed; irritations begin to surface, there are gaps in our dialogue, people waffle.

The leader tries to salvage the hopeless mood.

'We will sacrifice both profit and growth before compromising our values,' he says, 'and that's why we all work for this organisation. But I am worried about the times ahead.'

He speaks with a pathetic gravitas. We all know we are doomed.

'If we can succeed, it will be something that you will be proud to have been a part of, and something you can tell your grandchildren.'

There is an embarrassed silence, a shuffling of papers, the meeting ends. I can't move. My senses are dead. My wife wants us to have a baby and I can't even smell or taste. And now, here before me, this man unable to disguise the fact that the one supposedly compensatory thing in my life, my 'high-flying' career and the presumed groupshare of collective corporate purpose, is to me, nothing.

Once a week, I take the Metro to Montparnasse, and then a short walk. He is French, we speak French, we sit in his office. Sometimes he says something. 'Ian, people think that all this is about feeling bad, but often it's about feeling nothing at all.'

He watches me. We smoke. Next door, the sound of sobbing from one of his colleagues' rooms.

'I've been offered a transfer to London.'

'It's been a long time, no, since you lived there?'

'Ten years.'

He looks at me and checks his notes.

'Amsterdam. Brussels. Paris,' he reads. 'Now London.' He looks up, lights another cigarette. 'How do you feel about living in England again?'

His room is lit by a single desk lamp, the shutters always closed.

'I don't know why, but it's a place I don't want to return to.' I pause. 'Do you think we should go?'

'I think you should stop and find out why it is you cannot feel.'

Our last home had been a Montmartre apartment on a narrow, cobbled street. Our temporary apartment in London while we look for somewhere to buy is tiny and dark, where every morning the street awakes to the departing garbage trucks from the council depot at the end of a garden that isn't ours. Then comes the racing traffic, released in waves by the green lights on Kensington High Street, cascading down the road and washing up against the reds on the Earls Court Road, before slowing into a thick stagnant pool of unmoving fumes.

I want to cycle to work along the Prinsengracht and cross the Amstel by the old wooden swing bridge. Instead, I drive to an office in the Docklands.

On the daily commute to work, London looks so promising. I pass Kensington Palace and Gardens, next the Albert Hall and Memorial, and the turn into the park, slowing for the cavalry as they ride back to their barracks. On to Hyde Park Corner, Birdcage Walk, another palace, the Mall, the arch, the column and down to the river. If I glance left or right, into view comes the top of the Catholic cathedral, Wellington's memorial, the gallery, the war memorial, Big Ben, the funfair thing. Needles, boats, South Bank buildings, the Globe, the Tate Modern. A city's postcards and the mythology of a nation and me stuck in traffic, again.

'So, how're you finding it back in London? Missing Paris?' someone asks me as I make coffee. The milk in the office fridge is sour and there is a sink full of unwashed mugs. In Paris we used to go to the café Le Village in the mornings.

'It's great.'

The young executive director with the recently awarded bonus, I pass the office of the man who has worked for the newspaper for most of his life. He has been sacked as part of a process to save a few hundred thousand dollars, which will have no material impact on the future fortunes of the company, as a sop to our absent owners. Soon he will be gone. He has been fired based on a plan I have written. Make this plan save more, the leader had said, and I rewrote it and it did.

'Good morning,' I say to him.

A minute or so later he comes into my office, unannounced.

'Don't ever speak to me again,' he says, turns and walks out.

'There's no point hanging on until I collapse, there's nothing to hang on for. I've got to get out of this.'

'I know,' says my wife.

'We could use the bonus for a deposit on somewhere, buy it while I still have a salary to show the mortgage company, and then I'll quit.'

'I can support us, don't worry.'

'I could do some consulting.'

'You need to get yourself well.'

'Can we find somewhere quickly? I've got to stop.'

'I know.'

Our options seem to be a shoebox in a part of the city one might conceivably want to live in, or a yuppie cave in a strip of café-less, characterless red-brick nothing, near a drab, dank featureless patch of muddy green posing as a park. We decide that small where we sort of want to be is preferable to bigger in the outer zones of the tube map, hanging on to London.

Hannah finally finds somewhere, a modern, ex-council-housing two-bedroom maisonette, in the shadow of a six-lane flyover and opposite an ambulance station. The estate agent clings to the notion that it is in Notting Hill.

'It's a great buy,' he says. 'Can't go wrong.'

'Yeah,' we say.

I feel queasy; Han just relieved we've found something.

# CHAPTER I

# FIRST SIGHT

There is a childhood memory of an abandoned canal that runs through a valley. There is a pub nearby; a boy walking along a towpath with his father, and under the trees it is dark and cold. Water spills over a broken lock gate. It falls noisily into the basin, which is full of shattered stone and rotting wood. How can falling water move so slowly? The lock is deep and the bottom of it is a place from which there is no escape. My father will leave me here and I will be so very lonely and scared. That is my memory.

I can't understand why I want to go there. Am I drawn to the sadness?

Come on, I said. Let's go to the countryside for the weekend. You'll like it.

I said the same thing when we went to the Belgian coast. She didn't. Han is Australian and in January she wishes she were home.

We were exhausted as we drove to the west. Persuading ourselves we had found a home and had a way to pay for it was tiring. We repeated our plan to buy the almost-Notting Hill horror as though repetition would make it sound more sensible than it was.

Han was trying to be cheery; it was good to be away from London. My mother lived quite nearby, in Wiltshire, where we were staying in her house for the weekend while she was on holiday. But the Wiltshire of my town boarding school and short countryside holidays, holidays filled with seaside jaunts, trips abroad and days in London, spread south, away from where we were exploring, flat and muddy.

My teenage friends were, like me, not from one village or town and, for most of the year, we were scattered around the country in various boarding schools. During the holidays we would meet in the north Wiltshire pubs and houses of our families, in a space of our own; one which for many of us was more about a wider social network of shared class and background than the companionship of the kids of our villages, most if not all of whom we didn't know. The village where my mother lived was more hers and my much younger sister Frances's community; somehow never really mine.

Han and I had decided to spend a day in the Cotswolds north of Cirencester, a region of England that was just different, an area I had very rarely visited with my friends; not part of my memory landscape, save yellow fields and somewhere, something: a pub once?

'Do you think this is it?' Han said. We had stopped on a narrow stone bridge over a deep, tree-lined cutting that carried the canal. A pub sign hung from a tall thick post, but there was no pub. A dirt road went off to the left, following along the top of the cutting.

'It's been such a long time, I can't remember. It was in a valley, I think.'

'Let's go and look anyway.'

The grass verges of the puddled and potholed track were coated in car-sprayed wet mud, the canal mostly hidden by a steep, thin strip of woodland that dropped down to the brick-walled water. Emerging from the trees there was a strange pleasure in the way that the track rose up, offering at its gentle crest the climber's reward of a revealed view. In the centre of this view was a pub. But not the one I was looking for.

'Is this it?'

'No. But I remember this place, too.'

The track dipped down before widening and climbing ever so slightly, setting us down in front of a building.

Smoky flags of occupation flew from the pub's chimneys, and a tall, straight-backed, white-haired man strolled from the pub to a long, low barn that sat under the beech trees that lined the canal. He was followed by an Alsatian, trotting and unthreatening. The man seemed confident we would enter, indifferent as to whether we would. We had the sense we had stumbled into a private and undiscovered place.

I looked at the outside tables of cold, wet wood.

It is summer and I am outside at one of these tables, my father coming out of the pub, carrying a dented round metal tray of beer, orange juice and cheese-and-onion crisps. He has long, dark red hair and sideburns. I take the packet of crisps. It is sticky from the warm beer he has spilled which has settled in a rusted, paint-worn dip at the edge of the tray.

The canal had disappeared beneath us, and Han and I were drawn to see where it had gone. Some wide, worn and muddy steps descended to the still, spring-clear water of the canal, and above it was a Gothic stone portal at the mouth of the hill that had swallowed it. A rain-stained sign told us that the pub had been built to house and feed the late eighteenth-century navvies who had dug and blasted a 3,817-yard tunnel under the Cotswolds.

We leant round the corner of the portal wall into the brick-lined tunnel but saw only a gate, locked and barred, and beyond it, darkness. We shouted to hear our echo.

The pub stood on its own at the end of the track that led to it and it alone. With two storeys, a large central bay that faced towards the canal and gabled windows on either side, it was squat and solid, neither grand house nor humble hostelry. It sat in the weak winter shadow of a large oak, and they shared each other's age and shelter. Behind it was a wood, silent and tranquil, the tops of the trees visible over the two chimneys. With few cars parked outside, and unused picnic tables out front, the pub seemed as bare as a winter beech, but the light from the windows and the smell of woodsmoke told you it was still alive.

There was a heavy wooden front door that rubbed firmly on a flagstone floor, the latch purposeful and solid. Instead of the main bar, the door gave on to a tiny room, warm and fuggy, with some tables and a small fireplace. Like the rutted lane and the door that required a little effort to open, the ante-room seemed another device to slow you down and detach your journey before finally admitting you into the pub.

Walking through a short, dark, narrow passage, we entered the main bar, a space not much bigger than a generously sized living room and looking much like one. Only the short, stubby bar and, in front of it, a pair of tall barber's chairs protecting it from customers suggested this was indeed a pub. The barber's chairs were upholstered in plastic with a tiny teddy-bear motif, more suitable for a baby's high-chair than a boozer's bum.

Most of the room was filled with two long shabby sofas arranged on either side of a large log fire, deep armchairs facing it. The fire's grand wooden mantelpiece seemed to belong in a country mansion, not a navvies' canteen. Above the fireplace hung a portrait of a pretty young woman.

The other walls were covered with taxidermists' work of small wild animals and antique advertising boards from long-extinct Cotswold beer and tobacco brands. There were winners' cups, photos, statues of prize-winning horses and greyhounds, and hundreds of racetrack enclosure badges, signed English rugby team pictures, paintings, photos and memories; an organic collage of the pub's life and the people who lived there.

Only at the bar itself did the pub reveal more the signs of a hostelry than of a house. Hung next to it was a framed photomontage of raucous nights in the pub – pictures of flashed breasts, a stripper and a man's head some inches from the mooning buttocks of another. Postcards from holiday resorts, all puns and sand-on-oiled breasts, were pinned to the underside of the open bar hatch. Fixed from the ceiling above the bar was an upside-down card table, with card hands, beer cans and an ashtray and its contents glued to it. They hung as hints of what this pub might be like at night behind the calm of the weekend lunchtime.

After lunch ('Ham, egg and chips' and 'Probably the Best Chilli in the World' according to the chalkboard menu), we attempted to walk over the hill and through the wood to a village at the other end of the tunnel. For an hour we followed tracks through the tall, dense trees before emerging on to a road. But from it, instead of seeing the other end of the tunnel below us, Han saw the pub we had left. We had returned to where we had started.

We walked down to the car and drove back down the dirt road. At the lane by the bridge we briefly stopped. Left or right? We went right, never thinking 'how way leads on to way'.

The lane passed between two small grass fields before climbing gently up between high-sided banks topped by drystone walls. On the left side of the lane the walls were true, the fields large and open arable. They rolled gently away up to a Norman church and a castle-like manor house that stood next to it. The land looked businesslike and confident, with its well-ordered boundaries and neat clean lines.

On the other side of the lane the walls were crumbling and collapsing, the fields smaller, speckled with cows and sheep. The land's tattered patchwork seemed older and its run-down demeanour more in keeping with my jaded mood and my plans to drop out. Up ahead, on the right side of the lane that seemed to be a boundary for something we couldn't identify, was a turning down a short dirt track and at its end stood a lone Cotswold-stone cottage. As we passed it, with neither forewarning nor thought, I stopped, glanced in the mirror and reversed back down the lane towards it.

'What's going on?' said Han, alarmed.

'I'm just curious,' I said, pointing to the large 'For Sale' sign that hung on a post by the cottage's garden wall.

I parked the car and dialled the estate agent.

'We're outside this cottage and we were wondering what the price was?'

'Which cottage is it?'

'I'm not sure exactly. We're just near a pub called The Leggers' Inn.'

'Yes, that's Lettem Cottage.'

£229,000. The price was little more than for our London maisonette under the flyover.

'I know it's a bit short notice, but is there any way we could see it? We're just down from London for the weekend and we're actually right outside.'

'Let me take your number and I'll call the owner.'

Han gently laughed. 'You're not serious, are you?'

'No, no, I'm just curious, I suppose. You don't mind, do you?'

'No, fine.'

'We probably can't see it anyway, but, you know ...'

'Fine.'

A slump-backed old collie hobbled up the track to inspect us as we waited, her front feet bent, her paws exposed so that she seemed to walk on her ankles; a man tapped on the window, so close and quick it startled us.

I wound down the window.

'Hello, I hear you're interested in our house?'

'Er, yes, hello, yes, yes, we are.'

'Well, come in.'

Lettem Cottage dangled at the very edge of the village that was at the top of the lane, separated from the village and yet connected to it by some old farm buildings that lay between the cottage and the nearest other houses.

Set at the end of a long, bumpy track, it was a twin-gabled eighteenth-century cottage, built from South Cotswold stone once honey-coloured, now weathered grey, more golden on its less exposed side. At first glance it appeared to be a single building, but it was in fact two narrowly separated cottages and only number one, Lettem Cottage, was for sale.

The trackside roof was tiled in workaday Welsh slate and it showed its Cotswold-tile finery only on the garden-side gable. An old drystone wall, topped by a broken trellis and the bare and twisted winter remains of climbing plants, ran from a front porch along the side of the track. We were led by the owner down a short path and through a narrow garden gate to the front door.

We entered as curious tourists, worrying that our supposed interest would easily be exposed for the spontaneous intrusion it was.

The living room was long and slightly narrow, with a low ceiling and a carpeted floor. The end wall nearest the front door was of exposed stone, as was the large fireplace at the other end. The two double windows with black-painted iron latches set above deep, wood-topped windowsills showed a thickness of wall that no modern house builder would recognise; the ancient stone telling you it might be old but it wasn't infirm. The room's dimensions seemed ideal, providing as much space as they could without compromising the cottage's intimate proportions.

The door through to the dining room was at the end of the living room by the fire and was so low I had to duck my head. In the dining room there were exposed wooden beams and a glass-paned door that opened out on to a flagstone terrace and the garden. We had to resist the urge to break away from our host and see what was out there. We knew already it would be no view of a flyover. But he wanted to show us the bedrooms first.

'What is it they say? Save the best till last, or is it the other way round? There's that programme on TV, isn't there, tells you how to show your house off. Have you seen it?'

With rising excitement we went up some short, steep, narrow stairs. Stairs. It had been a long time since we had lived in a home with storeys and tread boards.

On the second floor there were three bedrooms, one larger than the others with a view out over the garden, and two smaller ones. From one of the two lane-side bedrooms was a long view to the west, over the hedge by the lane and across a large field, all the way to the beech trees that marked the dirt track to the pub and the wood behind it.

The cottage fulfilled every clichéd preconception of the English rural idyll that we didn't even know we held until confronted by its reality. Of course it had an ancient Aga stove; and the bathroom being downstairs and tiny seemed entirely right.

'Actually, it's quite handy having the bathroom next to the kitchen,' said the owner. 'Keep an eye on the kids while they're having their bath *and* get the meal going.'

The kitchen window looked out over a garden at the side of the cottage next to the track. There was a plastic children's swing, but I could tell that Han already saw rows of radishes and beanpoles. Beyond it were fruit trees, a rich compost heap, a smouldering fire and woodsheds leaning up against the ivy-clad walls of an ancient, roofless stone shed that bordered the garden. The shed partly hid an ugly caravan that stood large and obtrusively on the other side of it. But no matter: the caravan was empty, the owners reassured us, and soon to be moved.

It wasn't until we had been shown the entire cottage and come out through the stable-style kitchen door on to the terrace that we saw the view.

Beyond a small, lawned garden and a low moss-covered wall were rolling drystone-walled fields, a far-off barn, a church spire and an unobscured line of sight to hills that stretched across the horizon some twenty miles away.

'Is that the railway over there?' Han finally asked, pointing across the fields to the bridge that carried the railway over the canal and disappeared into a cutting through the hill.

'Yes. Runs up to Worcester. The kids love it. It's like living in *The Railway Children*.'

I leant forward and ran my hand along the moss that capped the garden wall, snowdrops at my feet, and breathed in the air. The smell reminded me of something, but of what I couldn't place.

It was the view that did it. The cottage's ken had seized me so forcefully that by the time we were back in the car, my mind, at least, was set. Han and I took the decision to buy Lettem Cottage within a day, made an offer on Monday on our return to London and heard it had been accepted on Tuesday.

# CHAPTER 2

# FIRST NAMES

I am lying in our London bed, listening to the garbage trucks starting their engines. Han sleeps next to me.

*What have we done?* I must have been drunk. We'll be living in a tiny cottage in a country I hadn't wanted to come back to (why is that?), career thrown away, drowning in debt. In the *countryside*.

What are we going to do with a bloody Aga?

Han will resent me and my weakness, my 'career' will be finished, my life unrecoverable, my friends and contemporaries living in a world I once had a grip on but which would now be for ever out of sight.

It was a long wait between the 'sale' and actually getting the keys and our joint decision to buy Lettem Cottage looked increasingly moonstruck. Desperate for change, Han and I had chosen to live in a place where we had little idea how our lives might be led. Our adult sensibilities were entirely urban; we had never even considered living in the English countryside until we stumbled across Lettem. Why that might have been, we ignored. The reasons I had lived for nearly a decade away from England were also overlooked, largely because I couldn't place what they were. Our return had been merely the following of tracks laid by my career and certainly not by any desire to leave Paris; why exactly my doubts existed remained unfaced. As for Han, she had done the London thing, and although she was happy to see more of her Australian sister who lived there, she hadn't harboured any longing to return to England: I think, when all was said and done, it was because of the weather.

Certainly my mother would be pleased. I had been a long-distant and hopeless son, for ever I think, our relationship circling in a little hoop of ever re-enforcing mutual disappointments, but still glued together by love and the hope that one day it might get better.

Somehow Han's and my nerves held, our course set firm by solicitors, banks and closing dates. 'Can you believe we are doing this?' we kept asking each other as we drove down from London the weekend before we were to move in.

We had bought the cottage on the back of one impromptu twenty-minute visit and it was smaller than we had remembered it. Han stared at the unmoved caravan, which still sat in front of the derelict, roofless barn next to the garden.

'I don't remember that caravan looking quite so big and white,' she said.

No. Nor did I.

Inside, the sellers were in a frenzy of departure.

'We haven't moved in ten years,' said the owner, almost apologetically.

Ten years? Where had I been in ten years?

Fransje's apartment above the gay bar when I arrived in Amsterdam; Tweede Jan Steenstraat in De Pijp, up endless flights of stairs that my American friend fell down carrying his chilli pot, stoned and happy; Swedish Ingela finding the apartment off the Overtoom and next the one behind a hairdresser on Beethovenstraat, where we awoke one night to find a junkie heaving a brick through the salon's window and removing their stereo. The worst. At last, Zocherstraat and its barbecue roof terrace looking on to the Vondel Park, with its winter ice-skaters, roller-bladers in the summer; and the man behind the trees, stopping to listen to my Dylan on a warm evening and calling up his requests.

Brussels next, above the Café Passiflore, watching the trams shake past the Parvis de la Trinité as Gabriella pulled up outside in her husband's BMW. Then finding my Australian at an English country wedding that only at the last minute had I flown in to attend and before we knew it, meeting her at the Eurostar, her life in her bags; moving into our run-down house off the Place du Châtelain with its Wednesday market, a house we still owned and rented to some French friends, which only just covered the mortgage.

To Paris, Villa Wagram St Honoré, the private road with its iron gates off the Rue du Faubourg St Honoré, before heading up the hill to Montmartre to an apartment bought from Claude Nougaro, the famous French 'singer of texts who can just about keep rhythm'. There, drinking hard at the No Problemo with Legionnaires, cops, fat Alain, the alcoholic Bertrand and a Scottish communist who never made it home after '68.

And back to London and a temporary apartment and somehow, inconceivably after all this, this little cottage in the middle of the Cotswolds.

'Oh,' I said.

'There is some oil still in the tank. We'd like some money for it.'

'OK. Um, how much is it?'

'Eighteen pounds and ten pence.'

'Eighteen pounds and what?'

'Ten pence.'

'Right.'

We can't belong here, can we, in the same house, the same village as these people? I felt embarrassed to think such a thing, but I couldn't let go the thought.

I walked outside with Martin. He and his family had lived here because of an office job in a nearby town; they were moving on and up for a better office job in another town. Perhaps they had already packed away all their pictures and possessions, their boots and coats, their rods and dogs, but there was something missing from their home. There was no sense of either the city or the country, just John Lewis furnishings and clean suburban carpets.

Walking around the garden I stopped and stared at the view.

'It's wonderful.'

'Yes,' he said matter-of-factly. He didn't sound as if he would miss it. I asked him about the pub.

'Oh, it's fantastic,' he said, his words implying he went there regularly, his slightly overeager tone suggesting perhaps he didn't.

There were voices over the hedge.

'That's a young guy who works for Norman.'

'Norman?

'Lives next door,' he said, pointing over the laurel hedge that divided the two gardens. Norman's cottage looked derelict and empty.

*Oh my God, we've bought a virtually semi-detached cottage and have no idea who lives next door.*

'Yes, and he's had some other bloke staying with him. I think he was in prison or something.' *Shit.* 'The bloke, I mean, not Norman,' added Martin.

'Really? What's his name?'

'I don't know,' said Martin, turning to go inside.

The following weekend, a heavy, cold April rain covered our journey from London, a moving van behind us. I did not feel well.

'Are you OK? You look like you're going to hyperventilate.'

'I can't believe we're doing this.'

We turned off the main road, drove into the village and turned down the track leading to the cottage. Parked outside, the 'For Sale' sign replaced with 'Sold', we paused and listened to the rain on the roof and watched a river of water flow down the lane. And then it stopped, quite suddenly, and it was time.

'Let's go.'

As Han tried the keys to the door, I stood immobile on the terrace at the back of the cottage, the stone paving wet and cold under my city shoes. In the garden there was a tree, leafless and large; low cloud over the fields. The smell was of wet grass and clean air. Han glowed and grinned in a fluster of excitement.

'You're sure you're OK?' she laughed.

'Sure.'

She turned and paused. 'Can you smell that?'

'Yes,' I smiled at her. 'I can.'

In the field over the garden wall, a small red tractor crossed the grass. A man wearing a baseball cap, waterproof trousers and a dirty raincoat got off the tractor and, leaving it in gear as it slowly trundled across the field, started tossing hay on to the ground from a transport box on the back. He was followed in his slow stream of feed by a herd of steaming, wet cows. He saw us watching and his arm shot up vertically, a quick and forceful acknowledgement closer to the raised arm of an eager pupil than a wave. I waved back and watched transfixed. That tractor was going to get away from him, wasn't it? But it moved at a gentle walking pace, and the man stepped easily back on to it once his hay was gone. Another shot of the arm and he drove away out of sight.

A minute later the tractor came up the lane, chugging noisily past. The man was younger than the pace of his work had suggested, perhaps in his early thirties, and he wore thick, unfashionable glasses smeared with water. He had the friendliest smile, reaching wide across his face, chin raised and held forward, not a glimpse of teeth. His arm shot up again, a nod and he was gone, up the lane to the farm buildings. He was singing.

Ten minutes later, he returned, walking down the track as we unloaded the car, still singing loudly.

'Hello,' I said. 'I'm Ian. We've just moved in.'

'Yeah, saw that. I'm Uglis, very nice to meet you, it is,' he said, sticking out his hand with the same energetic thrust as his salutes. His accent was thick, his voice loud, every word spoken with great emphasis and at even greater volume. We shook hands.

'Sorry, what was your name?'

'JUGLIS!' he repeated, louder this time. I still couldn't get it. One more go.

'Sorry?'

'DEE, OH, UW, GEEE, ELL, AYEE, ESS – JUGLIS,' he shouted, slowly and carefully for the benefit of the man moving in, so stupid, he must have been thinking, that he actually had to spell it out.

'Douglas, yes, of course, hello. Come and meet my wife.'

'Oh, that would be very nice, that would.'

We walked past the kitchen window and stood on the terrace. Douglas leant back, his hands on his hips, and admired the view.

'Oh, that's lovely, that is. Bootiful, isn't it? Bootiful spring day it is, bootiful. Who'd want to be inside on a day like this? My dad says you're better off outside, he does.'

'He's right.'

'That would be one of your Nuffields, that is,' he said, pointing to an old tractor parked on the bank of the second field from the house. 'And that's where I live, up there!'

We walked to the garden wall and I tried to make out where he was pointing.

'Where exactly?'

''Idcombe. Over there!'

'Where?'

'There,' he said, pointing vaguely to the top of the hill on the other side of the valley.

Han came out.

'Douglas, this is my wife, Hannah.'

'Hello, 'Ann'r, very nice to meet you it is. I've 'ad a check-up I 'ave. I 'ad a breathing problem. Doctors says I'm underweight, he says, he does.'

'That's no good, is it?' said Han.

'Do you like bikes?'

'Er, yes.'

'I like bikes. I make 'em, I do. Custom-made, highly specialised, they are. I'll bring you round some mag'zines, and all that. Very interesting they are, Ian, very interesting.'

'Thank you.'

'That's not natural,' Douglas said.

'Sorry?'

'That,' he said, gesturing to the overgrown pond on the other side of our garden wall. 'That's a steam pond that is. Man-made it is.'

'A what?'

'For the steam engines. They needed water.'

'Oh, I see.'

'Last New Year's Eve, me and Norman spent it together. Alone.'

'Oh.'

'That's an old 'arrow that is. Very old it is, we don't use it much. Bootiful day, isn't it?'

There was a rustle in the hedge that divided our garden from our neighbour and the haggard, limping collie we had seen when we first saw the house sidled on to our lawn. Up close we could see that her front paws were flattened at ninety degrees and she really did walk on her ankles. Without looking at us, she shat in front of us, turned and disappeared back through the hedge.

'That's Sukey, that is. Norman's dog.'

'Oh.'

'Better be off then, got my dinner to eat. You have a nice day then, and all that.'

As Douglas left, a figure strode towards us from the far field. He was wearing a tatty flat cap and was dressed in an ancient duffel coat and short, black, mud-covered wellington boots. Reaching a wall, he used a protruding flat stone built into it as a step, and climbed over with an ease that belied the wall's size. His gait was long-stepped, fast, head down, his upper body pitched forward as though walking into a strong wind. Long unwashed strands of hair protruded out of the sides of his cap. Sukey hobbled out to meet him as he came across the field.

We pretended to casually stroll over to our garden wall, trying not to look as if we were waiting for him. He looked at us as he approached, but said nothing and didn't wave. He just strode on relentlessly.

By his garden's wall were some bricks that made a rough step to climb up and over into his garden on the other side of the high laurel hedge that divided the two cottages. I was standing not more than two feet away and felt a fool. I had to say something.

'Hello.'

'Hello,' said Han.

'Hello,' he mumbled in reply, without stopping. As he climbed his steps, I tried again.

'I'm Ian; this is my wife, Hannah. We've just moved in.' I sounded like an overeager yuppie moving into his weekend cottage.

He paused on top of the wall and stared at me, bemused and slightly amused. His nearly toothless mouth was open in amazement, but what the source of wonder was I couldn't be sure. He was motionless and the silence could be filled only by him. There was a long pause as he stared at me. Finally he spoke.

'I've lived here all my life.'

*What can you say to that?*

'Those crows are enjoying your wheat,' I threw in, desperate to maintain momentum, pointing to a ploughed field black with birds.

*Probably not that.*

There was another pause.

'They're rooks, actually.'

'Oh.'

Long pause.

'It's barley. I've just planted it.'

*I'm struggling here.*

'Hungry little things, aren't they?'

*I can't believe I just said that.*

'I can think of other words for 'em,' he said, the slightest hint of a wry half-smile on his still-brown-in-winter skin. I was clearly an idiot.

And with that he was gone, over the wall and inside.

I am in Hong Kong, checking into the Grand Hyatt. My American colleague, dressed in Ivy League and MBA confidence, laughs when I say I am on the twelfth floor with a poor view of the harbour. She is on the twentieth floor and can see over the smog. Annoyed, I scowl, and wake up.

I wasn't in Hong Kong. Nor was it the sound of the garbage trucks from the council depot that roused me, but a deep, stilled silence. The view when I got up to look out of the window was filled by the looming tree and thick, thick fog that enveloped the fields as densely as Kowloon smog on a hot day.

Han joined me at the window and there on the lawn was a man, older than Norman, with thick glasses, an anorak and a beard. It wasn't clear if he was just having a look around, thinking we were not here, or if he had come to find us.

'Hello?' I said, going outside with some clothes dashed on.

He was a little nervous and for a moment appeared reticent about introducing himself.

'I'm Malcolm, Norman's brother.'

'Hello.'

'About that septic tank. It ought to be done, you know.'

'Yes.'

'All right. Goodbye.'

'Excuse me, but the caravan? Martin, the previous owner? He said it was yours and you were going to move it?'

The brother gave a dismissive snort as if to say he had said no such thing.

'It's my other brother's. I can't say.'

He mumbled a goodbye and left. It didn't seem the caravan was going anywhere. Han leant out of the window, grinning at what she had overheard. 'Shall we go to the pub tonight?' she laughed.

We did. The barman was called Liam and, partly to our surprise, more to our relief, was all gel and designer hair, camp, friendly and jovial.

'Oh, Londoners,' he said jokingly. 'I left there eight years ago and I've never gone back. So where are you living?'

'In the cottage up near the farm, next door to Norman Ludd?'

'Oh my God, Luddie!' Liam exclaimed dramatically. 'Have you met him? I met him once; he scared the *life* out of me. I was walking my dog in the graveyard one night, and all of a sudden this sensor light went on from the house next door, and there he was! Standing right next to me, just standing there! *Never heard a thing!* God knows what he was doing there. He terrified me! He's the scariest man in the village.'

Aside from meeting Norman and Douglas, and Liam at the pub, our sole contact with the village was a visit from the rector. No neighbour called with a pot of home-made jam; there were no invitations to drinks, nor little notes left in the postbox welcoming us to the community; and, equally, nor did we venture forth to introduce ourselves.

The Reverend Charles Stanton was in his sixties I guessed, well-spoken, tall and a little patriarchal. He lived in the new rectory at the top of the lane and was head of a parish which included six other villages and churches. His role as rector also involved something to do with the diocese in Gloucester, he told me. He declared his visit not as a welcome but for the purpose of dropping off the parish magazine, even though a copy had already been left in the postbox.

'What a marvellous view you have down here,' he said as we sat outside in the spring sunshine on the terrace. 'It's hidden from the lane, isn't it? One forgets it's here.'

'Yes, we love it.'

He had declined my offer of a drink; he seemed distracted and was gazing at the garden and the view.

'So, would you be based here or in London?' Weekenders, I think he meant.

'No, we're going to test this technology revolution and see if one actually can work from anywhere,' I replied, trying to adopt a jaunty, positive tone.

'Yes, my daughter-in-law would like to do that. She's an accountant, you know.'

'Really?' I closed the weekend gardening book that was open on the table in front of me, conscious there was neither a tool nor a sign of work in sight.

'City?'

He said the word so abruptly I wasn't sure what he meant. Was it some sort of a test, a question I was supposed to complete with some requisite, even standardised response, firmly denouncing the place and all its sins and omissions?

'Um, sorry, er ...? Oh right, yes. "*City*". Actually, no. No, I'm not in, er, "banking". I'm in, um, "newspapers".'

'Oh.' He seemed rather disappointed. 'Does your *wife* work?'

'Yes, she's a web developer,' I said.

'Oh, right.'

'Are you sure I can't offer you a drink?'

'No, no, I must be off now.' Only our professional and social status established, he was keen to go. There had been no invitations to come for tea or try out for the cricket team or join the bell-ringers. If he represented a community, he gave no sense of it. 'What was your surname again?'

'Walthew,' I said and, taking a cue from Douglas, I spelled it for him.

I had resigned the moment we completed on the house sale, the mortgage now secured. It had been agreed in May that for my lengthy notice period I would work progressively shorter weeks until I was finally to leave at the end of August. With Han continuing to work in London, I stayed at the cottage, alone, any midweek time I could.

I would sit on the garden wall in the spring sun, unshaved and out of place, staring mindlessly at nameless birds managing to balance on the tiniest bucking and rearing twigs of the big tree, whipped by the wind that flicked skittish clouds through the sky. The lawn was alive and needed to be cut, the garden an impossible space of things I knew nothing about, nor how or where I should start its care.

As each month of my notice period offered up one more day a week not to have to be at work, the freedom did not liberate me. It overwhelmed me, and at first I rarely left the cottage. I'd spend hours lying on the lawn trying to read, unable to move, morose and hot. Around me were sounds and smells I couldn't place or find my place among. The world beyond the garden wall, other than the lane that led to the pub and the road I took south out of the village back to London or Heathrow, remained green, pretty and vague.

My fear came from worries about who and what I would discover, and my likely inability to fit in when encountered. My other life, for all its urban hostilities and polluted air, was nothing if not familiar. I knew myself there. I didn't here. To live in this new world was going to require an effort and energy I feared I might never recapture. Only Han's steady confidence and excitement held me together.

Sinking hard, I found a doctor in a nearby village, a tiny surgery in the shadow of the church spire we could see from our garden. The waiting room was empty and disinfected-quiet and I sat staring at ancient NHS posters. An old woman who smelt like my grandmother came in and sat opposite me. Silence.

The country doctor was a dour but no doubt well-meaning Welshman and he wore his diagnosis on his face. It was a Friday, I was not at work, and I was too young and not ill enough to warrant his attention. And I had just bought a cottage here, weekender no doubt, and parked my shiny Lexus next to his old Peugeot.

I told him my symptoms: the permanent cold, the lethargy. I was going to tell him I was depressed and ask for drugs, but he struck me as too stern for a confession. He asked me about my job and my travelling.

'Without wishing to draw stereotypes, your condition is not atypical of your lifestyle. You smoke, you drink, you're single.'

'Actually, I'm married.'

'Oh?' He was openly surprised. 'To whom?'

'Um, to, er, my wife.' He didn't look like he believed me. I found myself telling him her name. 'Hannah.'

'Really? Well, anyway, what I mean is you are unsettled.'

Indeed.

We discussed my drink consumption (we absurdly settled, after a lot of reflection, on the maximum number of units per week recommended for a male of my age), my weight, my smoking. Hoping to win some favour, I told him I had quit my job.

'To do what?'

I couldn't tell him I had no idea.

'To be a consultant.'

'My brother works for an IT company that uses consultants,' he said, looking directly at me, 'and he tells me there are lots of jokes about the type of people who become consultants.'

'Right.'

He concluded that I was run-down; there was nothing he could prescribe. It had not been a productive visit. I came out and lit a cigarette and looked around at the Cotswold-stone houses and cars with pro-hunting messages stuck in their rear windows.

Back at the cottage there was a rare midweek visitor.

'Hello.'

A crude, prison-style heart tattoo on his arm, hands covered in varnish, the tip of one of his fingers missing, the man standing on the terrace was holding a large wooden chair. 'I've got your table.'

A house-warming present from my mother, the table was long and wide, sturdy and solid and came with two chairs, all made from dark brown reclaimed wood. She had come over when we moved in, seen exactly what was missing and now she had filled the space perfectly. The man and I carried it to the terrace where we sat at it for the first time. Later everyone would want to sit and look at that view, past the big tree, over the wall and out across the field, perhaps a brown cow staring back. The methodical sound of the cows' moving mouths across the thick spring grass always sounded reassuringly weighted between purposeful industry and gentle nature.

Hamish, the man who had made and delivered the table, asked me what I did and I told him I worked for an American-owned newspaper. He told me he had visited New York when he was a marine mechanic in the Bahamas.

'I met a girl from Brooklyn,' he said after a while. 'I love New York.'

'Yeah, so do I,' I said absent-mindedly. But I think at that moment, as the late-spring sun went down and the cows moved to the edge of the paddock to study us more closely, we were both glad we weren't there.

Norman and Douglas walked down the lane, heading back to the cottage for their lunch. We hadn't seen them since we had moved in a few weeks earlier except in the distance, Norman jumping into the paddock from the garden wall and heading off into the fields to do whatever he did there. In the first month we had been neighbours, no light came from his house, no noise, no radio, no TV. No car was ever parked out front, as though he lived somewhere else; or at least without electricity. Behind the curtainless, unwashed-in-years windows, on the trackside of his house was what appeared to be his sitting room, but never once showing a light, just like the rooms upstairs. All that could be seen was a row of empty, cobweb-covered bottles along the sills of the downstairs windows.

'That is a bootiful day, that is,' Douglas shouted, arm raised; Norman head-down, silent and sheepish alongside him.

'It's wonderful.'

'We can tell what the weather will be like. We don't need to listen to the forecast,' he said. Norman remained straight-faced. Douglas acted as though he, not Norman, was the man in charge.

'Going to be a hot summer, then?' The specificity of my question threw Douglas, who looked to the man who really ran the show. There was a pause, as we all waited to see what he would say.

'I reckon we'll have a drought,' Norman said quietly. His prediction was nonchalant and modest and I had complete faith in him.

'What was that round thing you were pulling behind your tractor?' I asked him clumsily, trying to make conversation.

Norman contained an embarrassed smile and narrowed his eyes. He was to look at me in this way many times to come. I think it was the look of a man amazed that someone did not know that the earth was round, and that if this strange person did not know this, Norman could not imagine why he could possibly want to find out.

Douglas launched into a long explanation of each and every farmyard tool, a trail that I failed to follow.

Norman, finally, shyly intervened. 'It's to keep the moisture in. There isn't much in that top field,' he said. And with that he was off. No farewell, not rudely, just gone.

'You can come and look at my tractor some time if you like,' said Douglas.

'OK. Um. Thanks.'

'Best be off for my sandwich. Nice seeing you, and all that.'

With the summer came my first guilty, tentative expeditions, Han still working hard days in the sticky city. The canal, I learnt, ran from the pub along the wide valley to the south of the cottage and was in fact entirely abandoned. Only the reach of water between the tunnel and the bridge on the lane had been properly cleared, and a wooden dam kept it full of water. Underneath the hill, the tunnel had collapsed long ago and on the other side of the dam the canal was full of brambles, bushes and trees. It had been officially declared closed since long before the Second World War.

The old towpath ran alongside it, at first clear and easily walkable. It passed a tall stone building, also long-derelict, with a missing roof and only holes where windows and door frames once had been. I showed it to Han one weekend and we took it to be an old lock-keeper's house. Beyond it, the path ran under the red-brick viaduct that took the railway over the canal, but further on the trail became overgrown and less easy to walk along. We didn't know that Norman owned this section of the canal, nor his views about its restoration and use as a public footpath, and so we innocently began creating ourselves a running trail, clearing the path along a stretch of canal that we later learnt some of the restoration club members were too scared even to walk.

From the canal I would jog up the footpath back to the village and home, stopping at a stone stile to look down over the fields to the green path of the canal that ran into Frimley Wood. I liked this intimate daily journey, seeing no one, just the same trees, the same fields, the same skies that were always there but always different. In the cities, it had never been the same places or people from one day to the next, but nothing had ever changed.

The few weekends that we were at the cottage, that first interrupted summer, we behaved as many weekenders do, putting on a show for visiting friends who couldn't see that we were as irrelevant to the village as they were. Naturally, we would take them to 'our' local, which was of course as much 'ours' as the village was. At the pub, I would act as if I belonged in spite of having no idea what there was to belong to.

Peg, the pub manager, was a short bubble of energy. In her fifties, with shortish straight hair, if she wasn't beavering around the place, she could be found somewhere with a cigarette in her mouth, her voice and her laugh deep with the rasp of tobacco but gentle with affection. She was welcoming and friendly in a way that seemed naturally predisposed to find the best in anyone. She was also the only person around who appeared actually to do any work beyond simply chatting with the customers, a fact that gave the pub's other bar staff the look of people more there for the laughing and the drinking than work. (Peg, I told Han confidently, was the landlord's wife.)

It was to be mid-July before we met the landlord, one grabbed Lettem weekend when we weren't away. Han came outside with him to where I sat, to introduce me. He was the tall, straight-backed man with the Alsatian we had seen the first time we had discovered the pub, ruddy cheeks and silver-grey hair.

'Ian, this is Geoff.'

'Hello, Ian, nice to meet you,' he said, shaking my hand, his firm voice softened by a delicate Gloucestershire burr. Geoff and I spoke only briefly. Perhaps I was embarrassed that it had taken us three months to meet him. I wanted to explain that we weren't weekenders, we *were* going to live here, but it was too complicated and felt like a lie.

He asked where we lived and when we had moved in.

'Next to Luddie? Oh my God!' he laughed, in what had become a familiar reaction. 'He hasn't still got that crippled dog, has he?'

I spoke properly with Norman just once that summer, only the third time we had exchanged words. It was the first time I came back from my run cutting off the footpath, and across the farm. He was at the gate at the top of the field I would come to know as the Humpty Dumps. Back then, though, it was just one of Norman's gates, broken down and held together by string, as all his gates were. It was July and it had been raining, despite his spring prediction of a drought. He didn't acknowledge me, but I was determined.

'Evening, Norman.'

He neither replied nor even looked up as he tried to close the gate he had passed through, but I stopped and waited.

'I hope you don't mind me coming over this way?'

There was a pause so long I began to regret my decision to follow the track that led towards the cottage.

'It's not a footpath, you know.'

'Oh, sorry,' I said, embarrassed.

'If you let people do it and you don't say anything and they carry on doing it, it becomes a right of way, you know, and I don't want that, people walking through the yard,' he replied, before sheepishly adding, 'but I don't mind you doing it, I suppose.'

When the gate was tied in a tangle of baler-twine, and he saw I was still there, to my surprise he spoke to me again.

'Not exactly haymaking weather, is it?' he said quietly.

This hadn't occurred to me. 'No, I can't believe it's July. Do you think we'll have a good late summer?'

'I don't know. No prospect of it, is there?'

I had no idea. Silence.

I pressed on.

'Who's that on the tractor?' I asked of the man making huge round bales of hay.

'Contractor.'

'Is that your field he's in?'

'Yes.'

'I saw someone cutting hay in the field between the canal and the road. Who was that?'

'Douglas.'

His one-word answers left me sounding intrusive, injecting questions into the slipping body of our conversation just to keep it conscious. I didn't want to sound like someone who felt he had a right to ask, or an expectation of being answered, but I found myself pressing on, nevertheless.

'So, do you reckon you'll get the hay in before it rains again?'

'Dunno.'

'You don't see square bales much any more, do you?' – saying something I thought vaguely might be true.

'Nope, nobody will do 'em. We used to do all small bales when Father was on the farm. But now I've only got Douglas.'

'Not enough?'

'Nope, he has to be home on time for his tea, doesn't he? Can't finish the job, so I don't dare do more than a few.'

'I'll help you,' I said.

'Yes?' he said with an embarrassed, or was it sceptical, grin.

'Sure. It's good exercise. If you see I'm at home and you're going to do them, just ask.'

'Yes?' His amusement was now incredulity.

'Sure.'

'I don't know if you live there all the time. Do you? Sometimes I have to guess.'

'Most of the time we're there.' I wanted this to be true. He didn't respond. 'Is that your field over there?' I asked.

'No.'

'Is it Goonetilleke's?'

'No. It belongs to the big house over there,' Norman said, pointing to Lettem House, a large early-Victorian house that was just off the lane that led to the village, but which was mostly unseen from the road. Between it and Lettem Cottage were Norman's yard and the house known as Syde Lettem.

'Do you know Goonetilleke then?' Norman asked, surprised and suspicious.

It had been Douglas who had told me about Goonetilleke, who lived in the house with the polo ground. He's an Indian, he is, Douglas had told us the night he came and ate with us at the barbecue we had built on the terrace. His kitchen is like a marble temple, it is.

'No, no. Douglas told me about him. He tells me he has a kitchen like a marble temple.'

Norman didn't reply, and another long pause surrounded us. The pause didn't seem to bother Norman; I'm not sure he even noticed it. I nervously broke it. Later, I would learn to savour them.

'Is it you fixing up the drystone walls?' I asked, pointing to a half-repaired, collapsed wall.

*I can't believe I've asked yet another question.*

'Yes.'

'That's, um, that's great. It's good to see them being kept up.'

*Tell me I didn't just say that.*

'You think so? We don't do much of it this time of the year. Winter job. Try to keep on top of it but haven't got the time.'

'I'd love to come and watch and see how it's done. Let me know and I'll come and help you.'

Bales and walls. Who on earth was I, out here in the middle of the week, running about on his land, asking endless questions and offering free labour?

'Yes?'

'Yes, that's if you wouldn't mind.'

This time the pause was even longer.

He wasn't going to say goodbye, or 'I better be off,' or 'Better get back to work.' I felt uncomfortable but peculiarly determined. Another question.

'So, you don't burn the fields any more after harvest?' I was thinking of stubble-burning and this was a hay field, which wouldn't be burnt anyway, but he didn't correct me.

'No. Not allowed to. That's why I reckon I've got so much rubbish growing in them.' The rubbish was the red of his poppy-splattered barley, a dash of throwback Monetesque vibrancy in a county sprayed sterile yellow with agri-chemicals. 'I reckon this country is going to the dogs, I do. It's the Common Market. They're ruining it.' He was looking at me closely to see how I would react to this.

'Yes.'

'There used to be dozens of small farms like me around here but they're all gone now. Tenancies came to an end, Marsham's agents were just told to take 'em back in. Rectory Farm,' he said, pointing to the village, 'that used to be a tenant farm. It's Marsham now.'

Marsham was Norman's shorthand for the Marsham Estate, owned by Lord Marsham and his family. It was said that the future of the Estate had at one point been threatened; that only the injection of City money and tougher, more business-minded agents saved it. Consolidation of the tenancies and the end of peppercorn rents for many of the Estate houses was seemingly the result. The Estate surrounded Norman's farm and included the parkland which ran north from Marsham House on the edge of Cirencester, our nearest town. The house, unusually close to the edge of a town for an estate mansion, was cut off from the town centre by high walls and an enormous yew hedge. The town's modern housing-estate outskirts were cut off from the town centre by a busy ring road. The centre focused on a small marketplace, used most of the week as a car park, surrounded by fine seventeenth- and eighteenth-century buildings which had been built on the region's wool trade. The movers who had brought our stuff from London had spent a night in Cirencester and had not liked it; 'posh' said one of them, 'rubbish' said his mate.

I had innocently tried to cycle through the park but had been stopped by an Estate worker. Cycling was banned, but I was free to walk until the park closed, a park which, he made clear to me, was in fact a very large private garden generously allowed to be open to the public between 8 a.m. and 5 p.m. I should have read the signs. 'He' didn't allow cycling, I was told. It was a shame, but if we let you in on a bike, we might get kids in. On bikes.

'Are you a Marsham tenant?' I asked Norman.

'No,' he chuckled, shaking his head at the thought. 'My grand-father used to be, but when he died the Estate ended the tenancy and that meant Father wasn't able to carry it on. Over that way it was,' he said, pointing to the east. 'But he got his farm here. All used to belong to Lettem House, all the land this side of the road.'

'Do you know why it's called Lettem?'

He stopped and stared at me. I wondered if I had asked a delicate question, or perhaps one too many.

'I do, actually.' He seemed slightly proud that he did and surprised that anyone should ask him.

'Why is it, then?'

'Do you really want to know?'

'Yes.'

'The Heathreys, they used to have lots of servants, but they docked 'em.'

'Sorry?'

'Ran out of money, let 'em go.'

Lett'em House it was then, or so the story ran.

'When was that?'

'Oh, about 1850,' reckon. Mrs Bruce, used to live in your house, told Mother that. She died the other day, Mrs Bruce; she was a hundred and two. She worked in Lettem House for thirty years.'

I realised that this was a moment when oral history was being passed on. Later I felt self-conscious at how momentous it had felt, embarrassed at how it revealed how little I must have engaged with the people around me in the cities I had lived in.

Norman stood silent, as did I.

'Well, I better be off. Probably holding you up.'

'No,' he said.

That first English summer had been mostly a long, hot farewell to a foreign corporate life I never wanted to see again. As it came to an end, so did the last strands of my connections with London and Paris and the obligations and rewards they offered. My salary stopped and my company car was returned, to be replaced at our own cost by a battered, ancient Golf. I had started taking off my management uniform at the annual board meeting in a Parisian June, and it was at the end of August before I finished up hot, suitless and recklessly drunk in a hip Soho hotel bedroom after my farewell party, insane with relief.

We had spent only a few long weekends at Lettem. Knowing now what lay ahead, I regret every minute I spent away. I should never have gone to New York, New Orleans, Budapest, Paris or any of the places I visited that summer.

Those last journeys overseas, wedding weekends in Devon and Dorset and trips into Cirencester, reminded me that our new life would now not only be entirely rural but also English. This was the country with towns reliant on private parkland for room to cycle, owned by people who didn't want kids on bikes; where the weekly market meant cheap clothes and plastic kitchen utensils; where it rained on the haymakers and the trains broke down or left you without a seat, where a seaside restaurant in Salcombe didn't carry shellfish, where a tiny Cotswold cottage with a downstairs bathroom cost nearly a quarter of a million pounds. Was this what I had left behind or was it something else?

Now that I had no job, so were the weekends and trips away going to come to an end. It was time to confront the reality of rural living – jobless, planless. The first signs, during the lengthening amount of midweek time spent at the cottage during the summer, had not been promising. Four months after we had bought Lettem, I was still sleeping badly and spending whole days paralysed with anxiety. I had had just one proper conversation with my neighbour and, with the exception of the rector's single visit, had met virtually no one from the village.

What are you going to do? a friend asked.

Recover, I said.

# CHAPTER 3

# HARVEST RAVE

From the first day I returned to Lettem after my last day at work and could finally call it our full-time home, it was sixty-one days and nights before I was to go more than four miles from the cottage. It was no longer my fears that made me not want to leave it, but my growing absorption with my immediate surroundings. As the leaves browned and the weather turned, the universe shrank to the manageable. Safe within its close borders and enveloped in the depths of its intimate detail, winter failed to threaten.

Early morning would find me in the same bed in the same room, not in London or Paris or some dislocating hotel, but at Lettem, the window open and through it the sound of two cooing collared doves that sat in the ash tree above the steam pond. Descending the same narrow stairs, passing through the same low-ceilinged dining room and coming out into the same garden was an ever more familiar pleasure, only intensified by knowing I was not about to drive to an office or take a plane to Frankfurt; that this was going to be another Lettem day.

Daily, we learnt the lie of our little land. Behind the cottage, there was our small garden and its mossy lawn, across which our city cat would pad, celebrating his liberation from endless apartments. Scully would lie under the Big Tree that stood over the garden by the low drystone wall at its end; on the other side, a paddock bound by similar ancient, crumbling walls.

Presumptuously, I gave these details names, without imagining they could already have their own. Home Paddock I referred to as the Garden Field. It sloped gently down, away from the cottage to a small stand of tall trees, with low beehives at their feet, that I named Bee Copse. Beyond Bee Copse lay a further paddock full of

dips and craters, the violence of the unknown acts that had created
them hidden with gentle grass and blackberry bushes. I called it the
Bumpy Field, when the Humpty Dumps was its actual, and much
better name. At the top of the Humpty Dumps stood a broken gate
and a smaller cluster of trees, bounded by another weary wall over
which the climbing sun would rise. Each day it pushed its weaken-
ing September rays towards the cottage, ever more visible through
the thinning leaves of Bee Copse.

Hearing the familiar morning call of a cock pheasant, I looked for
him on his customary sedate walk down the Humpty Dumps wall
and along the edge of Bee Copse. On the other side of the valley,
woodsmen's fires would sometimes burn, their smoke drifting slowly
eastwards. Each morning as autumn progressed, that view was there,
only richer in detail, and different as to the light or the weather.

Preparing for my morning run, I would turn and face the thick,
rough stone walls of the cottage, place my hands against them and
feel my home as I stretched in anticipation.

Warmed up, I would take the path that ran between the kitchen
garden and the cottage, pass under the dog rose arch that covered the
front door, unhitch the broken garden gate and stand in the empty
lane, looking down the hill to Frimley Wood. Unless Norman was
leaving his house to walk up the lane towards his yard, there would
be no one there.

'You going running then?' Norman asked me, the first time he
saw me dressed in my tracksuit pants and baseball cap.

'Yes.'

'Why?'

'For the exercise.'

Norman grinned and laughed quietly to himself.

'It's good for you,' I said.

'You're not *going* anywhere then?'

'Not really, no. Just up the track and down to the canal and
round.'

He walked off bemused as I ran down the hill.

At the bend in the road by the field I called Horse Paddock,
the fox heading for Frimley Wood often cut across the lane and
passed into the smarter land on my right. In Norman's fields by the
railway, the morning-sun-warmed rabbits scampered for cover as
they saw me approach.

Reaching the bridge over the canal I could either turn on to the towpath or carry on up the hill. The lane climbed up to the village where Douglas lived. Looking back down the hill was a view of the pub, beech trees along the canal cutting, the bridge by the track to The Leggers' Inn and the old canal Lock House in the valley below. On the other side of the valley the fields of Norman's farm ran up to Lettem Cottage itself. Over to the right was the footpath that ran up from the canal to the road that led into the village; in the far distance would be Norman, just visible on his tractor.

From the top of the hill the boundaries of Norman's farm were more easily seen, a patchwork of smaller fields divided by walls, trees and hedges. Some were stocked with sheep or cattle, others empty pasture, or harvested but still unploughed fields. The land that surrounded Norman's farm on all sides was pristine, composed of comparatively vast fields made large by the long-gone walls and ripped-up hedges that once had divided them. Those fields, already ploughed and planted with new crops of arable so soon after the summer harvest, stood in stark contrast to the unharvested, bedraggled barley in Upper Rathbury Field. The delayed cycle on Norman's farm only added to the sense that we lived in a different age from the modernity around us.

Other days I would run along the canal path, closed in and roofed by the trees and bushes on either side. Wood pigeons, fat and shiny from the last remains of harvest, rose as I ran. I ducked to avoid the branches that hung low above the towpath and jumped over the tree roots that crossed it. I never met anyone.

At the eastern edge of Norman's farm, the canal headed south along the edge of a wood. Here I would turn off the canal path and head north, up and over a small, almost overgrown bridge to the barn known as the Lambing Sheds. A mansion called Rathbury House stood somewhere within the wood, behind the high trees that clung to the primordial earthworks of a long-gone fort. Running in the evening, I would hear the racket of the rookery high above me in Rathbury's towering trees.

Cows that some mornings were in the Home Paddock to see me off, other mornings could be found here. They stopped their grazing of dew-soaked grass and looked intently as cows do, surprised and uninterested, all in one mournful turn, before their heavy heads sank back to their task. I ran up the edge of Pumping Station Field, named after the remains of a long-derelict canal pumping station shed, climbed over the worn stone stile under the crab tree and headed towards the road.

In the field by the road that led into the village, a dented and rusted combine harvester was parked between the wall and a small, square wood, a machine as forgotten as the uncut, rain-wilted barley that surrounded it. At the road, I would turn into the village, past the lumbering Victorian Lettem House and the 1990s neo-Georgian houses rudely built in its grounds; past the entrance to Norman's yard, through the gate and down the track back to Lettem Cottage.

Over the hedge that separated us from Norman's unseeable and unknowable garden, the wafting smell of bacon as he cooked his breakfast.

I would stagger over the lawn and stand under the Big Tree looking out down Home Paddock towards the railway track that led to the nearby village, where the London train stopped.

I liked to be standing there by my garden wall, the sweat of my run on my face, the thud of my recovering breath, in time to watch the morning train go by and celebrate that I was not on it.

By October, I was beginning to notice things in more detail, tried to remember when I last did and couldn't. A thick fog morning, so close I couldn't see across Home Paddock; cold clouded air I could blow as frosted breath in front of me as I ran down the lane, fences and hedgerows covered on every inch with glistening cobwebs; the slight sound of traffic I never noticed before, carried ever so faintly from far-off cars through the windless weight of fog.

In the evenings, the sun would set over Frimley Wood and throw a light over the harvested fields that was so animated I felt I couldn't hope to see it again. Shades of brown and green and yellow, each clod of ploughed earth, each stick of stubble catching and reflecting the light in a viscous coating of moving, vivid colour. But there it would be, the next evening, tinted by a slightly different prism. On rainy days, the clouds slid grey and hostile through metallic blue, blotchy skies to the Wiltshire Downs. The light of the late-afternoon sun would catch the occasional wet skin of a distant car on an obscured road, little flashes from a parallel existence where people drove home after indoor office days.

Han still continued to commute to London, while she tried to find clients that would let her shift her business west. She would come home from work and ask me what I had been up to and whom I had met, but it was only out running that I saw or met anyone and then only the few who had cause to pass Lettem during the day: Norman and Douglas, of course, and Geoff from the pub. He would drive past in his old BMW with his personalised number plate, a greyhound decoration on its bonnet, and the head of Pinto, his large Alsatian, stuck out of the window, mouth open, tongue out, ears blown back. As for the rest of the world out there, I had nothing to do with it.

'What do you know about these fuel protests then? They say the garages are running out of petrol,' Norman asked me one morning.

'Not much,' I said. 'Han and I haven't got a TV, and we haven't seen any.' We didn't read the English newspapers and listened only to the faded reception of the World Service; Norman was much the same.

'I don't have one either. Never have.'

'Never?'

'Nothing much on, is there?'

'No, probably not.'

The TV licensing people refused to accept what Norman and we told them. Each letter more urgently telling them there was no TV at Lettem Cottage would be met with a returned threat of ever-greater retribution.

'They think that people like us who don't own a TV are ...' I paused, seeking a word, not wishing to use 'freaks'.

'Outcasts,' Norman concluded.

Norman's father had lived in the cottage next to us since 1939, ever since he had come to the village as the tenant farmer to Lettem House, which, for reasons not clear to me, was not part of the Marsham Estate.

'Marsham own nearly everything that's not ours,' he said, waving his hand towards Tidcombe and behind us over the lane to the fields up to the church. Norman referred to Marsham as 'they', not 'he', and to his own farm, Parish Farm, as 'ours', not 'mine'.

In 1939 Major Cholsey, who at that time owned Lettem House,

Parish Farm and the houses on their side of the road, including Lettem Cottage, had been obliged to get rid of the manager of Parish Farm. The Cholseys' manager lived in a fine house up in the village, Parish House, but his skills as a farmer were considered inadequate to the task of feeding the besieged Britain. 'He was also a major or something, he didn't know much about farming. Always hunting.'

The Ministry of Agriculture had insisted on a new tenant and Norman's father was given the opportunity. He still hoped one day to take on the tenancy of Norman's grandfather's Marsham farm.

An inscription on Mrs Cholsey's headstone in the churchyard marked the Cholseys' son's death during the battle for Normandy in 1944, on 19 July, serving with the Royal Artillery. Mrs Cholsey died three days later, her husband as yet unaware of their son's death.

'They were lovely and pleasant in their lives and in their death they were not divided,' read the headstone.

Major Cholsey remarried, keeping Norman's father as his tenant, until he died and left Lettem House, its houses and farm to the second Mrs Cholsey. In 1965 she decided to sell everything and build herself a new house in the village, which she called Lettem Barn.

'Mrs Cholsey wanted to sell the house and the farm as one. She always said, "This house is a white elephant, it is,"' mimicked Norman, using a high, loud, strident voice. '"It needs the income of the farm," she always used to say. But she had promised the farm to Father.'

Contracts had been prepared: one for the sale of the house to a Mr Simpson; another for the sale of the farm to Norman's father. But somebody pushed harder and Mrs Cholsey sold Lettem House, Parish Farm and its cottages to Simpson. Only Parish House, in which the hopeless farm manager had lived, was sold separately and was now lived in by people who seemed to be weekenders.

Simpson was a colonial farmer obliged to flee Kenya because of 'all that trouble', Norman relayed.

'The Mau Maus?'

'That's it.'

According to Norman's father, Simpson's purchase of Lettem House and the farm caused a great row, so great that Norman assumed I would know about it.

'You've probably heard about it then?' he asked suspiciously.

'No.'

Mrs Cholsey's failure to sell the farm to Father was the source of an ongoing battle between Simpson and Father over the future of the farm. Norman thought that Simpson finally avoided the arguments and any problematic inheritance disputes between his stepchildren by selling the farm to Father before he died, worried Father would outlive him.

'Father got it in the end, you see. He worked this farm as a tenant for forty-two years. He was seventy-three when he got it. I actually said that at Father's funeral, that he got what he always wanted. His independence. He farmed this place till he was eighty-nine. Marsham's son was there, Lord Rodley, and I looked directly at him when I said that,' Norman said.

'Why was Marsham's son at the funeral?' I asked; perhaps a mark of respect I wondered. 'Did he know your father?'

'Not really, no. He was just having a look at what's going on. Father said they'd always have liked to get their hands on Parish Farm. But they've done well out of us, Father said. Father fighting with Simpson, Simpson having the highest rents around. Father had a terrible time under Simpson he did. He always believed that Marsham's old agents used that to fix higher rents on the farms around us, he reckoned.'

Norman didn't know for sure if that was true and there was no way of being certain, but he did recount a tale of how, as a young teenager, he was doing some fencing one summer evening for Mr Simpson, and he had seen the Marshams' then agent enter Lettem House soon after Father and Simpson had been to arbitration to settle the rent. Through an open window Norman overhead them discussing the outcome. Later Norman spoke with a mate, the son of another Marsham tenant, and they swapped rent stories: the two boys reckoned that the Marsham tenants' rent had been increased to the levels settled by Simpson for Parish Farm.

As Norman told me this, I thought it was more the cereal subsidies that now artificially inflated both rents and land values, but I didn't dare say this to Norman.

Norman's father stayed on the farm a total of fifty-nine springs, summers and winters, and then went and lived with one of Norman's brothers for his last three years. He had died just that August, aged ninety-two, while we had been away.

'Father came and saw me he did. Ten days before he died. He told me to leave the farm and get another job before I was too old. There was no future in farming, he said.'

'You don't want to do that, do you? You'll be farming until you're eighty-nine too,' I said hopefully. The death of his father, the death duties that would soon no doubt have to be paid, and two older brothers who didn't appear to be interested in the farm, all suggested the possibility that the farm might have to be sold.

'I don't know about that,' he replied with a chuckle.

Norman could be chatty and friendly, but on his own terms and by his own definition of those words. He was too canny to show his interest in Han or me and it was to be a long time before he judged the moment right to ask me much about myself.

Once he overcame his initial incomprehension that anyone might be interested in him and his life and the history of the land he knew so well, he was open and generous with his knowledge. He was always telling me something but never too much, and never in a way that was to show off. But he was cautious too. Everyone wanted Norman off that farm, was the impression he gave. Maybe this strange neighbour from London who didn't seem to go to work was no different.

From what was said at the pub, then and later, my experience of Norman was completely at odds with that of the people in the village who knew him, or rather knew of him. Undeniably, despite his handsome face, he did look wild and unkempt, with his mad hair and missing teeth and shabby work clothes. It was also quite evident that he could see in the dark and that he had an unnatural ability not only to detect the movement of any living creature on any inch of his farm, but also to come up on them, unseen and unheard. If you were on his land and off a footpath, it was not going to be good for you.

His house was quite normal by the standards of the age when his father had taken it on, but weirdly unlit and uncared for by the home-improvement standards of today. Sukey, permanently guarding the track that led down to our cottages or the gate into his wild, untended garden, only added to the hermit-like aura of this strange man who lived all alone at the very lower end of the village.

Norman seemed to have little time for interaction with anyone, especially when driving his escaped cows up the lane and home to the yard, bent forward over an old red and yellow mountain bike, probably made by Douglas. As the ever-crap-splattering cows took up the full width of the lane, the passing jogger and the occasional car would be forced on to the verge. Cars would wait as Norman obliviously wove his way towards the cottage, the bike moving so slowly behind the cows that he struggled to keep it upright. People in waiting cars would wind down their windows expecting a cheery hello, a thanks or even an apology to accompany these charming but irritating rural scenes. Norman, however, would pass by drivers not more than a foot away as if they were invisible. There would be looks of dismay as the drivers' faces shifted in a second from forbearance to outrage.

Other people who sometimes took time to help him bring in his escaped animals, including neighbouring farmers and members of the Marsham family, would seldom receive more than a mumbled, often inaudible, thank you. Norman was proud, taciturn and sometimes shy; a man who lived alone and largely had only himself for company; he did not endear himself to others. It wasn't clear to me whether his reticence was partly deliberate, just for devilment, or whether there was merely some embarrassment that others should ever be needed to help him. Certainly I saw no signs of spite or resentment; if he had such feelings they were entirely private.

One evening, a fifty-something gentleman cyclist stood waiting by the canal bridge as Norman came towards us with his cows.

'Are you *with* those cows?' he demanded of me.

'No, they're with the farmer on the bike behind them.'

'He doesn't *say* much, does he? Has he lost his *tongue* or something?'

'No, he's just a quiet man, I think.'

'I've said hello to him *six* times,' the man said indignantly, 'and he's never said a word.'

When I first heard of Father's death and Marsham apparently hoping to pick up this two-hundred-odd-acre irritation in the heart of their Estate (at least as Norman saw it), I didn't understand anything about Marsham to be worried about their possible wants. But in two short months, my one-sided conversations with Norman and my understanding of his land and its stone-walled and animal-grazed charms left me rooting for the underdog. It took that little time to realise that Norman, with his near-derelict cottage and hopeless farm, was exactly the neighbour we wanted. That October, when I saw a man in a Range Rover drive slowly up and down the lane, eyeing Norman's yard with all its potential for Cotswold converted sleeping quarters for London commuters, I glared at him and hoped he wouldn't return.

Norman wasn't ready to share with me what the future of the farm would be now that his father had died, nor I ready to ask him, but finally I couldn't resist asking Douglas what he knew.

'Malcolm's solicitor reckons old Norman should sell the farm,' Douglas said of Norman's older brother.

'Oh yes?'

'He doesn't want to do that does he. He doesn't want to go and live in town and be on the dole, and all that.'

'Surely his brothers wouldn't make him sell up?'

Douglas looked confused. I had reached the end of his knowledge of the subject.

'Don't know what I'd do,' he pondered. 'Probably go and work for Marsham, I s'pose.'

'What would that be like?'

'They'd probably sack me.' 'They're upper class aren't they.' He paused. 'Did you know Marsham are trying to get rid of all the working-class people round 'ere?'

'Really? Who's saying that then?'

'Oh yeah. They don't want 'em, my dad says. They don't. Which class are you then? I'm working class. Are you working class?'

'No, I'm middle class, I suppose.'

'Middle ... right.' Douglas was clear on the notion of working class, and indeed upper class. Middle seemed to throw him.

We stood on the terrace in silence. Douglas seemed as nervous contemplating the future as Han and I were. We wondered about death duties and how Norman and the brothers would pay them.

'Better be going then,' said Douglas. 'Go and have my dinner. I'll be seeing you then.'

Douglas went out over the garden wall and into Norman's garden.

'All right, Norman!' he shouted even more loudly and cheerfully than his normal booming voice. 'What a lovely day, Norman! Bootiful.' Our conversation had to be dispelled, Douglas wanted everything to be this way for ever.

Burning leaves. On a Sunday. I remember something sad about burning leaves, something sad about autumn. Winter will follow. Dark short days, and the drive back to school without my father.

Han ordered logs and we stacked them in our woodshed, and had the Aga serviced and the boiler repaired. As the golden sunsets over Parish Farm fell earlier and more days drew dulled by cloud, perhaps it was time to show that we weren't just summer visitors but winter stayers. It was time to go to the pub.

I had seen Geoff the day before the late-September harvest festival. I was cutting the grass alongside the track that led to our cottage when a long procession of children, ponies, dogs and adults passed down the lane. Pinto, Geoff's Alsatian, ran excitedly with the other dogs between the ponies and the children, but there was no sign of Geoff. This strange outing had the air of an event, a ritual rather than a ramble.

'We're collecting flowers for the harvest festival,' said one of the mothers.

Harvest Festival. I hadn't heard those words since the days of my school chapel with its loaded boxes of tinned food and bought apples for the local old people's home. Standing on Norman's farm, the phrase sounded different, better.

Geoff drove slowly through the strung-out crowd and stopped in front of the cottage when he saw his errant dog. He got out of the car, and in front of me and the gatherers, fiercely shouted at her.

'Come 'ere, you bloody animal!'

The dog ran off a bit, cursed anew by Geoff, red and fuming. He grabbed hold of her and pushed her into his car. Everyone was staring, not least me.

'Never work with children and dogs, isn't that what they say?' he joked, but some of the more genteel mothers looked aghast. 'How are you then? Settling in all right?' he asked.

'Yeah, good.'

'Come down and have a drink some time, won't you?'

'Yes, of course.'

I was embarrassed. We hadn't been to the pub since we had moved full-time to the cottage, except for one quick pint when neither Geoff, Peg nor Liam, the only three people we would have recognised, had been there.

Han and I went down the next night.

'Hello there,' he said, standing up from one of the barber's chairs to greet us. 'How nice to see you. What can I get you?'

Standing at the bar he was chatty and warm, not the man I had seen in that single, fleeting instant with the dog. He was tall and imposing but he smiled and he laughed, and stood so confident in himself and his world. Peg was there too and she joined him for a meal when he sat down to eat. Geoff always ate in the pub from the tiny kitchen, we learnt, with Peg or May, often entertaining others as he did so. He liked to say his pub was a 'pub with food', never a restaurant or a place where the drinking did not come first.

We talked about the cottage and those who had lived there before us. There were the people who had sold the house to us of course, and neither Norman nor Geoff had had much to do with them. Before them, a doctor who was always rushing out in the middle of the night to go to a heart attack or something, according to Norman. Then there was the man who Norman had told me had worked for an airline and who had taken on the tenancy of The Marsham Arms at Little Mayford, south of Cirencester; from Geoff, it turned out, who had been born and raised in that village. And there was a secretary who worked in London or somewhere, according to Norman.

Geoff asked whom we had met in the village. We had arrived with our urban reluctance to introduce ourselves, unreasonably relying on visions of people stopping by and introducing themselves, but it hadn't happened. We hadn't met anyone.

'That doesn't surprise me,' said Liam from behind the bar, familiar with the experience himself.

'You're not missing much,' Geoff reassured us unreassuringly. 'Have you met Proctor in Lettem House?'

We had got the impression from Douglas that the man who lived there was not Mr Proctor but a doctor, but we hadn't met him.

'He's a property developer basically,' said Geoff. 'He was the one who built all those bloody ugly houses there on the corner next to his house. You've met the vicar, I suppose?'

'Yes, he came by with a copy of the parish magazine when we moved in. We haven't seen him since.' Nor had we been to church.

'Doesn't surprise me much. When I first came here, he and I got off on a bad foot, you might say. I tried to organise a bit of a disco; you know, bussing the kids out here from Cirencester. That Stanton, he fought me every inch of the way with my licensing applications. Anyway, I was at church that Christmas with my father. You never met my father but he was a wonderful man.'

'Oh, he was a wonderful man,' added Liam.

'Stanton starts going on about Christmas and Jesus and Jesus not needing discos and all this sort of thing. It was embarrassing for me with my dad there. At the door on the way out, he shook my dad's hand and turned to me and said, "I suppose I better shake your hand too."'

The talk of the rector in the pub, and the church decoration gathering the day before, prompted our first visit to St Michael's. On Harvest Festival Sunday we walked up to the village, another world, for all its half-mile distance away.

The village had two distinct halves, and a small copse that stood between them only accentuated their separation. In the church half were most of the 'big houses'. Clustered around the late fourteenth-century church stood the castle-like manor house, Rectory Farm, with its satellite barns and cottage, and the Old Vicarage. This elegiac early-Victorian vicarage, its garden hidden by impenetrable hedges, had been sold off as a private home long ago.

In addition there were several other large houses set back on the left-hand side of the road that led to the church and which included Mrs Cholsey's less attractive 1960s Lettem Barn. Their large gardens were just so, with tall, clipped hedges and tree-lined drives, one with flowerbeds on a carefully tended suburban verge. That Sunday morning all was peaceful, only the sound of the steady scratch of a rake and the smell of burning beech leaves.

The new rectory, where Stanton lived, was a 1950s house that stood near the copse that divided the two halves of the village. Much of the garden was taken up with stabling for the tiny ponies the rector's wife and her helpers would lead past the cottage carrying underprivileged children. The rest of the garden was scattered with chicken coops, pigsties and rabbit hutches, a little farm for the village children or perhaps just a larder for the rector. A small table sat outside the gate, with eggs for sale and an honesty box. The new rectory had been built near to the church in the church half of the village, but as close to the other half without actually being in it.

As for the 'other half' of the village, it was a place that by the end of my first autumn I had difficulty even visualising. Han and I never walked up there, and rarely drove through it. There was a village hall, some Estate cottages and some council houses built after the war, but what lay beyond was not entirely clear to me. I had seen an old school building, a war memorial, some cul-de-sacs and some more council houses, but I had no sense of who lived there or how the village was laid out. With no shop or post office, we had no reason to go there and it was as anonymous and meaningless to me as it probably would have been if I were a weekender living in the twee end of the village.

Our arrival at church ill-equipped for the 'bring and share' post-service harvest lunch plunged the lady by the door into something of a fluster. In the confident manner of an Amsterdam nightclub bouncer assuming his tip, she put out her hands to receive our contribution for the table of Tupperwared and foil-wrapped food, but we had nothing. She tried to say something reassuring but terribly embarrassed for us and for herself, her words ingested themselves in her own discomfort. We loitered by the door, for some reason sure that form called for a worthy member of the congregation to identify us as newcomers and usher us in with a well-chosen question and a soft-armed welcoming steer to a pew with a view. No one greeted us and we took seats a modest five rows back but far enough forward not to be seen as lurking.

In the front pew sat a priest, introduced to the congregation by the rector as a trainee who was spending a week with 'us', finding out about the life of a parish priest. Behind him sat a couple of around our age with four young children, one a baby. The father was dressed in a tweed jacket, cords, brogues, a tie and a checked shirt. The trousers were just a little too tight and just a little too short. The mother wore a navy blue jumper, a navy blue long skirt and a long black overcoat. The children, all girls, wore navy blue too. Han nicknamed them the St John Smythington-Smythes in honour of her Australian brother-in-law who loved to use that name whenever he talked of Han and me living in the Cotswolds.

The rector was as I remembered him, only a little younger, perhaps. Clipped, public school, Stanton was so finely balanced between being aloof and warm that my first impression was that he had achieved a rather disconcerting ambiguity. I think he was a man of the Church from an older, more formal time, who perhaps struggled a little with the new twenty-first-century Church. It was as easy to imagine him being caring and kind, as it was to see him as being unintentionally scatterbrained, not sure who his flock were, their names or needs. But there was not a hint of malice or pride; he struck me, as much as I understood the phrase, as a good Christian.

He wore a microphone to address the forty-some people gathered before him in the small church. Most of the congregation were of an age that many no doubt benefited from the sound system. His service and his manner were an unfamiliar mix of Sunday chapel formality, with prayers for the Queen and her government, and a leavening of 'action hymns' and inclusive, fun, child-friendly sermon which the children loved.

He began with neither welcome nor prayer but a somewhat leaden list of un-harvest-related practical announcements that seemed ill-placed as the opening remarks of a festival. A gentleman at the back of the church was invited to tell us about a forthcoming Gilbert and Sullivan evening to take place in Cirencester.

As we stood and sang, pretending to be ploughs and scattering seed, I wondered who present worked on the land. In this Cotswold church, surrounded by acres and acres of farmland and little else, there was no sign of Norman, or of men who looked like they worked outside. The rector's sermon did refer to 'farm managers' who reported to 'him', but it wasn't clear if 'him' was Marsham or Him.

The festival was to come with lunch after the service, to be eaten on a stone seat that ran round the south aisle. Again we had our absurd preconceptions of cider and home-made apple pies, children running outside in the filtered sunlight on a stubble field, tables made of straw bales and perhaps a fiddle. Instead, it was pasta salad and cold Waitrose quiche served inside in the darkest, coldest corner of the church.

We didn't stay for lunch, but perhaps we should have. Belonging to a community means taking part it in it, but Han and I weren't there yet.

If there was an autumn festival, 'Get Twisted' the following week-end was surely it. Geoff told us he held raves in the pub's barn and he had invited us to the next one. Neither Han nor I could quite visualise what he had described taking place at his quiet, hidden pub, deep in the countryside down an unlit, unmade dirt road.

The driveway and the garden were full of the very young and the very excited, smoking, laughing and flirting as loud house music pumped viciously out of the barn opposite the pub. Outside the barn were the money-collecting and rubber-stamping bouncers, and Geoff took us in past them. One of the bouncers, dressed only in a Gloucester rugby shirt and jeans, no coat despite the cold night, short-cropped hair, his thick arms dangling from his side like a bodybuilder's, nodded good evening as we approached, and Geoff introduced us. I think that was the first time Han and I properly spoke with Spider.

The heat, the noise, the music and the dancing were as intense as at any urban club. There was hardly room to move, dancers on tables and benches that lined the walls, smoke and fluorescent lights being waved in our faces as we pushed our way to the bar. Han loved it, not without some relief at the idea there could be something as fun as this at the end of our lane. She was seized by our new life at Lettem as much as I was, but I think she needed to have just a slightly clearer glimpse of the shore as we bobbed away from the lands and lives we had known.

We were excited, after our autumn isolation, to feel all this man-made sound and energy and fun. Conscious we were a little older and a lot more sober than the crowd, we bought some drinks and downed them fast.

A tall, lean man – a little older than me, I was sure, dressed for the rave in a thick white shirt, green moleskins and walking boots – stood near the bar rolling a cigarette, moving rather than dancing to the music. I'd seen him before in the pub but he had never spoken to me.

Han and I danced and drank and talked with whoever we could above the noise of the music. Liam was there, open and engaging, and he seemed to know everyone. His parents, we learnt, were Methodist ministers and his mother worked in a Christian healing centre near Tewkesbury. He had been living in Brighton before he moved to the Cotswolds.

'You know, drugs, drink, lots of crazy problems.' One night at 4 a.m., he rang his mother. 'She was waiting by the phone. "I dreamt you would call me," she said.'

Liam moved to Gloucestershire and had lived in the village for seven years. 'Oh, you get that, do you?' he said about the parish magazine when Han mentioned it. 'When I came here, we were the gay couple who had to run after the vicar to get him to give us a copy. "I didn't think you'd be interested," he said.'

Liam pointed out the 'kids from the village', as he would collectively refer to them and their mates from town. Geoff and Spider knew they were all under-age, but it troubled Geoff not one bit; he kept a fatherly eye on them and they were always under his close supervision. The girls were all flirtatious and giggly, confident and alert to their scantily dressed teenage charms, the boys loud, or brooding and confused with the possibilities. Liam assured us it was all way beyond possibilities.

'They're all at it. Everyone's shagged everyone. It's DISGUST-ING!' he laughed.

Outside under the dazzling stars that in the city were invisible, joints were smoked and couples headed down to the canal path, there to conduct transactions, sexual or hallucinogenic and sometimes both. The headlights of arriving cars picked out the beech tree branches, and the grand oak stood floodlit up against the pub as the music thudded away in the barn. Our coming to live here had been so accidental; these new moments of happiness for us seemed somehow undeserved.

# CHAPTER 4

# RAIN

A brutal early-October gale spun and bickered across Frimley Wood, over the farm and up against the cottage. My sister Frances was visiting, and we opened the top half of the kitchen stable door to listen to the storm; the noise of the winter wind in the Big Tree snatched our shouted concerns and threw them away into the evening. If the tree fell, it would fall into Home Paddock, we hoped. Back inside we heard the chimney's lamentings, but the fire burnt strong and it was quiet in this thick-walled house, too old to be troubled by even the most evil night.

The trees on Rathbury Road could not say the same, and the branch of a large beech tree blocked Frances's way out of the village. The noise of the rain and falling branches was exciting, but later the road cleared and back by the fireside, soaked clothes drying on the Aga, I remembered our father and the fallen tree from another October gale.

The next day the storm left, but the rain stayed. It was to be the wettest November in three hundred years. It rained unrelentingly, the lane outside the cottage more waterway than road, carrying the water down to Horse Paddock Bend where it filled the dip in the road. The wet and cold drove Sukey from her spot guarding Norman's gate, inside somewhere we hoped. Everywhere was mud and rotting leaves and more mud and more leaves, the trees stripped and beaten. The rutted tracks in Frimley Wood turned to impassable ditches.

The canal, though, welcomed the rain. It filled the overgrown and neglected channel so deeply that water lapped a foot over the top of the long-broken stop-lock and covered the towpath under the railway bridge. It was a canal again, a navigable piece of water. Standing on the stone bridge and looking down the canal, one could imagine a barge of Shropshire iron or Welsh coal from the upper Severn emerging from the tunnel.

The rains brought out men with beards, anoraks and green Northleach Canal Trust sweatshirts. They would stand by the side of the canal in dreamy reflection and tell you what they knew about the canal, especially about the man who now owned this little stretch.

'A few years back, this farmer round here dammed the canal and no water could flow. He's ruined it,' said a Canal Trust member from Nailsworth. 'You're a brave man clearing his towpath.'

Landowners like Norman, through whose land the path of the canal went, were one of the principal obstacles to the Trust's dream of seeing the canal fully restored, but what this member had said wasn't true. The water could pass under this dam, which was in fact more of a causeway built by Norman to cross the canal, or so he said. There was a pipe underneath it and water the other side of it, and I offered to show this to the man. As we walked, I asked him why he thought I was brave clearing the path.

'Don't you know? Up until three years ago this path was completely overgrown. We had great battles with the farmer to get it opened. He owns it, you see. A terrible man. He's terrifying, he is. Foul-mouthed if he catches you off the footpath. You want to be careful,' he confided, lowering his voice. 'He's got eyes in the back of his head. He just comes out of nowhere. You won't hear or see him until he's there, right by you.'

A Yeti-like figure emerged up ahead. He had come out of the bushes and stood on the path. It was Norman. He took one look, turned and vanished round a bend ahead.

'I told you. He's got a sixth sense, he has. He comes and goes like a ghost.'

We walked on to the dam, but the ghost was nowhere to be seen.

The water had flowed through the dam and we continued to the bridge by the Lambing Sheds. It was here that the canal disappeared into Rathbury Wood, and the public footpath climbed up off the towpath and followed the edge of the trees. I asked my companion why the path here no longer went alongside the canal.

'That's because his land ends here. The other side of the bridge, the canal belongs to this bloke called Goonetilleke. Goony everyone calls him. He's Sri Lankan.'

'Oh.'

'That's why the farmer got so upset you know. He didn't see why the footpath should be open on his land but not on Goony's. It's terrible what this farmer's done,' he said, pointing at the old tyres, baler-twine and black plastic tipped over the bridge into the canal, which here was empty of water and any dreams of Severn traffic.

The winter farm was sodden and muddy and Douglas moved around the fields dressed as a North Sea deckhand. Norman just looked endlessly wet but was never deterred by the rain. My stoic neighbour remained both fascinating and mysterious, as was his life and its cycles and those of his land. He would leave his cottage every morning and walk past our windows up the track and on to the lane that led to the yard, never even once casting a curious eye towards our house; the same when he would return at lunchtime, always at more or less the same time, although he didn't carry a watch. Up the track he would go again in the afternoon but we would seldom see him returning at night, not a light nor a noise to indicate his homecoming.

Norman entered his yard through a badly hung door that led into a long low barn that ran down the side of the lane a couple of hundred metres or so from the cottage. Behind it could be seen more barns and the other two cottages which had originally made up Parish Farm and which, like ours, had once been the homes of the workers of Lettem House and its land. They stood the other side of a deep-in-cow-shit yard and had views out over Bee Copse and the Humpty Dumps; but the cottages were only just visible from the end of our garden. In one of these lived Stephanie with her small child, in the other, we didn't know. Stephanie was young and pretty with long dark hair and a sad face. Once a day she would come down the lane carrying a meal. Her rent included the task of cooking one meal a day for Norman.

What took place behind that limping door into the yard, or what was there, few people knew. There was no reason to enter nor invitation to do so, and the same was true of Norman's house. From

Lettem, looking out over Home Paddock, we could see Norman or Douglas drive one seen-better-days tractor or another up the track that climbed over the Humpty Dumps. Once through the gate they were gone, unless they were working in the two fields that could be seen from the garden, that ran down to the canal. We had little idea what they did out there in the fields, either. Twice a day, cows that didn't look like dairy cows were led to the yard for what could only be milking. In winter this took place in the dark, and on a moonless night, standing on the terrace, there would be just the sound of the moving cows but no sign of Norman or a flashlight. He was presumably out there, but gliding, invisible and silent, with his supernatural night vision.

The yard was an alluring place, known by its comings and goings, smells and sounds, but in my mind it had no interior. What did they do all day, where were they, what was up there?

Curiosity finally overcame me and I dangerously took a walk through the yard, approaching on my return from a run along the canal and back over the fields to the Humpty Dumps. Like my illegal crossing of the park by bike, my straying off the footpaths was, to me, a seemingly harmless and altogether too enticing prospect; I was still very much the townie.

I had always cut off the track before reaching the yard, climbing the wall into Home Paddock and towards our garden wall, but this time I kept going, up to the broken gate held up with string and wire that marked the rear entrance to the yard.

The yard was centred round a large Cotswold-stone barn, with tall, wooden double doors stretching nearly the entire height of the building's two extended gable porches. Like all of Norman's gates or barn doors, they were broken. The barn was connected to the lower stone buildings that ran the length of the lane. On the lane-side they were windowless and fortress-like, but on the yard-side one could see through collapsed doors and open windows into cowsheds thick with manure or into open barns crammed full with every manner of stuff: old carts, tractors and tools, an engine-stripped van, ancient clothes ripped for rags, sheep hurdles and water carriers, broken mopeds and bikes, fertiliser bags and open paint cans, syringes and shearing equipment, old generators and junk; a half-century of working life.

In the yard itself stood a large Dutch barn with a corrugated-iron roof and high open sides, stacked with hay; but the roof of a smaller lean-to barn was hanging by a single remaining beam and threatened to fall on to the rusting hulk of a combine harvester underneath it.

Indeed, none of the buildings in the yard was looking its best. They ranged from the fully collapsed to the slowly collapsing.

Behind the Dutch barn, and separated from the main yard by a feral forest of nettles and brambles, was a paddock full of smashed cars, half-stripped Land Rovers, vans, ploughs and unused machinery. If it was unrepairable or unusable, here seemed to be its final rusting place.

Scrap metal, wood, asbestos sheets, corrugated iron, punctured tyres and the old and the broken lay everywhere in the yard. One large pile of rubbish was mostly plastic: empty feed and fertiliser sacks and twisted heaps of black plastic once used to wrap large round bales. Against the wall of the main barn, growing up out of high nettles and weeds, stood pieces of rotting timber, broken posts and gate rails, put aside long ago in the hope they might come in useful one day. A corroded diesel tank sat on a pile of stone, dripping fuel on to the ground. The remains of knocked-over sticky oil cans and splashes of diesel mixed with the rain water and cow shit creating whirling rainbows in the muddy puddles.

The yard was faultless in all that it was not: sold off and converted into executive barn homes in a picture-postcard rendition of a Cotswolds that never was. This was a working yard, and among all that chaos was Norman's own precise order of value, which was that everything has some value. It was not how I would have my yard, but it was not my yard.

As the days shortened into stumpy reminders of autumn evenings sitting on the terrace, we often splashed down the flooded lane and branch-strewn way to the pub. We sat by the fire in the main bar and put names to faces, and faces to names, slowly acquiring the little details and moonshine that filled out our small world map. There was Geoff and the tiny, ever-friendly, ever-smoking, ever-busy Peg. Peg, we finally learnt somewhere along the way, was not Geoff's wife, but the pub manager.

We were yet to meet Geoff's actual partner Laura, who lived much of the time in Portugal, holidayed in Florida and came home

to 'do the books'. I guessed that doing the books was about recon-
ciling, for the benefit of the taxman, Peg's efficient management
with Geoff's rather casual relationship with the till.

May was the chef, and she was large in every way, enjoying her
food, her drinks, her laughs and her life. She came from Indonesia.
The rhythms of her mother tongue had mixed with the sound
of Gloucestershire, producing a voice that was both exotic and
familiar. May had originally come to England to work as a nanny for
a Member of Parliament, and somehow she had never returned.

On Fridays, Saturdays, Sundays and a Tuesday or a Wednesday,
Spider, the bouncer from the rave, would be there. Spider was perhaps thirty, wore his hair cut para-commando short and worked on a
farm 'over Chedworth way'. Rain or shine, Spider walked to the pub
from the village, hands never in his pockets, chest out, back straight,
arms held out in a slightly ape-like curl, a Gloucester, England or
Lions rugby shirt always on his back.

Spider was proud of Gloucestershire. An 'old boy' who had served
with the Gloucesters in Korea had given him his regimental tie and
Spider wore it to the old boy's funeral.

'"What are you wearing that tie for?" these old Gloucester boys
asked me. "He was fucking proud of it," I said. "He gave it to me.
Now I'm fucking proud of it," I said.'

On November the fifth Han and I went outside the pub and
stood with a small gaggle of drunken students from the local agricultural college to watch fireworks launched into the wet night by
Spider and Geoff. We seemed such a modest group of people for
such a generous display. The explosions lit the tops of the beech
trees against a black sky of low, skittish clouds, and the noise echoed
deep into Frimley Wood. Back inside, Han was asked to be the
timekeeper for a quiz between two teams, one representing The
Leggers', and I was asked to read the questions. We sat and drank
in the snug bar, and in so doing passed a certain threshold.

The pub had two bars, and two lives. The main bar received
the agricultural college students ('the aggies'), the passing trade of
ramblers and canal explorers and the weekenders who sat there, like
us, with their weekend guests; but it was the snug bar that was the
inner sanctum of the pub. It was here that the familiar faces would
be found. Spider and Knoxey (the name nearly all the locals used
for Geoff, after his surname Knox) were the two fixed points of

reference, Knoxey eating his dinner in the evening, offering his red wine and cheese, Spider at the bar with his Becks. 'All right, Spides!?' Knoxey would say when Spider came in. 'All right,' Spider would mutter back gruffly, stretching his neck to work out an ever-present back problem. On a big night, life would spill and mingle across these two spaces but it was clear which zone was for the regulars. The snug bar served variously as Geoff's and Laura's dining room, a place for staff to come and sit while on the job, drinks always on the house for them, and occasionally a refuge from the term-time aggies with their loud voices and ways.

Apart from Spider, two of the main stalwarts were Liz and Dave. Liz was an attractive, slightly scruffy woman with a big smile and a deep voice. Leant forward, with one long, thin leg tucked in over the other, a pint of beer in front of her and her outdoor hands always rolling or smoking a cigarette, she was sometimes a little nervous, sometimes very mellow, but always friendly and chatty. She lived in a rented semi-detached house next to a horse yard she managed, along with her spaniels and her boyfriend Jeremy.

Dave was in his forties and lived in a rented cottage in Tidcombe. A witty and entertaining ex-solicitor from Wales, he was a big man who now worked as a law lecturer at a local college. He doubled up as the local point-to-point, agricultural show and polo match commentator. He always seemed to be wearing rather expensive-looking 'country-casuals' which I think he got via some sort of promotional deal with a gentlemen's outfitters in Cirencester.

With Knoxey as patriarch, the pub had all the appeal and foibles of an extended family; many of the regulars and the people who worked there were also the friends and relatives of other people who worked there, especially Peg's and May's. Lennie, in his early twenties, who worked behind the bar with his girlfriend Nancy, lived in Cirencester and was a friend of Peg's son. May's teenage daughter Kelly was often at the pub, waiting tables and occasionally drinking in front of the bar she was too young, legally, to serve behind. She was a tall girl with her mother's exotic looks, her father Bob's Gloucestershire accent and both her parents' laughter.

After the quiz, we talked of the village and 'Luddie', as Knoxey called Norman. It was said that Norman was still an excellent boxer, and a top-class runner when he was at school in Northleach. His brother, they were sure, was a bank manager; they were sure, too, that chickens used to live in their kitchen and that the farm would be sold; they were sure of all of this just as they were sure that Goony – as everyone referred to Goonetilleke, but never to his face – or Marsham would get hold of it. I said that that would be a shame, that I liked Norman and having him as my neighbour. I don't think anyone had ever said that before, judging from their bemused reaction. Does Norman ever come to the pub? I asked. No, never. He's a hermit, isn't he?

The speculation about the farm was troubling. We had seen Norman's eldest brother Malcolm when we had met to talk about our shared septic tank.

'It's a very simple system designed for farm cottages,' he had explained, implying that our lifestyle of dishwashers and clothes washers and daily showers was beyond what the tank could be expected to carry. 'We were fixing it with your predecessor,' he added, reminding us that we were but the latest of those who would come and go and worry about septic tanks and eyesore caravans before returning to where we belonged, places with town sewage systems.

After we had finished inspecting the tank, I told him I had been sorry to hear about his father's death. I hoped it wouldn't change anything here, I had said.

'Well, we'll have to see about that. It's the solicitors, you see. The solicitors are the hard men.'

Winter was long and dark and wetter still. We were invited by old friends of mine, whose parents lived nearby, to attend a local hunt ball. In a dinner jacket that didn't fit, I drove our scrappy little car to a marquee in the middle of a muddy field and we parked alongside Range Rovers and BMWs and entered another English rural world. I had lukewarm associations with the idea of a ball, the result of many a teenage outing: staying in houses with impossibly soft mattresses, slightly damp sheets and coarse blankets; where the hosts only occasionally put on the central heating despite the fact they could seemingly afford it. Han had Australian memories of drunken 'Bachelors and Spinsters' balls and was sceptical, too, about going.

Norman had told me he wasn't that fussed about the hunt – they seldom caught a fox, but it was something he had to support, for reasons both practical and political. 'It's about doing what you want on your own land,' he would say. 'You can't 'ave 'em telling you you can't do this, you can't do that, it's not right.' Pause. 'And they take away my dead animals for the hounds.'

This was the Beaufort Hunt Ball, and although I didn't meet anyone who looked like they had had a dead animal hauled away recently, our table was a fun mix of local hunt supporters, if perhaps not actual members, and their guests from London. As the evening progressed and the tables broke up, Han and I circulated, even though we didn't know anyone there, save our hosts.

At the bar I started chatting with a woman, younger than me, who lived in Hammersmith, Gloucestershire at the weekends. She immediately asked me what I did and where we lived. I told of my pottering around, pretending to be a 'consultant', some efforts to be 'creative' and slow days. She held my arm, leant in and told me confessionally how her husband got up at 5 to be at work by 6.30. He was a banker. He came home between 8 and 9 p.m., later on Thursdays. The children were asleep by then. On the weekends in Gloucestershire (his wife, the children and the nanny went ahead on Fridays after school) he slept until noon. Her need for something, *anything*, seemed visceral. I thought of my life at Lettem and I didn't know what to say to her.

At dinner, the conversation had been much like that at any 'smart' London dinner party might be, jovial and light, but there were fragments that I overheard as I moved around the marquee that I hadn't heard in nearly twenty years. I was struck by their brashness, how little their tone had changed when so much of the rest of England seemingly had. Most of the people were very loud and self-assured. Nothing was being said that needed to be whispered.

'Anyway, this horrible, grockley-looking little man and his family park outside our house in their Fiesta and start having an ice cream.'

'Unbelievable. Who do these people think they are?'

'Exactly. Daddy went up to them and asked them to move. Do you know what he said? "When me and my family have finished our ice creams." So Daddy hit their car!'

A man in his late forties asks what *I DO*, always the first question, and seldom posed with much finesse. Maybe it was having lived in places where this question might emerge mostly after at least a few minutes of conversation, and without the full frontal pigeonholing-ness of it all, that made it jar.

I said to the man how busy my days seemed to be.

'*Really*? How can you fill them? Does enough happen in your life down here?' he asked.

As we drove home, Han compared the evening with our time in Paris and asked me why so many of the people she had met had posed similar sorts of opening questions in the same sharp way as the man I had encountered.

It was especially a certain type of older woman, someone whom she had never met before, which she found the trickiest in parrying their eager opening thrusts. She was reminded of younger versions of this type of English person that she had met in France, frequently Eurostar weekenders, whose first question was often, '*So, how's your French?*' She had answered this question several times at the ball when asked about her time living in Paris. It was, she felt, in Paris and in England, more about their determination to find out if she was one of '*us*' (i.e. that her French was poor and she had no French friends), than a gentle discussion about living abroad and having to use another language. Her speaking no French and it all being a terrible problem would have been much more reassuring, just as it would have been if I had replied to the man that I was bored stupid and deeply regretted moving to the countryside.

Being invited to the Hunt Ball was a reminder that a parallel social universe existed all around us at Lettem, even if it remained largely invisible. Dave the law lecturer would speak jokingly of a 'county set', but Han and I, now reminded that of course it did exist, instead spoke of the world of the 'supers' when we wanted to shorthand the type of people we thought he meant. As in 'Yes, that would be *super*,' or 'Oh gosh, yes, you must meet them, they're *super*.'

Actually the term was just a well-meaning joke among Han's Australian siblings to shorthand a wide array of Brits, known separately and at various times as the nobility, gentry, the upper middle class and even Sloanes; but who were in all cases (young or old, rich or of more modest means), posh, public-school-educated people who would all agree that posh is not a term they would use themselves, except ironically.

It was as a minor super that I had grown up, and our credentials that would allow us to enter this world (special dispensation for

Antipodeans) were in order – other exceptions perhaps being made for people of some quirky interest. Older class divisions of course remained. Han and I were probably just being naïve in our surprise that in the twenty-first century, the world I remembered of the rural 'supers' still appeared to be firmly defined by 'background'. Neither wealth, profession, intellect nor affability seemed to be much of an entrée.

Neither of us felt any special need to be a part of it; in general they weren't people whom Han could easily relate to, coming from Sydney and the life she had led there. As for me, during my many years living abroad, I had been struck every time I had returned to London by how many of my childhood peers seemingly led such socially monochrome lives (segregated drinks with work colleagues excluded), despite no Richard Curtis *Notting Hill* movie being complete without Hugh Grant having a gay, a black, a disabled and a working-class friend. I perhaps unreasonably believed that the socially static situation in the countryside could only be worse, and as a result I approached any invitation into this world with unjustified trepidation.

As it happened, we had little occasion to meet these people: we didn't hunt, neither did we have young children whom we would send to the private schools that served them. Nor did they hang out with Norman and Douglas and Spider, and nor did they, by and large, come to the pub ('Admittedly some of them aren't very ecumenical in their social views,' as Dave once put it). As a result our contacts were limited. We saw their children, students at the Agricultural College, but they went home at weekends and holidays and generally avoided the snug bar. My mother and her friends often mentioned that there were *lots* of interesting people of our age we could meet (specifics were always somewhat vague), but again we weren't sure these dinner parties were quite our thing, however uninformed – perhaps even prejudiced – our views were.

Back at Lettem, away from the hunt balls and glimpses of these other social circles, England seemed kinder and calmer. There we didn't see the people in the big houses in the villages I ran through, or listen to the pantomime hostility to politicians of every persuasion or people who stuck their necks out ('So what makes *you* think *you*

can build the fastest round-the-world yacht *ever*?'); an aggression that seemed to shape the *Today* programme on Radio 4 and from there, as I loosely imagined it, all the media and the country itself.

Mostly I saw Norman, and Douglas, who would stop by with copies of mountain-biking magazines and talk bike parts. Apart from them we saw only Knoxey and the small cast of people working and drinking at the pub: the regulars, the occasionals and single conversations with the passing-throughs. The young kids from the village would hang out in the bar by the fruit machine, still only faces and nods rather than names and hellos. And in the lane I would see the old man who shuffled along past the cottage once a day, ruffled and dishevelled, with his little dog. My world here was small and I liked that very much.

Standing in the rain one day, as we helped Norman herd some escaped cattle, Mr Proctor from Lettem House and I blocked cars on the lane as Norman brought them on.

'I'm terribly concerned, of course, about Norman, terribly so,' Proctor said as we waited. He was extremely super and probably in his seventies. He didn't know my name, though I supposed he knew who I was. 'I don't know if you would know this, but he works all the time. The vicar and I wanted to send him on holiday to New Zealand. I was going to pay, but he wouldn't go.'

The cows in, I asked Proctor and Norman inside for a drink. It was just before Christmas and I felt festive. Proctor declined but Norman, to my surprise, accepted.

'Thank you,' he said quietly. As we walked down the lane I asked him if he wanted to make it lunch.

'Thank you.'

Greeted warmly by Han, he came by a little later wearing neatly pressed grey flannel trousers, a clean shirt and a round-necked navy blue jumper, all rather new-looking. On his feet he wore a pair of lace-up shoes. It was a tidy transformation of some contrast. He lowered his head instinctively as he passed under our low doors, and for the first time he sat in our sitting room by the fire, drinking a glass of beer. He sat steady and sure, his hands face down on the chair arms. He seemed so gentle and just ever so slightly formal.

'Proctor seems a nice man,' I ventured.

'Yes. He's all right. Wants to buy the farm. Offered a million pounds, he did.'

Norman wasn't going anywhere, least of all to New Zealand, not with the brothers around and a county full of property developers.

Over lunch he told Han and me in his calm, matter-of-fact way where Mrs Bruce used to have her fireplace in our dining room and how he sat on the window bench as a child and watched her knit as she watched over him. We talked about the farm and the weather, and Sneaky the cow.

Sneaky was always getting out. There'd be a knock at the door and there we'd find a terrified and hysterical town-dweller on his way to a country pub for a 'ploughman's lunch' who had seen an ESCAPED COW! Sneaky would be out again and Norman would be nowhere to be seen. The closer to Christmas, the more she escaped; perhaps she thought she was a turkey.

I loved getting Sneaky back in, pulling on my boots and getting my stick and chasing her down the lane, working my way round her, holding up a car, tapping her haunches and shouting, 'Get on there, you bastard!' Sometimes Sneaky would go back into her field through a gate I had opened, sometimes she just jumped over the crumbling tops of Norman's drystone walls or crashed through a hedge.

Normally she'd escape at dusk, about the time of day I might have been in a business lounge checking that my ticket had been registered for frequent-flyer points.

The hand-painted Christmas tree signs pointing to the house of a local man who sold them were the village's equivalent of Christmas lights – the first reminder that Christmas was coming. You could buy your Christmas tree in the supermarket car parks but driving along the Cotswold lanes to his welcoming village home was more of a *Christmas Carol* expedition. His garden was full of trees, and mistletoe hung from the home-made hanging racks leant up against the Cotswold-stone walls, surrounded by buckets of freshly cut red-berried holly from secret corners of the local woods.

The pub's Christmas dinner in mid-December was held in the barn and Liam, dressed up in drag to shock and entertain us, acted as our hostess. We sat with a group of women on a girls' night out who welcomed us. One, a local farmer's wife, told me she hated farming and married her husband only on the condition that he wouldn't farm. Happily for her, he and his brothers were busily selling their land to developers. She was going to get a nice new five-bedroom house out of it.

We ate prawn cocktails and school-dinner turkey with vegetables, Christmas pudding and rapidly congealing custard. The entertainment was Kotswolde Karaoke and, pulled up by our drag-queen compère, I sang 'Perfect Day' by Lou Reed and Han, 'Killing Me Softly' (Fugees version). The singer after me, out on the office Christmas party of a local Northleach firm – his case pending, we were told, for intent to supply Ecstasy and spiking a girl's drink with it – sang much better than me.

Han decided to call it a night. She was tired, but told me to stop on. I walked home later, happily pissed and stumbling up the dark lane with Spider. Spider spent most of his days driving tractors and combines, the work of most farmhands in the now mostly arable Cotswolds. He lived at home with his parents in a late-forties ex-council house in the village. He wanted to buy somewhere, but he couldn't afford it and there was no way he would live in town. The sort of landowners for whom he worked had long since sold off or rented out any housing once given (or provided at peppercorn rents) to their labourers, and the Marsham cottages were rented on an open market that didn't appear to favour farmworkers over white-collar workers, at least the ones I knew of. Lennie passed by in his old Mini and scooped us up and dropped me off home. Under acres of liquid stars, I stood wobbling on the terrace before making it inside and falling asleep in front of the fireplace's dying embers.

At church on Christmas day it was strangely quiet. I remember a Christmas morning past, not wanting to go to church, my older brother persuading me I should; could I have been four or five, he seven or eight?

Stanton informed us that it was the first time he had done a Communion on Christmas Day in our village, and hadn't known whether 'to expect ten or a hundred, but I think we have ended up somewhere between the two'. In all there were six families present, one of them the rector's and heavily represented, plus a scattering of widows, and Han and I before we drove to my mother's house for lunch. The rector's two daughters were home for Christmas. They read from the Bible and sang beautiful descants and a duet of 'The Holly and the Ivy' accompanied by the organ.

After weeks of dripping grey, the sun came out on Boxing Day and Sukey hobbled out to see what was about. Skies were blue and the ground was frozen. The next day snow fell and Parish Farm woke up white. Standing at the wall under the Big Tree we stared in cold, speechless wonder. The world was motionless, save for its sunrise, a bowl of blue-rimmed orange that slowly climbed up over Bee Copse.

Two inches of unmelting snow lay on the ground, and in its traces we learnt where our cats went at night and how close the foxes came to the garden. It was a precise map of everything that happened out here in the dark and the early dawn, out of sight and unreported; a thousand comings and goings of foxes, badgers and birds, cats, dogs and deer. Where we thought of only one route past our house, the snow showed a myriad of intricate paths and diversions, main thoroughfares and the amblings of solitary travellers.

My own feet scrunched in the snow beneath me as I ran, my frosty breath blowing before me, my fingertips cold, my heart excited. A landscape now so familiar, so known, was transformed in this most comprehensive of redecorations that left no inch unchanged, and with the cold of the day, there the snow stayed.

This was no snow to be seen briefly on the way to the Metro, the pavements already turning grey when you surfaced from an underground journey. This snow sat untouched and inviting, ready to be run on under a brilliant sky with the excitement of a child, not gazed at wistfully from an office window, wondering if it would be there at the weekend. Damp autumn doubts were gone, every decision made faultless because it had led us here.

Frimley Wood was stilled by the weight of its snow-covered branches, with sudden quick flurries of crisp powder when one of them could no longer support its burden. Even the thinnest of twigs would bear its thin ridge of white above its brown underbelly. The long straight tracks that ran through the woods stood as white-turfed fairways, the deer easier to see against the snow as they moved through the trees.

Norman said he didn't much mind the snow; perhaps it was a relief from the daily mud. The cows still had to be fed and this was no amount of snow that would prevent that. The hay would be tossed on the snow and the cows would tramp over to eat, clouds of frosty air from their big, wet noses. What Norman made of us as we made a snowman and threw snowballs at passing cars, he didn't say.

At the pub we warmed up in the snug bar and hoped and hoped for a blizzard that would cut us off. Knoxey told us of the time when the snow fell so deep it filled the deep-cut lanes and how the pub was cut off for days.

'Oh, I hate the snow,' he said to my surprise. I thought everyone loved the snow. Then he remembered a story about his father and forgot the empty car park and the quiet till, and smiled with the pleasure of it.

His father had come home on leave from the First World War. It was winter and he arrived by train at night to the now long-gone Cirencester station. His home was in Little Mayford, five miles away, and he would walk. He gathered his kitbag, got off the train and stepped on to a platform covered in thick winter snow. There on the platform, he saw a single set of footprints leading out of the station and into town, heading in his direction. Gathering his things and hoisting his bag over his shoulder, he set off after them. It was cold and late and the town was quiet and empty. He lost the trail as the single footprints mingled and merged with a hundred others, but leading south out of town on the lane to his village, he picked up the track again. The footprints of a single person continued to lead all the way through the night, an invisible man marching a few steps in front of him. He thought of his brother, whom he hadn't seen since he'd emigrated to Canada, where it snowed all the time, and he remembered the nights they had made the walk home together from town, penniless but warm with beer and tales of their evening.

When he reached his village, he was sure he would say goodbye to the gentle support of the invisible companion who had walked with him and eased his solitude, but to his great surprise the tracks turned off the main road, crossed the bridge over the brook and continued up the narrow, steep lane into the very village that was his home. The footprints led to a garden gate, his garden gate, and a front door, his front door. He went inside the house and there, sitting in the kitchen, was his émigré brother as his mother cooked him bacon and eggs. He had joined up, crossed back over the Atlantic with a

Canadian regiment, fought in France and taken his leave back in Gloucestershire at the exact same time, on the exact same night, carried by the exact same train as the brother who thought he would never see him again.

Back at the cottage we sat outside at the ice-frozen table, snow brushed off the chairs. Han and I talked about the English health system we had returned to and what lay ahead. We very badly wanted a child, but still we were waiting. We had had tests in Paris, we had had tests now in Cheltenham. And nothing. Nothing wrong, but nothing going right.

All the time working in a city and travelling and flying, there had been this sense that there was something out there that made me too sick to have babies. Looking out over the snow-covered Home Paddock, I didn't feel I could be ailing now.

# CHAPTER 5

# ENGLAND

Laura, Knoxey's partner, had returned from Portugal for Christmas. She was warm and friendly and called everyone darling. Like Knoxey, she laughed a lot, and like him said 'Love it' when something made her laugh, clasping her hands and beaming. Her winter tan, fine looks and elegant jewellery gave the snug bar a touch of sophistication and gentility it sometimes lacked, without in any way tempering the banter and consumption habits. She was the young woman in the portrait that hung above the fireplace.

At a dinner party Geoff and Laura held at the pub, we sat at a long table laid out in the snug bar, the food cooked by May and served by one of the girls who worked there. That Laura and Geoff were so independent made their closeness as a couple seem even tighter. Geoff was a man so very much at ease with himself and his life, made all the more attractive because I felt that this had not always been so. A woman married to one of the pub's regular quiz participants told Han that Laura was eighty; that she had been married to one of the Marsham family who lived in a big house in Little Mayford; that Knoxey had been her driver, and that the Estate had given Laura 'The Leggers'' as a divorce settlement. Later that winter someone told me with equally inaccurate conviction that Knoxey had been her butler, not her chauffeur, when he was sixteen, and it wasn't at Little Mayford but at another village. I doubted any of it was true. I had not ever imagined Laura could even be sixty.

On New Year's Eve, Knoxey and Spider set off fireworks at midnight. The jukebox was turned up, chairs and tables were pushed aside and a dance floor materialised for an exuberant night of drinking and dancing.

The agricultural students and the weekend explorers were gone for Christmas. The pub was left to its locals, the kids from the village, Kelly and their friends out from town, and friends of the pub from further afield, like the couple from Cheltenham who had come back to the pub they had courted in when they were married to other people and hiding their affair.

Han and I met John, a gamekeeper-cum-drystone-waller who lived in the village.

'I saw him looking at me,' his Canadian girlfriend shouted at us above the noise of the music; they had met at a Leggers' rave when she had come down from London one weekend. 'Then he just came over and kissed me and that was that.'

'Yeah,' said John, 'I looked at her, thought she looks a bit of all right and I went over and kissed her.'

John lived in an isolated rented Estate cottage down a long track on the far side of the village, which he shared with a bloke called Tom, whom he presumed I knew but whom neither Han nor I had met. Another old Estate cottage he knew of in the area was rented, or had been sold, to an aromatherapist who was said to spend a great deal of his spare time out and about driving one of his collection of four-wheel drives to take part in various pheasant shoots and other field sports. Han said that was a first for her: a field sports devotee aromatherapist, but so it was.

'Hardly anybody works for the Estate any more, not full-time on the land at least. It's all machines now so they rent the cottages to anyone. You don't even have to work for the Estate,' John told me at the bar. 'To tell you the truth, I don't know if there are many country people left.'

Han and I walked home at three, weaving under the stars, and made snowballs in the garden, giggling and waiting to ambush revellers coming up the lane back to the village. I think of New Years past: in Amsterdam, my ears ringing and the streets red with the paper detritus of a million firecrackers; in a bar in Spain, served free drinks by the Dutch owner because I spoke to him in Dutch. I think of cities and crowds.

In the cold, still night we hear the voices and laughter of our intended victims far out in snow-covered fields, and realise they have gone the back way, through the woods and up behind the church.

The snow did melt but the winter went on. However, with the New Year came invitations. Whatever we had done, or whatever period of requisite time had passed, they marked an acceptance of some sort.

Some came from the pub and those who had now accepted us as a part of their community; some from the big houses, from people who thought it might be time to see if we might be part of theirs. And so we were to see more closely what to me had been the forgotten, to Han the suspected and to everyone else it seemed, simply how it was: that our part of rural England had not one community, but at least two. These two seldom met, save for one to clean the other's houses or at a scattering of village festivals and events, participation in which was no longer for everyone the intuitive act it once was.

From the village came an invitation 'for drinks' from an elderly spinster. She was the friend of a friend's mother, with whom she had served in the Wrens in the Second World War. They had met in 1943 on a train en route to their training in Perth, and had served together in an old Napoleonic-era fort looking out over Milford Haven, communicating in Morse with the convoys and their escorts who crept out into cold Atlantic seas and returned battered and thinned.

'I can still remember the call sign for Milford Haven, you know,' she told me.

Miss Dibden's family had lived in this village where she was born – gentry they called them in those days, a term Norman liked to use, nostalgically and with a glint of irony in his smile. Her brother had died in France and his name was on the war memorial next to the cul-de-sac that was built in the gardens of her family home when it was sold off. Miss Dibden, still in the village, still alone and unmarried, now lived in a seventies bungalow filled with the paintings and furniture of a life that was gone. Yes, she knew the Cholseys who used to live at Lettem House. She and her brother had been great friends with their son, and he had died, too; two young men from two Cotswold gentry families from the same small village.

We drank sherry and ate little pieces of sliced bread with salmon on them, and crisps passed around in a small silver bowl. I wondered if she and the boys had ever walked down the lane and had a drink at The Leggers' or met for tennis in the grounds of Lettem House before they went away and died.

Miss Dibden had wanted to introduce us to some people from the village, she had said. There to meet us were a couple in their fifties, the Larches, who lived in Lettem Barn, which the second Mrs Cholsey had built and moved into when she finally sold Lettem House, empty of its male heir. I had the impression that Mrs Cholsey had either sold it to the Larches and moved on, or had died.

Miss Dibden told us that Peter and Penelope Larch had added greatly to the village. Fresh blood, new ideas, energy. Even though they had lived in the village for just three years, Simon, who had retired here after a career in management with an engineering company, I think it was, was already a churchwarden and 'very active', as well as being a parish councillor. I had seen him driving his Land Rover down to the canal, where he used to walk his Labrador. Penny had generously taken over the editing of the parish magazine.

'It was a dreadful rag before she took it over,' Peter said proudly, in his burgundy cords, tweed jacket and tie, 'and now it's wizard, twenty-eight pages, isn't that right?'

'Well, twenty, I think,' said Penny modestly, with a kind smile. Penny looked older and tired; she had not been well I found out later.

'Last night we spent all evening batting ideas around for the next edition, you know. It gets quite heated sometimes,' he told us.

It was a marvellous village. A few old stick-in-the-muds fighting progress, of course, like his idea to erect a mobile telephone mast on the church tower (which had stood there for six hundred years before he arrived), but generally very nice people.

'Penelope is a wizard gardener,' he said. 'She brought with her from her mother's garden all our cuttings, and it is just marvellous what she has done in three years.'

The garden did look lovely, Han and I agreed.

'Have you met any nice people?' he asked.

Yes, Han told him, but he didn't seem to know any of the people she mentioned, and I had the feeling he meant people more like him.

'And Norman, of course,' Han said.

Norman he did know, by reputation.

'A *very* strange chap,' Peter pronounced. 'He can actually *talk*, can he?'

Yes, he can talk.

'We must get you over for supper and introduce you to some people, mustn't we, darling?'

'Yes, we must,' she said. They were very friendly and open and in charge.

The Larches were on the phone within the week.

'Michael is hosting a bit of a do for the Conservatives next Friday. Fund-raising sort of thing. I do hope you can come. Local great and the good, got to work jolly hard to get this lot out,' Penelope said, referring to the upcoming election. 'Thought you might like to join us for dinner afterwards. Our MEP is coming too, you know.'

'I'm sorry, er, Michael ...?'

'Proctor, Michael Proctor, I'm sure you know him, lives at Lettem House.'

People making assumptions about our political loyalties was something neither Han nor I were quite up to speed on; at that moment I was so thrown I didn't know what to say without appearing rude. I presumed the invitation had been made because we were thought to know Mr Proctor and that we were naturally supporters of the Conservatives, despite the fact Penelope and I had never talked politics.

'It's jacket and tie, by the way,' she said.

We couldn't make 'the do' but we were able to make it to dinner. Strangely, for a dinner with our local MEP and her agent, we didn't talk politics during the entire evening, except briefly and privately with the Tory MEP. I told her we used to live in Brussels and that in all my time of living there, and in Amsterdam and Paris, I never once met that Continental bogeyman the Tories liked to speak of (of which there were apparently whole nations) – someone who genuinely believed in or wanted a federal European superstate.

'Yes, I agree,' she said.

I asked her why, then, the Tory party claimed these sorts of people were everywhere and she smiled and pointed out that Penelope was ushering us through to dinner.

There was no need to talk politics any further because our politics were a given. Instead, we talked a lot about the Second World War, seated at a dining table under a large, heavily framed painting of a Lancaster bomber that dominated the wood-panelled dining room, with well-polished naval swords and framed medals and Second World War military paraphernalia decorating the hallway that led to it. Peter told us how his father had won bravery medals serving with the Royal Air Force in the Far East, and Proctor told of how he had taken part in a landing party to secure the Cocos Islands.

'We were all blacked up, charging up the beach, machine-guns in hand and there was some Aussie air force chap who said, "Glad you could make it for dinner." That was a cock-up to end all cock-ups.'

Proctor didn't address me throughout dinner. The MEP looked tired and bored, and her overweight agent sat mute and rigid. He was from the Midlands and one of Thatcher's new Tories, and he looked sullen and uncomfortable in the rural grandee heartlands.

We set off for home, walking down their drive, leaving behind the crude glare of the security light that lit their Sunday-best garden, and wove, slightly pissed, up the lane. It was crisp-cold, the star-stippled sky above and layered darkness around us. Somewhere out there we could hear Norman's tractor, the sound of its clunky, unmuffled exhaust sliding sharp through the frosty air. The cows in the yard mooed and stomped and splashed in their shit. Norman was often out past midnight without any lights, chugging around. It seemed normal.

As we walked home I thought back to the ball and birthday dinner parties of my late teens, where we sat in rooms like that dressed up in black tie and passing the port. My friend Guy looks around a dining table and wonders if we all realise that there isn't a single boy there who hasn't 'got off' with Clemy Nicks. Everyone is laughing, the girls too. There was nothing to talk about, everything was normal. Our families were all normal, even mine I supposed.

It was presumed, of course, by old friends of mine who now happened to live in the area that we would want to meet other people 'like us'. Han wasn't quite sure what 'like us' meant, and again she would gently take the mickey out of me. Aside from Miss Dibden's invitation there came other early probes by people in the area who were the friends or acquaintances of people we knew, thoughtfully put in touch with us in an effort to introduce us. Having been away for so long, the houses I was returning to were those of the next generation: I sat once again in homes that looked no different from the houses of their sixty-something parents. There would be lots of wedding-present china and table settings and dozens of silver-framed family photos. Isn't it great? said one host showing me around; it so reminded him of his parents' house.

Men younger than me dressed like old men, and we'd drink port and have the same conversations I imagined their parents did. There was some drinking, and lots of smoking, with Han and me catching each other's eye just to check that someone had actually said what we thought they'd said.

The people were either a little younger or a little older than me, but either way, and through no fault of their own, I felt lost. At the younger end of the 'set' was a crowd made up of young public school rural professionals and their friends down from London. Sometimes these evenings were fun, sometimes they were excruciating.

'Bloody hell, my parents will see pictures of me at my thirtieth birthday party, smoking! There I am, cigar in one hand, whisky in the other, lashed, bird under this arm, bird under that arm! Bloody hell!' one dinner companion told us.

Later, a drunken broker shouted long and loud stories of boozy escapades, including how he had been out – in black tie, pissed, dressed in fancy dress – when he was knocked down by a bus. He had spent four weeks in hospital, had a metal pin in his arm, and received 'thirty-five K' compensation which was a deposit on a 'bloody nice flat'.

For me, little had changed. For the younger ones it was hours of 'stories' and 'that reminds me'. At one slightly older gathering it was little bits of gossip about people we didn't know, Labour bashing and, in a way that echoed that particular type of *Today*-programme-style interviewing that was new to me, aggression. Efforts at conversation that particular night seemed doomed. Ideas were seldom discussed, and if they were they would be met with blanket agreement or vehement opposition, seldom a question or a modification.

There was also something about the way the Prime Minister was often castigated as if he were a truly despicable man, attacked not for his politics but to the core of his very person, as if they were speaking of someone they personally knew. Their vitriol seemed to demand more questions about them and their hatred than it did of this politician none of us had met.

Old Labour had their reasons to distrust him (and later, for many, there would be the war in Iraq), but it's difficult to remember that time when not everyone hated the Prime Minister. But these people, then, what was it *they* found so unnerving? I wasn't sure.

When the UK ruling party had last changed we were living in Brussels and the new Prime Minister of England meant little more to me than the prime minister of Spain. But even from a distance, he had always struck me as being rather like an old-style Tory: well-spoken, privately educated, oozing with confidence. He looked like them, he sounded like them, he had been to their schools and was married to a barrister.

Back in England I gradually realised that despite all this, the people who had most in common with him hated him in a way I don't think they hated the old Left. Their complaints weren't of raised taxes or the state of the economy or of public services getting worse (they might not have got much better, but no one suggested things were worse). The PM's greatest crime, these people agreed, was that he was fake, that it was all spin. His 'feelings weren't feelings', they were a lie.

I had no idea if the Prime Minister was a phoney or not; perhaps he was. (Certainly Bernard Ingham, I recalled from the years long ago when I lived in England, could say a word or two on spin.) I just sat and listened, reflecting on my own childhood, where feelings, if not fake, were certainly hidden, at least about the things that mattered most to me.

As we left, our host, who had sensed that perhaps this particular dinner hadn't been quite our thing, made a joke about it all, and Han told him not to be silly; it had been fun.

'So go on then,' said Han as we drove home. 'What did you make of all that?'

'Interesting,' I said.

It had been strange listening to the sorts of people I remembered always being reluctant to speak of 'feelings' so readily criticising those that did.

For many of the people like this that Han and I encountered, whether sophisticated and charming, or brash and loud, there still seemed to be an underlying self-belief in their place within a homogenous law of social physics that placed them not so much at the top of society, but at its centre. That they ran England was clearly no longer the case, but the perception remained nevertheless that 'everyone else' was still a collection of minor planets orbiting their certain sun.

When I had left England, there had been something in that cliquish world that had troubled me and shaped my views about it, beyond just their politics and their studied determination to self-associate. I realised now I was back, that, yes, my opinion was unfairly collective, but still it remained, touching something deep inside me. I just couldn't remember what this something was, or why I still felt it so deeply.

We had liked our hosts, but we didn't extend our own invitations through these generously opened doors, and for the time being that was the end of our flirtation with the 'county set'.

Winter pressed on, and in the midweek evenings the pub would be quiet as we toughed out these last pared months of dark. On occasion, if we were the only customers in there on a cold, drenched night, someone working behind the bar would crack and start bitching to Han and me about Knoxey, or Knoxey would bitch about the staff to us. It seemed part of the winter sadness and we didn't take it too seriously, nor the rumours about how far foot-and-mouth disease had entered the county.

It made it as far as Frampton-on-Severn, making the parish a threatened area. The rector told us that, like in the last war, we would all have to play our part in 'defeating the enemy'. When Han and I went out running or walking, we would pass farms with hopeless defences of thin strips of disinfected straw, the richer and more organised ones with elaborate checkpoints and perimeters of stacked straw bales.

The Right and the Tory media blamed people in government offices in London for a disease that was certainly spread, even if accidentally, by farmers and transporters in the provinces.

Locally, the wife of Lord Rodley, son and heir to Lord Marsham, appeared to lead the anti-government outrage. Lady Rodley was frequently in the public eye berating the government for their sins and raging against the Prime Minister. It wasn't clear to me why exactly it was the government's fault, nor why its extraordinarily generous compensation programmes were never much appreciated.

As for Norman, no farmer in England had signs up announcing

the closing of the footpaths quicker than he and Douglas: this was an opportunity to bar the people who wandered around his farm and complained about the state of the gates, or reported him to the RSPCA in lambing season if they saw a dead lamb, or knocked on his door to tell him that his crippled sheepdog was limping. Mostly, the signs were made by Douglas: crude, hand-painted boards or oil drums blocking the canal path and left there long after the crisis was over.

Nor could the local hunt now cross his land and churn up his sodden fields, something they regularly did but which he never complained about. I hoped that on the days when other landowners might ask the hunt not to go over their land because it was too wet, they wouldn't show up and hunt Norman's land instead, because Norman would never dream of saying no.

More importantly, foot-and-mouth put a stop to the huntsmen being allowed on to the farm to take away dead carcasses, which, unlike the hunt's negligible fox-killing successes, was a valued and important service, and one they offered for free. So Douglas dug a 'dead pit' in the Humpty Dumps where a dead sheep or lamb could be tossed. There, they would slowly decompose, helped by the foxes who roamed around the pit at night. If the wind was right, the smell of carrion carried over the fields and the faintest whiff of it could be smelt from our open kitchen door.

Norman's main concern, however, was that he couldn't take his animals to slaughter with all the restrictions on livestock movements. Given that cattle had to be killed at under thirty months old (the result of another recent chapter in British farming, mad cow disease), and that few people liked to eat mutton, it meant that the farmer was left with the cost of feeding and maintaining stock that would have no value unless they were diseased, in which case he would receive compensation.

A weekday morning started with one of those panicked knocks on the door from a near-hysterical passing motorist, whose fear of disease and the dangers of moving animals had been so heightened by the media that seeing an escaped animal on the road was tantamount to seeing a maniacal axeman.

'Are those your sheep in the lane?!!!!!'

But it was too late; by now they were on the railway it seemed.

Next to arrive were the police, wearing fixed combat expressions suitable for such a dangerous and terrifying situation.

'Do you know where Mr Ludd is?'

Spider said that given Norman's track record for escaped animals, there was now a more-or-less permanent police presence in the village keeping an eye on his crumbling walls. Norman was, of course, nowhere to be seen. Some locals were sympathetic to Norm's travails to keep stock in behind the walls and fences he had neither the money nor the time to properly maintain; others were angry and annoyed at the way the cows slowed or blocked their cars, and then there were those who reported his escapees to the landowners on to whose land his livestock had escaped before Norman had even been given a chance to rescue them, admittedly not something he was overly prompt about, nor expansively appreciative over; such were Norman's ways.

Parked under the railway bridge were two four-wheel-drive 'Rail Track Incident Response Units' and the police Land Rover. Up on the embankment, men in fluorescent jackets tossed dead sheep off the track and down. The entire flock of escapees had been hit and killed outright by a train.

Later I found Norman driving Sneaky up the lane and told him the news.

'They're only old hoggets,' he said calmly, with perhaps even a hint of relief. The nineteen sheep 'should have gone to market long ago anyway, but what with this foot-'n'-mouth can't do that'.

'Will you get compensation from the railway?'

'Get something I reckon,' he said quietly, his face poker-straight; long reflective pause. 'New railway fences, too.'

For owners of the expensive pedigree herds bred over generations, the wholesale slaughter was indeed a heartbreaking tragedy to watch unfold, and Lord Rodley was a devoted owner with his own pet herd of pedigree Gloucesters to worry about, as well as a dairy herd, despite the fact the Estate were trying to get out of milk production. Nevertheless, Lady Rodley's position on foot-and-mouth, given that Marsham was mainly arable land, struck me as being perhaps subconsciously linked to a wider need to keep alive the notion that farming should be subsidised, just as much as her position was a reflection of her seemingly genuine social concern for affected small farmers (of the type that ironically the Estate now had few of ). The small-field, mixed farming of Norman's type, with his sheep and cattle, was a long way from the spreadsheets, labour reduction and chemicals of England's industrial farming, all built on an extravagant infrastructure of subsidy.

Knoxey, despite having been brought up in the countryside and having lived there most of his life, didn't much care for farmers, rich or poor. The rich were greedy and destructive subsidy chasers, smashing down miles of drystone walls to create their arable prairie fields, sprayed year round; the poor farmers too stupid to find easier ways of farming than keeping livestock, and too cruel to look after them well.

Knoxey's concerns were more to do with his business. The closure of public footpaths had slowed trade. He had returned from his holiday at Laura's house in Florida to find his takings had dramatically shrunk, and he threw himself into his own PR campaign that made Lady Rodley's efforts seem tame. He rang the 'London newspapers', as he called them, got written up in one of them as a suffering rural landlord and managed to get a handsome spread in the local paper, with a photo of him standing outside the pub. Given that the purpose of his campaign was to spread the word that the pub was open, and welcoming all comers, the pose he adopted of a scowling, arms-crossed nightclub bouncer seemed a little at odds with the message, but he was very pleased.

The rector took something of an Old Testament position on the national pestilence, and spoke of the Sodom and Gomorrah landscape that was England, with its piles of burning, diseased animals. Foot-and-mouth, he said, was the direct by-product of a 'greedy desire for cheap food, for profit margins and fat dividends', not the result of an act of God or even Parliament. The rector encouraged us to keep in touch with those affected, specifically 'by phone'. Dropping in, for some reason, was not the suggested methodology, despite the fact that this village of some 170-odd households could boast only a handful of people who worked on the land.

'I would prefer it if the vicar came down here once in a while and spent some bloody money,' Geoff said.

'Doesn't he ever come, then?'

'Yes, once a month he comes at lunchtime on our one-pound-lunch days. He buys half a pint, which isn't actually the idea behind the one-pound lunch, is it?'

It wasn't just the winter and foot-and-mouth and some nagging memory of my formative teenage years that unsettled me about England, I soon realised. It was that much of the country we now lived in seemed so troubled. Even the rector talked about the endless disasters of flooding and pollution and horrible train crashes. The parish magazine wrote of the 'ongoing problems with youth in the village', listed as: general noise, bad language, appalling litter, criminal damage and the dangerous use of motorbikes along the main street. We were happy we lived on the edge of the village and saw and heard none of it.

At the pub, Peg's son's friend Lennie was watching a game of football on the TV from behind the bar. A minute's silence was held for the victims of a collapsed bridge in Portugal. The Porto crowd was completely silent and the English club's players wore black armbands alongside their hosts. The week before, during another game, an English crowd tried to be silent after a train crash. There was shouting and talking until in the middle of the minute a man's voice was clearly heard.

'Shut the fuck up!' he yelled.

Towards the end of February I travelled to give an unpaid speech to a newspaper conference in a half-hearted attempt to drum up some consultancy work, invited by people who still imagined I was part of their world. On the short trip away my delayed train crawled out of the Cotswolds.

'Ooohh, my belly button is sore, I've just had it pierced you know,' said the woman opposite, a Welsh woman on her way to Scotland for a blind date.

'I sometimes wonder if Britain isn't just broken,' I said absent-mindedly, looking out of the smeared window into the rain: the wrecked greenhouses, graffitied fences, litter-filled canals, rusting cars, empty warehouses and derelict factories; wasteland and dirt and endless rubbish heaps down the sides of once-used cuttings and overgrown embankments.

'Ooohh, I know, I mean, look at all the immigrants we've got now.'

I turned to her. 'I think that's the least of our worries,' I said, but her head was buried in a copy of *Hello!*.

But where the sadness of England most got to me was where it coincided perfectly with our own: time spent with the 'once-proud

NHS' about our failed attempts to have a baby.

Han went to see yet another doctor and left in tears when her *seven* minutes was up.

'How soon would the referral be?'

'Oh, months,' the doctor had said, seemingly unconcerned, telling us the tests we had had done in France were no good, only English tests would be good enough. 'You could go private, of course,' she added, without looking up.

On a blustery March day, we drove in silence to a private specialist in Cheltenham, the very same one we would have waited three months or more to see in the NHS. Up through the villages and lanes that wended across the high ground, we arrived at the top edge of the rolling plateau that was our home and looked west to Wales. Then we followed the road steeply down the hill into the town below and a parallel universe of health care. The private consultant we met and the expensive IVF treatment he proposed cast a long comparative shadow over the pressed NHS service we had previously received; he reminded us of the unrushed, generous health systems we had experienced 'on the Continent'. The fault lines of English society seemed to fall unnoticed in such divisive areas, like health and education, and were as stark and abrupt as the western escarpment of the Cotswolds; as clear to us when we spoke of a German friend having her IVF, paid for entirely by a very different health system.

In the last days of winter the council workers came in a tractor and cut the grass verges in preparation for spring, and there beneath the cut grass lay miles and miles of litter. On the quietest of lanes people had systematically thrown their rubbish from their car windows: cans and bottles of every type that had accompanied the sandwiches and crisps and cigarettes. I imagined these people as a handful of passing salesmen, en route from one meeting in one town to another meeting in another, who turned off the main roads into our world, to sit in a quiet Cotswold lane and eat a lunch they had bought at a petrol station, and to mark their passing with their wrappings.

The man in charge of roadside litter at Cotswold District Council had two thousand kilometres of lanes, roads and dual carriageways to take care of, and a hundred and fifty villages. For this job, he had two men. He was a decent man and would like to help, but he said the problem was the people who live in the Cotswolds, most likely the people who lived in the villages around me driving to and from work. He was probably right: blaming 'town folk' for the litter, as one letter-writer to the local paper did, was akin to blaming immigrants for the fact the trains didn't work.

What started with picking up a can here and a crisp packet there soon turned into an obsession. One day I cracked. I came back from a run, took a roll of large, black plastic sacks and walked a two-mile stretch of lane, down one side and back the other, filling eighteen sacks.

'It reminds me of the sort of thing my dad would do – make us go out for a walk and pick up litter,' said a woman in her thirties through the lowered window of her people carrier.

'Oh?' I said hopefully, looking at her children slumped in the back of her car on this dry, clear winter's day, as she looked wistfully down the lane.

'I'd do it myself, of course, but I have children you see.'

'I'm running a bit low on bags actually,' I hinted.

'We must write you up in the parish magazine,' she said, raising her window. 'Keep up the good work.'

Later, a woman in a BMW roared past and gave me a thumbs-up sign. Oh piss off, I said to myself, by now tired and irritable.

Come dusk, a second car stopped, and inside was Alan, who lived in Storeton. Alan Kerck, or Kercksey (everyone it seemed was given their own affectionate nickname, something that struck Han as very Australian: the adding or deleting of a vowel) was a Gloucestershire woodsman. He was short, with a thick mop of slowly greying curly brown hair and outdoor skin.

'Who organised this, then?'

When I told him, he was visibly shocked and truly grateful. There was so little hands-on individual initiative these days, he said.

'The subject of roadside litter is always coming up at the parish council and gets discussed, but nothing ever happens. The thing is, it always ends up the same few people doing all the work, if someone brings it up.'

A little while later Alan returned with the log-dented truck he used for his wood deliveries, and he drove as I leapt in and out and tossed the bags into the back.

'Most of these people who come and live in our villages, they don't get involved except complaining about something or telling us what to do. You know they complain about harvest trucks, don't you? They're always inviting each other to dinner parties. Not me, though.'

It was so warm I had asked Douglas to fix up our bikes to be ready for long sunny rides, and he'd brought them back, gleaming and oiled. He handed me a carefully handwritten receipt for the work he had done. 'You wanna keep that. It's like a guarantee, like, proof, and all that,' he said.

Alan, however, warned me of false springs, with their warm blue days but cold, frosty nights. 'Don't get your hopes up,' he told me as we stood there in the lane at the back of Frimley Wood, the setting sun so hard in my eyes it was difficult to see him. He had turned off the engine of his truck, and I had stopped my run. It struck me what a generous gift time was, a proper weighting of priorities. 'People are fooled by this weather, you know. I can tell by the way the phone stops ringing and they think they don't need any more wood, but I tell 'em it'll still be horrible, even in May.'

A Second World War vintage Dakota circled overhead, heading for Hamden airfield, once an RAF base and built in the 1930s, and we talked about the war.

'It was at its busiest during the war, you know. Americans every-where round here. I told my daughter about the two large American army Nissen hut hospitals that used to be in Cirencester Park. They used to fly them Dakotas right in there from Normandy and land them on the grass gallops, near Rittleton. She did her school project on it and we got this old aerial photo and went over there and we mapped out on the ground where everything was, all the planes and all parked under the trees, camouflaged. It was huge.' We watched the plane and stood in silence in the empty lane.

I ran home over the March fields and along the edge of Frimley Wood, the sunset behind me casting long shadows before me. Through the cooling evening air came the call of wood pigeons and the quick flutter of birds sprinting from tree to bush; snowdrops in the hedges and the first green shoots of daffodils. Tidcombe stood golden grey in the late-afternoon light with the first lazy-rising smoke of evening fires. Back towards Lettem along the lane, past

Douglas on his tractor, and a wave to Norman in the field and home, as the sun went down over the wood.

False start or not, spring was on its way. This English winter, with its doubts and darknesses, seemed to be over. We had come out of it with friends and a sense of place that had not been there in the autumn. Douglas had even invited me to build a drystone wall. We stood by the lane and sorted stone before finally beginning to build. It was slow work; Douglas was unable to talk and work simultaneously. He'd try, but he couldn't, and as each unrelated, non-sequential subject came to mind, he would stand up, put down his stones and address me, loudly.

'My dad gave up his job at the factory, and all that,' he told me, referring to a local light-engineering firm. 'It's too fast, that work is, my dad says. Doesn't stop. Like a production line it is, and all that. You can't ever stop, he says.' He looked at me, slightly confused by the way I continued to work as he talked. My simple job was to place the fillings of small stones and rubble as Douglas selected and raised the face stones.

'Trick is not to rush there, Ian. Just go nice and slow, and all that,' he counselled wisely. 'He's working now in the mortuary at Cheltenham hospital he is now.'

'Really?'

'He has to measure the bodies and all that. You know why they measure the bodies?'

'No.'

'To fit the coffins.'

Another stone laid and then he stopped again to discuss the farm and what was going to happen.

'You know something, Ian?'

'What?'

'Someone posh from the village offered Norman five thousand pound for one of his barns so that he can have picnics there,' he told me. 'That is *ridic'lous*,' he said. It was, given that converted barns sold for £400,000 or more and picnics seemed an unlikely motivation, but Douglas was more dismissive of the idea of using a working barn for picnics than of the price offered.

Douglas knew that working for Norman was how all jobs should be. A Land Rover drove past us as we worked; it could have been anyone.

'You know who that is?'

'No.'

'Marsham bloke. Checking. Checking they're working. We're different over here, we don't have none of that. Norman, you know what he said?'

'What?'

'You work when you like, that's what he said.'

It was different over here, as we stood on the Ludd–Marsham border, well-maintained walls and perfectly maintained fields on one side of the lane, and Douglas and me fixing one of a thousand collapses on the other. Our side had hedges and coverts and sheep and cows, birds and wildlife and workers. The other had open ploughed fields, no stock grazing them, little cover for any animal running down the few remaining walls; and perhaps even a man in a Land Rover, checking.

At the last turn of winter, on the very eve of spring, Spider invited me to go with him on the train to Gloucester and watch his team play rugby. It seemed a reward for standing firm through winter as we drank beer and cheered in 'The Shed'.

Travelling to the match on the wobbly two-carriage shuttle train, Spider told me that his father had been a building-site manager who worked for the company that built Glebe Field Close, the modern cul-de-sac of tightly packed houses in the village. His dad had been against it, had asked not to be site manager on that project. And the houses, where he now lived with his parents and which were built for returning servicemen? Only one was ever lived in by a service-man from the village.

On the way back to Hamden, Spider told me that as a lad on the train home from Gloucester, as it approached The Leggers' in the cutting in Frimley Wood, he and his friends had once pulled the emergency stop. They had leapt out of the stopped train into the dark, scampered through the woods and stumbled into The Leggers', avoiding the long walk back from Hamden station.

That night, after the game, the pub was busy, full of spring and smiles. Knoxey had taken Han to Ascot. According to Lennie, Knoxey had spent two hours shining his redbreast-scarlet Corvette in anticipation of the day out and it gleamed and purred, and so did

Knoxey in jacket and tie. Han told me he was Mr Racing, known by everyone at every turn at Ascot, it appeared. He had delighted in having Han on his arm, and being able to tell them that Laura was in Florida without ever explaining who Han was and letting them all think it was the old Knoxey, still up to his ways. Laura, despite the fact she was in Florida, had been tipped off before Knoxey and Han were even home. She had rung Geoff on his mobile asking him who the brunette was he had been racing with that day. Geoff laughed at that. 'Love it!' he said. 'Love it!'

The night turned into a celebration, a spring festival of sorts, and during the evening there was both banter and confessional. John, the gamekeeper and waller we had met at the harvest rave, merry and high on the feeling we all had that spring was finally here, told me how he loved the English countryside, how he could never work indoors; about his love of fishing, his certainty and fear that the seasons and the climate were changing, but also how Canadian Vicky had opened his eyes to a world beyond this island.

He confided in me.

'There's other places than this wet, grey, crowded, shitty island, but you know that, don't you?'

I saw Spider listening to us, but he didn't say anything.

Knoxey was on a roll, happier and more relaxed than I had ever seen him. He told Leggers' lore and stories everyone had heard a hundred times but which only got better in the retelling. We got talking about Laura's mother.

'She fucking hated me,' Geoff said. 'One day we had this bloody great stand-up row, face to face we were, so I said to her, I did, "When you're dead, I'm going to dance on your grave." And you know what she said? "Aha! I've got you, then, you old bugger, because I'm going to be buried at *sea*!"' Geoff roared with laughter. 'Oh, she was something,' he said, with a respect and warmth that belied his earlier words.

He turned a little mournful, took another drink and continued. 'When she was dying, Peg's ex, Mike, who was living down in Portugal near to Laura and her mum, had been very good to Laura's mum, driving her around and stuff. Anyway, she'd been in hospital a few days, she was pretty bad, and Mike rings me up. He says, you better get down here, he says, she's about to go and Laura's pretty upset and all. So I drop everything here, get up to Heathrow, get a plane there, get a taxi, go straight to the hospital and there she is. Laura goes out of the room and there I am with her, and she's completely out of it. Then you know what? She opens one eye, looks straight at me, know what she says? "What the fuck are you doing here?"'

Long after the pub should have closed that night of tales and laughter, we finally made it back to Lettem, Vicky slowly driving Han and me, and Spider and John walking ahead of us in the headlights, unsteady but trying not to show it.

Back at Lettem Cottage, Vicky dropped us off and Han lit candles to place on the garden table. It was the first still and mild night of the year. Spider, John, Han and I sat outside. There was no moon, darkness, the cows in the yard bellowing through the night the only sounds. Then, as we sat and drank in silence, came the sound of Norman on his tractor somewhere out there on the farm, way past one o'clock in the morning, headlightless, invisible, working on some inscrutable late-night task.

'What *is* he doing?' asked John.

'I don't know, I really don't.'

Spring night, our first spring night. We sat in total silence, listened to the night and revelled privately in our own intense privilege.

After they left, Han went to bed and I stayed outside and thought back on the long winter that had passed and all that had changed for the good, despite our anxieties over a baby and my nagging doubts about England. I thought of the moon that I had seen rising over the cottage one winter's dusk as I walked back up the lane with Douglas after an afternoon on the walls. It was full and burnt red from the palette of the event that had caused it – a solar eclipse, Douglas told me – with wisps of dusk-lit clouds gently brushed across it, as if placed by a painter. I had never seen the moon so close to earth, so giant, so corporeal, so shockingly wondrous, and I was there, at the exact place, the exact time to see it ascend over Lettem, the only place on the planet the moon could have chosen to rise.

Han and I were on the verge of this terrifying venture to try and have a baby, a treatment that we couldn't afford financially, nor its failure emotionally, and we were living in a country that we still couldn't fully embrace. But at that very moment, England seemed the calm centre of the world, and we were within its safest heart.

## CHAPTER 6

# SPRING DAYS

Spring was to see an important new arrival at Lettem Cottage. Malcolm, Norman's older brother, had found Norman a new sheepdog, a five-month-old Border collie called Maggie. She was delivered in the back of Malcolm's little Renault and put directly into a kennel built in Norman's garden. The kennel was made from some old rusting pieces of rigid mesh fencing tied together with baler-twine, and a piece of broken plywood as a roof. There she stayed, whining and whimpering.

'How's the training going?' I asked Norman as he climbed over the garden wall into Home Paddock. Maggie was straining on a piece of ubiquitous baler-twine, Norman's multipurpose tool for gate latches, fixing fences, holding up trousers, leashing dogs and lashing wet-weather fertiliser bag leggings to his thighs.

'You don't want to know,' he said, looking down at her. 'She'll learn,' he added in a not very convincing attempt to sound stern. Norman let Maggie off her leash and she promptly jumped over the garden wall and cavorted and rolled across our lawn, ignoring Norman's whistles and surprisingly gentle calls.

Old Sukey wanted to join in but she could only hobble through the hole in the hedge, flop exhausted under the cherry tree and study the young pretender. She took Maggie's arrival well enough, knowing that she could not compete, and she surrendered any pretensions to ever being able to work again. Norman bent down and stroked Sookie as he looked at Maggie.

'I'm not quite sure about her breeding,' Norman said as Maggie charged around looking very unsheepdoglike. 'Might have to go back,' he muttered. Then he grinned. He wasn't sending her back anywhere, even if her breeding was all wrong and she wouldn't work properly.

Douglas joined us at the wall and we all stood and looked out over the farm.

'Now that, Ian, that is a bootiful day, that is. Think how lucky we are, not to be in cities. Or cars. Yes, I like bikes, Ian, I like to see all the moving parts, and all that. Don't like cars much, can't see much moving.'

A youngish couple with two cars and two young children had moved into Syde Lettem, the house in the shadow of Lettem House. Someone drove a new, green Range Rover and there was a Japanese sports car too, Douglas told us. Norman had seen the husband and I'd seen the wife. I had stopped in to introduce myself but she'd not come round to us. People don't do that any longer, do they, we agreed.

'Do you know what the people before them paid for that place?' said Norman, using one of his quiet fact-dropping 'questions'. At first I thought they were actually questions, and tried to answer them, but now I just let them hang in silence until he told me what he wanted to tell me. His voice was slow and gentle, as if he was worried I might not be interested.

'£72,000. That was 1991.'

Pause.

'They say they paid £400,000 for it, these new ones.'

'That is unbelievable, that is,' chimed in Douglas, incredulous.

'I can't understand how people get that sort of money,' wondered Norman.

The three of us stood in silence and thought it over, I looking down rather uncomfortably at my boots, not explaining that I could comprehend entirely a world where people could raise £400,000 without so much as a blink.

'Better be going,' muttered Norman finally.

'RIGHT! You have a nice day then, Ian!' boomed Douglas. 'Spring! Bootiful.'

Spring. That morning, mist had filled the canal valley and rolled up and over the lane on the hill that ran to the station, where I had dropped Han. As I stayed at home, still without the consulting work I had promised to deliver, Han was off to London again for the day, working for the last of the Internet wannabees before that whole first bubble finally ran out of air. We had sat outside the empty ticket office awaiting the 0715, talking about our plans to start IVF.

On my way back to Lettem I had stopped the car at Tidcombe, turned off the engine and watched the sun come up through the slowly clearing mist to reveal the cottage and the farm. I didn't know what, but something powerful and able had made all this and given me this moment. In this spring it seemed impossible that nature could not work for us too.

Three hours later, Han called me from London on her way to a client meeting. We didn't need IVF. She was pregnant.

Han's pregnancy seemed but a part of everything that was around us. It was spring, we were at Lettem, of course she was pregnant. The sun finally shone and Scully stretched out on the warm flagstones, too content to hunt. The collared doves, never seen further away than the ash tree over the steam pond all winter, flew down and settled on the lawn. Norman's newborn calves sniffed and explored Home Paddock in front of the cottage and there were eighty-five lambs down in the Lambing Sheds.

Like the damp, misty mornings, nature wasn't always easy or obvious, and just as each day we would wait to see if the sun had decided if it was to be a warm one, we waited to see if we were going to pass through those first few weeks without loss. Norman would tell us of calves that had died, or lambs that had been taken by the foxes, which this year ran plentiful, their own breeding undisturbed by ramblers or hunters. Life seemed promising, but not certain.

The night before we go to hospital for a scan, I can't sleep.

I wake in the middle of the night, the room flooded with full moonlight, and I stand naked and shivering at the window, watching single, silver clouds blow brusquely through the sky, thinking of my father and my family thinned.

The dog rose was set to flower and we needed to train it. At the sawmill hidden in Frimley Wood we picked up trellis and posts.

'It's not from Frimley Wood, you know,' said the man who worked at the mill and who sharpened our posts. 'There are products that come from the Marsham woods, but most of it comes from abroad now. These gates come from Wales I think. A lot of Frimley wood's for pulping.'

Frimley Wood Sawmill gates came with a discreet Frimley Wood Sawmill badge tacked on to them, because for a certain type, having one's gate from the ex-Marsham-owned sawmill was as important as having a real Barbour jacket. Was the input from Frimley Wood really nothing more than some bloke tacking on the Frimley Wood Sawmill badge? It seemed hard to believe that most, or even any, of the Frimley wood ended up in a pulping machine. We liked the idea of our fences and gates coming from the wood we could see across the field. It seemed a shame if they didn't, and we'd rather not have known.

Down at the pub some young kids from the agricultural college were drinking in the bar next door. Knoxey and The Leggers' had had a long relationship with the aggies. Knoxey embraced them and their families' money with gusto, and Spider would always go and inspect the new crop. Spider judged intakes of aggies like wine vintages, and would speak wistfully of how the year of nineteen-eighty-whatever were 'a great bunch' but ninety-something-or-other were 'complete prats'.

The Leggers' reputation for hedonism and fun and Knoxey's tolerance, combined with the pub's isolated setting, pulled in both customers and criticism. Not everyone wanted to sip a pint next to the aggies and their raised voices and brash ways. They had names like Binkie, Roo and Flic and when drunk, the boys, aside from crashing their Golfs into the canal bridge, often liked to undress in public; but they seldom came in numbers that overwhelmed the pub, not at least in the years we were there, although this had not always been so.

What we always saw from Peg and Knoxey, Laura and May, was marked good humour and tolerance of the aggies and their friends. They knew they were mostly children but treated them respectfully like adults and equals. If they got out of hand, Peg would step in and talk to them like their mothers, and they would feel guilty and help her mop up.

The group next door were doing shots and lager and had drunk so much they ended up giving us their last undrunk pints, red-faced and flushed.

'That Ginny Brimley girl used to drink here,' Geoff told us, speaking of one of the aggies' cousins. 'Some snooty little girl came to me and she said that Captain Brimley – who the bloody 'ell keeps their army rank when they leave? – "had a message for me": she said he didn't want his daughter drinking down here any more.'

'What did you say?'

'I told her to tell him to fuck off and if he had a message to give, he should come down 'ere and tell me himself.'

It was Knoxey's pub and he ran it as he pleased. He was not a man to doff his cap to anyone.

There was a census enumerator at Alan's door when I dropped in one morning to say hello. I warned Alan not to tell him anything, he's a government spy, I joked.

'They've been saying the same thing about a lack of confidentiality since 1801,' said the enumerator defensively, 'and it's rubbish.' Back then it was little more than a headcount, but a hundred years from this census, who did what in the village would be common knowledge, just as I had been able to find the details of the 1871 census on the Internet.

Back then there were 452 people in the village: 236 males and 216 females. Of these, about 160 were 'scholars' or other children of pre-school age. Of the remaining 300-odd people (including many children who worked as nurses, ploughboys and farmworkers from as young as ten), over a third worked in agriculture. Ploughmen and ploughboys, poultry managers, shepherds and undershepherds, oxmen and a couple of farm bailiffs accounted for about twenty of them. The great majority were plain agricultural labourers, or 'farmworkers', as the women and children who worked as agricultural labourers were called.

If you weren't working on the land, you were likely to be engaged in domestic service to one of the handful of prosperous middle- and upper-class families in the area. There appeared to be seven households in the village who provided such jobs. There was the 'landowner' from Norfolk, Grenville Inge, thirty-three, and his six children at Rathbury House; the reverend in the Old Rectory and the four farmers (the Priests – 745 acres; the Jeffries – 586 acres; the Gleases – 650 acres; and the Howmisters at Rectory Farm – 490 acres). In addition there was the family of Michael Knight (aged twenty-eight, profession, 'none') who employed a governess from Lancashire, a footman, a cook, a housemaid, a nurse (fifteen-year-old Elisabeth Renny) and a kitchen maid from Tidcombe.

There were footmen and butlers, housemaids and house workers, cooks and kitchen maids, washerwomen and laundresses, lady's
maids and house peers, nurses and governesses, general servants,
plain servants, domestics and charwomen and last, but not least,
Alfred Carnblade from Ashton Keynes, aged seventeen and a boot
cleaner in the employ of Mr Lavery's hotel on the Northleach Road.
In the grounds of the big houses were the gardeners and grooms,
coach drivers and coachmen. Forty women in the village were
described as housekeepers, most keeping the house of families other
than their own.

Beyond domestic service and agricultural labouring, job oppor-
tunities were limited. The canal employed just one person from
the village, a labourer, perhaps explaining the already declining
condition of the canal's bed. The railway, which back then ran to
Cirencester, employed a policeman, a porter, an engine driver and a
labourer. The roads offered employment to just one labourer and a
toll collector, as well as, indirectly, to the three hauliers and carters
who lived in the village.

There were, of course, the tradesmen: a bricklayer, a plumber
and glazier, three carpenters (one of whom was also a wheelwright)
and a father-and-two-sons blacksmith operation. With all those
drystone walls there were just five stone workers in the village: two
stonemasons and their labourer, a stone breaker and a quarryman,
who was perhaps responsible for the craters and cuttings in the
Humpty Dumps. So few men with the word mason to their name
suggested that, just as Douglas did the repairs on the walls today,
the drystone walling was the work of all those agricultural labourers
and a skill most men would have had.

The village was rounded off by the schoolmaster (Mr Seelig, who
was also the parish clerk and income tax collector) and his wife, a
Methodist preacher, a shopkeeper, a midwife, a coal merchant and
half a dozen women who worked as dressmakers and seamstresses.

The only innkeepers I could find were the Laverys up on the
Northleach Road. Who ran The Leggers' back then, I could only
guess at.

When the census enumerator had gone, Alan and I drank coffee
standing in his exposed-beam kitchen with its smell of woodsmoke.
It was, by his own admission, untidy. On one side of the room were

shelves with jars and jars of pickled eggs, onions and chutneys, and at the end an open fire burnt on the floor under a wide, tall, corbelless mantelpiece. There was an old wooden kitchen table, scattered with plates, knives, a shotgun cartridge, bits of string and old bills. The table seemed to be a workbench, a dining table and a desk. He'd been restoring this house for seventeen years, and did a bit here and a bit there when he had money and time.

'One of the things about living on your own is that you can do just as you like. I'm too old now to be told what to do, so any woman just has to put up with it. Help yourself to milk and sugar, there's a teaspoon in the dishwasher. I didn't get a chance to empty it today. Mind you,' he laughed, 'it takes me about three months to fill it.'

Over coffee we talked about farming, the village and how it had changed. I had heard of Marsham's plans to convert some farm buildings.

Someone else had told me that they needed cash to do the works, and accordingly rumour had it that they had identified all the land they owned in the village that could potentially be used for development and which they might possibly sell.

It was said by others that another family, who owned most of a village a few miles from Northleach, had made a million pounds converting some barns behind the church and also that they informally interviewed people who wanted to live in the village. ('Doesn't matter how much money you've got, if they don't like you, you're out.') Someone had even told me the front rows in the church were still reserved for this family, but that couldn't be true *today*, could it? This type of talk was common, and it was impossible to distinguish reality from perception, but it was perception more than facts that shaped how we all saw each other.

But mostly what I heard about as I drank tea and pints was the huge farms that now only employed one or two people per thousand acres and how the cottages that used to be for farmworkers now sold for at least fifteen times a farmworker's income. The homes they and their children would have lived in had been sold or rented by the landowners to executives from Swindon or London solicitors who wanted somewhere for the weekend, or newcomers who picked up litter for free.

'I knew people in the village who could remember the kids that used to join their parents for an evening picnic as they harvested, but now you go to harvest festival with an apple bought at a supermarket; no one knows what farming is,' said Alan wistfully, as he spoke of how the few farm labourers left worked ever-longer hours, with ever-increasing productivity targets, seated all alone in the air-conditioned cabs of the monster tractors, with only the radio for company. That was just the nature of modern farming, he said. I thought of Spider endlessly ploughing, drilling, spraying and harvesting huge acreages of crops that only the subsidies made any sense of.

There was talk too of the newcomers and the 'dinner party lot', the people who didn't send their children to the community schools of the communities they claimed to belong to, who complained if the church wanted to build affordable housing in the village, who wanted street lights outside their executive homes. The same people always asked the locals for their fields for their ponies, or their teenagers for babysitting, but never asked them in for a meal or even a drink.

'They come in and buy up all the houses and all our kids have to go and live on a housing estate in Cirencester or Swindon or somewhere,' said Alan, 'and then they tell us that nothing should change and how we can't do this and we can't do that and the Estate can't have tractors coming through the village at harvest time.'

We sat in silence for a moment, long enough for us both to know that I was one of those house buyers, living in a farmworker's cottage that Spider, aged thirty, had to pass each evening on his way back to the home he shared with his parents. But Alan was too polite to go further and I too embarrassed to help him. We had another cup of coffee.

. I ran home, past Norman planting his linseed. He'd told me it was only for the subsidy and that he'd probably never even harvest it. Maggie ran out with Han to greet me as Peg called in on her way down to the pub. We stood at the garden wall and watched a young calf, only minutes old, stagger after her reluctant mother, who was on her feet and eating, oblivious to her offspring or her trailing afterbirth.

'Oh, it's so beautiful here. I remember when my friend lived here and she used to have these great parties and we'd come round all the time.'

Peg, like everyone, was curious to know how we found it living next to Norman.

'The last time I had any dealings with him,' she said, 'was when he came steaming into the pub, enraged, he was, that his tractor had been burnt! I told him to calm down and not to speak to me in that way. It wasn't my fault his effing tractor had been burnt, I'm not responsible for what people do when they leave the pub. "Yes you are!" shouts Norman.'

It was getting chilly, and we came inside and lit a fire. She spoke of her time running a hotel in Weymouth which she bought with her ex-husband, a famous English rugby league player of the sixties who ran off and left her, in her opinion, with a great deal less than she might have expected.

Peg now lived in an ex-council house on an estate in Cirencester and wanted to buy a house in the countryside with a bigger garden, but couldn't afford it. After Weymouth she and her husband had moved to the Cotswolds. They used to live in a village near the pub they ran in Little Mayford. 'When I lived there, it was still a working village. It had a school with two classes, seventeen kids in all, and the main farm was run by the Tucks. They had teenagers and they used to have these wonderful parties at the weekends. But they left. They'd been the local estate's tenants for years. They put up the rents I s'pose. All the people who worked on the farm, all the land, it all changed. There's a lot of weekenders there now.'

'Do you think it might come back?'

'No, it's gone for ever, I think,' she said.

On Easter Day the rector's children were visiting again. As it was the second most important and second best attended religious festival of the year, one of his daughters, her hair tied back and dressed in a tight skirt, knee-length boots and a clinging woollen jumper, was once again invited to read the lesson.

Stanton gave a sermon about how, as a young boy, he had broken a china model of Lord Nelson that had belonged to his grandmother. The model had been his great-great-great-great-grandfather's, who had served with Nelson at Trafalgar. Never before or since had the rector felt as utterly ashamed or guilty as he did that day. I reflected on what a good life he must have led for this to be so, and the shame of my own life, scattered with broken china I'd rather forget, dropped in the corporate life I had led or in the closer confines of my family.

Later, he spoke again of Sodom and Gomorrah England, and then kindly showed the children a tiny chick. We prayed to 'dear Jesus, who loves all the little animals', for the safe return of Tiffany's kitten (who Norman later told me had probably been taken by a fox), and then we prayed for the Queen. I prayed for Han and our child-to-be.

The late-April days were washed blue but a cold strong wind remained, bullying the daffodils. Warmth, where are you? we would wonder, don't tease us like this. In response came a burst of winter weather; at least Norman called it that. It poured the same pitiless rain we had seen all winter, chilling the ground and dampening our spring steps. No April shower; this was winter water.

'I lost two lambs on Sunday. They came out expecting spring and they landed in winter. I've lost three calves now, too,' he told me matter-of-factly.

But then May came and the world exploded. One day nature was budding and hopeful and the next it was rioting, rampant green; celebratory flags and streamers of leaves hung in every tree and hedge. The cherry-tree blossoms had come and gone and the daffodils had passed their best, but the tulips flowered in the garden, the verges spotted yellow with spring dandelions and the gardens pink with apple blossom; everything was emerging from winter and leaping towards summer.

The blossom on the hawthorn that lined the road down Tidcombe Hill burst most gloriously of all, a wall of white exuberance and musky scent, bushy and fat, covering the hill in a spring snow of flower.

'That's May blossom,' Norman told me, curious that I should mention the obvious. Surely I had seen and noticed May blossom before? Surely I hadn't. The Big Tree, so long leafless, was suddenly alive.

'You know the story about that tree?' Norman asked me. 'Old Frankie, he was the one that done it.'

I looked up at the tree's thick trunk and fat branches and made myself wait.

'Frankie Bruce, he was the gardener at Lettem House, he put it up. Old Mrs Bruce, she was in charge like, she said to him one day: Frankie, get out there and put me up a new clothes post, that old one's no good. So Frankie went over to that covert there and cut a shooter off one of them lime trees, came back, he stuck it in the lawn.' We were staring up at it in awe. 'And that's it there now. Why couldn't you get me a proper oak post, she used to say.'

I was learning to notice, even anticipate, these moments when a piece of oral history was passed on, to invest them with the weight they deserved. It's said that oral history is notoriously inaccurate but that only made it more interesting, observing the tension between what might have been and what we want it to have been. A story told is the rebirth of something nearly gone and, like a spring tree after winter, slightly different each time but still there.

I felt silly about my reverence when I doubted Norman would ever think of these small conversations of mundane detail as anything other than that. But something had changed. When I had come here a year ago, it had been the Big Tree, and then I learnt it was a lime tree, and now it was Frankie's Tree, and through knowing this, a tree somehow becomes much more than a tree.

It wasn't just the flowers that appeared. The criminals did, too, and a crime wave swept our world like the return of a campaigning army that had wintered at home quarters. Winter was too cold and wet for stealing, too dull and heavy for the smashing, but spring changed all that. It started with a vandalised pub sign and spread. Two metal exercise weights that had sat outside our cottage all winter, wet, rusting and unused, were gone, taken from the terrace. Norman lost a jerrycan of diesel and a welding kit, pinched from his shed in the middle of the day.

Someone had seen Murray walking down the lane with a jerry-can and asked me to ask Norman what colour his missing can was. Murray was an easy suspect to some who didn't know him so well. He was a young man who lived with his grandad over Storeton way; his teeth, eyes and accent as wonky as the unreliable moped he drove. He would show up in the middle of the night and knock on Norman's door, or do a little work here and there for some of

Norman's odd change; few people would employ him. Then he'd disappear for weeks and re-emerge, hustling for a few quid. On occasion the police would come round in the night asking after him, and we would tell them we had no idea where he was, even when we did.

Norman wouldn't be having the idea it was him; he trusted him implicitly.

'That Murray doesn't know where he is half the time, let alone steal anything,' was Norman's verdict, admitting that one of the reasons Murray and Douglas were the only people he'd have working for him was because all the other kids he'd ever had there couldn't stop pinching stuff.

'It's people from Birmingham that does it, you know,' Norman said, telling the tale of how his cottage had once been broken into. 'They drive out in the day, into the villages. There's no one in half these villages in the day nowadays, you see.'

Rural burglary happens in daylight, and starts with a knock on the door to check that no one is at home. Except this spring I was, and when I went down I found him at the back door, armed with his excuse: a big fat man in his fifties with the thick brogue of a traveller of some sort.

'Oh,' he said. 'Hello.'

'Hello.'

'Sorry to be botherin' you but I t'ink I just hit a cat up t'ere, up in the village. Ran right out in front of me, she did.'

'Oh no? Where was that, then?' I said, getting a coat and coming outside.

We walked round the side of the house, up the track and out into the lane.

'Just up there it was.'

Through the rain I noticed the bonnet of a car peeking out from a gateway, engine idling. And that's when I got it.

'What colour was it?'

'Ginger.'

The hidden car pulled out, turned down the lane and pulled alongside the pet lover, who quickly got in the back seat, impatient to get away. I leant down and put my hands on the wound-down window of the driver's door. In the front were the two young men who were there to rob me blind and would have done so in a second;

hard faces, cropped hair, one with a hat pulled down over his brow, eyes set straight ahead.

'There's only one problem,' I said, taking courage from seeing Norman coming down the lane, displaying his uncanny ability for sensing when someone was about. 'No one's got a ginger cat around here.'

'All right, Jimmy,' said the young driver to me, coldly and menacingly, hinting none of us wanted trouble. 'We'll be off, then.' And with that he pulled smartly away.

Norman raced off to get his car from the yard to follow them, and I went inside and called the police. Norman could smell blood and his missing welding kit, and he tore past the cottage in the car, Maggie sitting up on the front seat next to him, his hair and her ears flying in the wind through the open windows, at a speed I didn't know Norman's old Land Rover could go.

The police were not interested. Did they break in? No. Are they still there? No. Do you have a car registration? Yes. Well, we'll keep an eye out for them.

I hung up and jumped in our car, wondering if they might have gone to The Leggers', and were robbing it now. I drove down the lane and bumped into Alan Kerck. Alan was as enthusiastic as Norman about getting them.

'Bloody bastards,' Alan said. 'They're always around this time of year, like bloody vultures, they are.' And with that, he too tore off in his wood truck for a drive around. I wouldn't want to be a robber stuck in a narrow lane with Norm coming up on one side and Kercksey the other. It could put a man off thieving.

The chase and search were futile and later that morning the police did eventually show up, so slow and jaded that I wondered what the point had been of calling them.

'These days they can pretty much do as they like, nothing we can do.'

'So I'm a sitting duck, then?'

'People put in burglar alarms, but who's around to hear them?'

'Right.'

'Have a nice day then.'

Perhaps our visitors were the ones who stole Spider's moped from the barn at the farm where he worked; he stopped to tell Norman and me about it.

'Got to use the company car now,' he said, nodding at the wheel of his enormous tractor.

It was dusk, the sun going down over Frimley Wood and Spider had turned off the tractor engine. We all let Spider's words hang in the warm evening air. I was still mastering the art of not being the one to break the silences and the pauses, and I was pleased when it was Norman this time.

'You ever find a fellow looking through your window?' said Norman.

Spider and I waited for it. Just when you think he won't, he starts.

'I followed him up the lane and I said, what are you doing looking through my window? Oh, I wanted to know the way to Northleach,' imitated Norman in a passable version of a thick Irish accent. 'You don't want to know the way to Northleach, I said.'

There was another pause as Spider and I thought about what we would have done, and after a long pause Spider told us his approach.

'If I find the fucker who took my bike, I'll bury the c—t,' he said, pulling out a large machete knife he had in the cabin of the tractor. Later, when the insurance came through, Spider bought himself one of those new silver Italian Vespa bikes, and Knoxey thought that was a laugh, Spides on his Italian-city-boy scooter. But according to Spider you could get it to do over seventy miles an hour (downhill), and that was pretty fast.

We stood again in silence, Spider sitting high above us in his monster tractor, in his camouflage trousers, wraparound shades and airborne haircut. The long leisurely gaps in our conversation did not signal an end to an encounter, but here in the Lettem lane, were more time to consider what had been said, what might be said next and to enjoy standing still.

Finally: 'I suppose you finished all your drilling, have you?' asked Norman with a laugh.

Spider straightened himself up and stretched his neck, pulling back his arms and pushing out his chest. He had, ten, twelve days ago, but Norman didn't seem fussed, just chuckled to himself.

Another long pause.

'Reckon it'll still be a hot summer.'

Pause.

'Yup.'

Longer pause; I sensed it might be my turn to say something.

'That lady who keeps horses in Tidcombe, she stopped by today, Norm. She wants you to chain-harrow her field.'

'She's no lady,' grinned Norman. 'Getting a pony doesn't make you gentry.'

Finally, Spider pulled himself up ever so slowly from his position of leaning on the wheel, adjusted his shades and stretched again.

'Better be off then,' he said regretfully. He fired up the big £42,000 Massey and powered up the lane past Norman's yard full of his 1950s tractors that he jump-started on the banks of the Humpty Dumps. Two generations, two worlds of farming, meeting on a lane as I cut the grass and clipped the hedge on a spring evening at Lettem.

Of all the spring criminals the most notorious was Sneaky. Douglas called her Sneaky, but Norman thought it was ridiculous to give cows names; still, he knew all the ones Douglas used. Sneaky could escape from anywhere. If she'd made just a few breakouts in the winter, by spring it was a couple of times a day and people weren't amused. Some suspected that Norman's less-than-perfect walling and fencing weren't entirely haphazard: with a shortage of grazing always a concern on Parish Farm, a couple of miles of uncut verges running alongside the fields and pony paddocks made unavailable to Norman were not too bad a pasture. I had been on enough exasperating, time-consuming rescue expeditions with Norman to know that not to be true, but one could understand the suspicion.

'For a cow, she's a bit of an escape artist, I have to say,' Norman would note about Sneaky, and Norman had seen a few. 'She can jump walls, proper ones. And fences.'

It would start with the knock at the door and the outraged motorist. Norman would be nowhere in sight and I would head off with my stick. Sneaky was thin and brown and would be grazing the verges somewhere, more interested in her tummy than her calves. Finally, one afternoon she escaped three times. The first time, she was herded back into the yard, the gate shut behind her, but by the time I was back at the cottage she was out again. She'd made it around to Home Paddock, and there in front of me, she skipped over the broken-down wall like a dog. I herded her back in, but later in the afternoon she was out again, this time with a partner in crime.

Knoxey knew to drive slowly round the corners near Norman's farm and he was laid-back enough, but this was getting too much, even for him.

'It's bloody ridiculous,' he said in the pub that night. 'I came round the corner and there's that bloody cow again, that bloody brown one.'

'Sneaky,' Han offered.

'That'd be right, Sneaky. There's going to be a bloody nasty accident one of these days, I tell you. And what happens if one of them diseased animals has got foot-'n'-mouth, then what?'

'Apparently she can jump fences, and walls, proper ones,' I said.

'Don't be bloody ridiculous, anyone could jump one of Norman's fences. Half the fucking things are pieces of baler twine tied round a rotting post,' he retorted. A week later it happened again, and this time someone complained to the police.

There was one particular piece of wall that Sneaky did use as something of a gateway, and I hinted to Norman that maybe it might be an idea to get it repaired. I'd help.

'That won't stop Sneaky,' he said.

'That won't stop Sneaky,' said Douglas. 'She can jump walls and fences, and all that. Proper ones, and all that.'

But a week later and a dozen more escapes, there was a knock on the door. It was Norman.

'You busy today?' he asked.

This was new. This was him asking me for help, not me offering and him wondering why or how a man offered his labour for free.

'Why?' I answered, after what I hoped was a credible delay and with a wry enough smile.

The police had been round, someone had complained, the wall on the lane needed to be fixed.

Sure, I said.

Douglas came round at ten to pick me up and the three of us spent the morning on the walls. We talked the normal wall talk: bikes, class structure ('Don't let Douglas talk politics,' Norman warned, 'he's a socialist, ain't he?'), cars, the trains (identifying the makes of the passing trains, of which there were only two: Intercity

125, he would knowledgeably point out; yup, I'd say, that'd be your Intercity 125), and stress and cities.

'Stress is what kills people, Ian. Stress. And cities. Factories. And all that. I tell you what, my brother, works at that place where my dad worked, he says that working on the farm is boring. But he's working in a factory, standing in the same place doing the same thing all day. How boring is that? Now that is stress, that is.'

'Don't you ever stop talking, Douglas?' asked Norman, steadily working away and giving me a smile.

'Why, what's the matter, can't you work and talk?' said Douglas, pulling himself up in surprise.

'I can work and talk; I just can't work and listen.'

Our lunch break, taken at the table on the terrace at the cottage, was exactly one hour. Douglas timed it from the minute we sat down to eat and not before and noted it precisely on a piece of paper, carefully folded and put away until it was carefully unfolded and the time our lunch break finished noted too.

After lunch Douglas and I were up at the yard, getting the tractor to pick up some stone. A sheep had escaped and fallen into the slurry pit. Its two shit-covered young lambs bleated, panicked, scared and hungry, as their mother's thick wool coat got heavier and her body sank more with every effort to free herself. Douglas said he hadn't noticed until I pointed her out.

'Oh, Norman can do that. He'll be back soon.'

It's not my place to say, I'm a city boy, but this is two tiny lambs watching their mother drown in a slurry pit, something has to be done.

'Get them pieces of corrugated iron then,' Douglas instructed me reluctantly. 'Put 'em on the shit and then you can walk over them and get her.'

'Are you sure that'll work, Douglas?'

'Yeah, go on, then.'

I put the first one down and it lay promisingly on the shit, a walkway to the now near-hysterical ewe who thrashed and tried, but sank back more exhausted with each futile effort. It was not looking good. I put one foot on to the metal and it sank instantly under my weight; I swung back up to the side of the pit just in time.

It was clear. Someone had to go in the pit, waist deep at best, up to the neck maybe, and get the ewe. Or she was going to drown.

And that someone was not going to be the socialist timekeeper. At which point, like a miracle, Murray showed up.

'WHATHEFUCKKINGELLSGOINGNONNEARREN?' he shouted.

'It's a sheep, stuck in the slurry pit, Murray.'

'I can fucking see that,' he said, and without a word of discussion or invitation, jumped into the pit and disappeared up to his waist in shit. Lord knows how he did it but he waded through it and started shit-wrestling the animal, so much more terrified now at the company of Murray than by her previous predicament that I was certain she was going to drown herself.

'Come 'ere, you fucking thing. Jesus, I fucking hate sheep,' he shouted, as he struggled after her. 'Fucking stupid animals, what the fucking 'ell did you jump in 'ere for?'

I couldn't look, not knowing whether I would laugh or cry. This was obviously not going to work and Murray was going to drown and I was going to drown saving him and all the time Douglas would be doing what he was doing now, giving a lot of useless instructions.

'Come 'ere, you fucking bastard!' said Murray.

I tried to get Murray to stand still, to stop. We needed a plan, we needed a rope, we needed competent people, we needed help, but Murray was having none of it. As the lambs were going berserk, the ewe made one final bleat before entering a stage of catatonic, wide-eyed terror. Murray was swearing and screaming and then somehow, *somehow*, I don't know how, he lifted the animal to the side and up and out and it was the most incredible feat of strength and perseverance I had ever seen. The ewe collapsed on its front legs, her lambs came hurtling over and then she was up and they were away.

'Jesus, I fucking hate sheep,' he said as he climbed out. He was truly covered in shit.

'Murray, *that* was fucking well done. Listen, er? Do you want to come back to the cottage and change, you know, maybe have a shower?'

'No, don't you worry about that,' he said, wiping the shit off himself with his hands and then dipping his hands in the cattle trough. 'Where's bloody old Norman 'en? He owes me some money, two quid.'

'I don't know actually, Murray.'

'You tell 'im I was here and I'll come round later. Going into town now, I gotta pick up grandad's paper.'

'OK, well, thanks then.'

I looked around, checking to see if there was anyone there who could confirm what I'd just seen: Murray, covered in shit, on his moped heading off to W. H. Smith.

'Better be getting back to that wall then, Ian, and all that,' said Douglas.

Norman joined us back at the wall, and at the end of the day, as we walked home, he remembered some time when I must have told him that I keep a journal.

'So, what will you be writing in your book for today, then? That you spent it with two old locals?' We laughed.

I told him, jokingly, what I would write about his observation about my journal: 'That Norman, he doesn't miss much,' and Norman chuckled.

Douglas came and had a drink, that would be very nice, that would, thank you very much.

'Now that is bootiful, that is, Ian,' says Douglas sitting at the table, looking out over the fields. 'Beats being in an office all day.'

The next day, from the field with the new, beautifully capped three-and-a-half-foot-high drystone wall, Sneaky escaped.

The days got longer and the mood lighter as spring moved along. Down at the pub, Knoxey bantered crudely with a barmaid about her sexual appetite, history and skills, joking that the only reason she'd have sex with a condom would be for her to avoid giving away one of her sexual diseases.

'Too bloody right,' she joked back. 'I'm not giving them away for free after all the work I put in to get 'em.'

The news was on and it was footage of a building being blown up in San Diego.

'I was in San Diego once,' said Lennie distractedly to no one in particular, his chin cupped in his hand, his elbow on the bar. 'Got beaten up. By a lesbian.'

'It's difficult, that,' said Geoff, 'being attacked by a woman. I got attacked once by this old bloke in Little Mayford. He was about seventy. I hated him. He always used to bash me when I was a kid.

I was coming up the hill one night and there he was talking to some bloke. As I walked past I leant in and said to the other bloke, "You don't want to talk to that old fucker." Next day he comes up to me and he says, "What did you say yesterday to me when I was talking to that bloke?" I said, "Don't talk to an old fucker like you." He went bloody berserk he did, kicking and punching and I don't know what. It was bloody difficult, I can tell you. I mean, what can you do, you can't hit an old bloke like that, can you?'

Before settling down at The Leggers', Geoff had moved back with Laura to the village of his birth, Little Mayford. As rumour had it, it was with Laura's divorce settlement from her ex-husband (whoever that was depended on which of the dozen versions you believed; one such had it that it was a high-ranking Scottish peer) that he or she had bought the lease on the local pub, The Marsham Arms.

Knoxey, the kid who was bashed, became the man who ran the pub in the village of his birth, and I was never sure if that decision to return to Little Mayford was because of demons he was trying to exorcise or a happiness that he wanted to return to. Geoff was a Gloucestershire man, and Little Mayford was his family's village, but it was here, finally, at The Leggers', that he had chosen to make his home, at the end of a dirt road, outside the view of any village. He or Laura had bought the lease to The Marsham from Peg and her husband after he ran off, eventually to Portugal. Several years later Peg came into the fold of the The Leggers' after Laura had sold the lease of The Marsham to the man who had lived in Lettem Cottage and whom she initially worked for. At least that's how I understood it. No one ever told me a complete history; just small pieces of conversation that somehow made a picture.

Geoff was a late child to an older father, also born and raised in Little Mayford, and how he loved his father. His father had joined up aged sixteen in 1915, just outside the pub his son (over half a century later) would become the landlord of. Geoff's father served as an engineer attached to the Scots Guards.

He survived that war and came home and worked as a drystone-waller and mason. Geoff said his memory of his father was of a man who was always, always working.

'There wasn't much fun in Little Mayford in those days. Everyone just worked,' Geoff would say.

His father would rise at six, go to the yard and see his boss to find out his job for the day, to which he would then cycle ten miles or more and work on the walls all day. After a ten-mile ride home, he would be back by five, have a cup of tea and head straight to the garden. Then he would eat his evening meal and go up the church to cut the grass or rake the leaves. He was always working, and I think that's probably why Knoxey wasn't.

Peg did most of the work in the pub. She was the manager, Laura did the books, May did the cooking and Knoxey did not a lot. He did the welcomes and the jokes and the tales and the drinking and the spoofing; the racing, the Corvettes and the rugby and the golf, and all the things everyone else never had the time to do. If they were too busy working on the land or studying at the college or fighting at the office, Knoxey was there at the end of the dirt road, free of all that, and if you went down there and joined him, you would be too. And perhaps that's why everyone loved The Leggers' and a lot of people loved Knoxey.

At the beginning of May, there were leaves on Frankie's Tree, and great swaths of yellow came out as the rape flowered. The Bee Man, a friend of Norman's from over Burford way, arrived with the bees for the hives that stood in Bee Copse. It was Norman's father who had planted the low fruit trees along its edge, and the hives had been there for nearly twenty years. Where the bees had been for winter we didn't know, but they were back to pollinate the Marsham rape that stood opposite, its scent enveloping Han and me as we walked down the lane.

'Watch out at night,' the Bee Man warned, 'when you're walking to the pub.' He left us with visions of killer swarms, but they never bothered us.

For the first time in months I could run the waterlogged canal path, now finally dried out. The canal trust had been at work on the Lock House, bricking up the windows and the doors to prevent the kids, I guessed, from having their fires and parties inside it.

Norman and Murray came for our first barbecue of the year, at lunchtime, sitting on the terrace in the sun. Norman was already complaining about the weather, not enough rain. He remembered Sidney, the old man who used to live in the Lock House up until 1959, he thought. Down the overgrown path, long after the canal was dead and long before the trust was clearing, fussing and remembering, he lived all alone. Once a week, he would come down the path to the lane, cross the canal bridge and slowly, slowly wobble his way up to the village, using two sticks for support, a battery on his back. His battery was his only source of power and used solely for his radio; his only reason for coming to the village was to have it recharged at the garage that used to be there.

'Opposite The Butcher's Arms it was.' (The beer shop in the centre of the village, long now a private home.) 'Used to have a school then too. All gone now.'

I had to go away, to Turkey, only for a few days. I was to be best man to my Wiltshire childhood friend Scott who had lived in Istanbul for many years, and this was to be his stag trip. Spider and Dave joked that they were sure I was a spy, resting after a troubled assignment, occasionally called upon for a dangerous mission. To Istanbul, for example.

I didn't want to go. I'd miss a day at Lettem and then I'd miss it all. I'd come back and it would be summer and that moment, that exact moment when you first say summer is here, would have been and gone.

Knoxey stopped by in his car, on his way to the dog track, and wished me well on my trip. We stood and talked in the lane in the late-afternoon warmth, Maggie straining to get up and lick his face. We'd told Knoxey that Han was pregnant and not to tell anyone else and soon everyone knew. He felt pleased and involved, and remembered the drunken day at Ascot when Han, already pregnant unknown to us, told him we had been trying and he had told her it would all come out right.

In the afternoon I headed down the lane, the Lock House peeking through the trees as the leaves thickened, running with Maggie. Sukey sat in the dirt by Norman's garden gate and saw us off, maybe thinking about the time she could run and her paws weren't flat. It was an evening of brooding clouds that never delivered rain, the warm air so busy with fragrance and diffused evening light that everything seemed blurred.

Coming home that afternoon past hedges of white blossom, we stopped at the top of Tidcombe Hill and I dreamt of living here for ever. Of the caravan being moved, and tidying up Norman's yard; of winning the lottery and fixing all the crumbling walls, of driving ancient tractors and finding escaped cows with Douglas and rescuing drowning sheep with Murray. And of sinking deeper into this place, and once in a while hobbling down to the pub with two sticks for support.

## CHAPTER 7

# SUMMER

The lawn is parched and brown, the courgette crop so bountiful my father swims naked in a bright blue swimming pool washing his harvest. He lies back in the water, laughing, his face held up to the sun, surrounded by the floating courgettes.

The summer of '76.

The roots of the trees along the road loosen in the dry cracked soil.

The memory of a single summer of drought served as a reminder of the possibilities of the one to come. For Norman and Knoxey, their memory of summer was not of a single year but of an entire childhood. They could tell of Cotswold summers that once were days on end hidden in the shade of a hayrick, with a Rosie or a Jo, but no one could tell me when all that had ended and this all had started: the cold bank holidays, the washed-out Wimbledons, the motorbike crashes on the main roads south to the coast, the sporting defeats and the barbecues surrounded by people wrapped in June jumpers.

I longed for a southern summer, weeks running into weeks of heat and hugging shadows and hoping for rain, a single sheet on the bed and a shaded depression in the lawn under Frankie's Tree, too hot to roll out of.

Douglas announced summer with news of an accident on the summer's first bank holiday; his father had been called in to work to take care of the bodies. 'Both killed, they were. In'suntly. The helmet cracked open, you see, no car involved or nothing. I wonder why people go running off everywhere on bank holiday weekends, and all that. Can't understand it.'

Summer in the village was advertised by an invitation, a photo-copied note in the parish magazine. The owners of one of the big houses had invited people from the village to use their swimming pool and tennis court once a week throughout the summer: Tuesday afternoons from one until seven. I mentioned it to some others from the village in the pub that night. Some hadn't got the invitation in their copy, they said. It was hinted that the invitation hadn't made it into every copy of the magazine delivered, and probably not to the council houses at the end of the village. I wondered if this selective delivery was true and hoped it wasn't, because it was a kind and generous invitation that few would make.

Spider had prepared the cricket pitch for the season on the last remaining patch of infill land off the village lane, a spot otherwise waiting to have concrete poured over it and another hundred matchbox houses built on top. Of eleven players on the team for that season, only one lived in the village, and Spider seemed to be a defender of a space and an institution that was hanging on to existence. That summer, the English lost the test cricket series to Australia, nil–three. Perhaps the Australians simply had more small cricket pitches that their winners grew up playing on.

For the early-summer elections, we ambled up the lane to the village hall and cast our votes. An Old Etonian from Norfolk called Geoffrey Clifton Brown (or 'Clitoris Brown' as Knoxey preferred to call him) was elected our Member of Parliament. He had become the constituency MP in 1992, aged thirty-nine, prior to which, according to his biography on the Conservative party website at the time, he appeared never to have had a paid job outside of politics. The Labour candidate had been into the pub once, Geoff said; a young lad, from Stroud or somewhere. He came third.

An English summer is a single day that we cast as the memory of the season's weeks and months. The day before is chilly, pale and blustery, but the next will be the day, the moment when we say, 'Now this is what we mean by an English summer.'

This day – of which there are few but of which winter's expecta-tions and longings tell us there are many – takes place under an immense blue sky with a few solitary puffy white clouds there to remind us of its alternatives.

It is hot but the heat is clean and fresh because there is but the gentlest breeze, too weak to disturb a hair or move a leaf but strong enough to gently circulate the air. And with all this heat and sun and sky, nothing is brown or parched or cracked. Instead, everything is heavy with green. We are refreshed by the rain that came yesterday and reassured by the rain that will come, but which today seems impossible. The landscape is fat with verdant hedges and huge, leafy trees, and underneath them soft, knee-deep banks of grass and shade.

And with it comes the smell of heat and cut hay or harvested wheat, sun cream and the sticky, warm remains of a bottle of once-cold beer, each smell separate and distinct but only one small part of summer's scent. Your eyes close under the rose hedge, Han sitting reading on the lawn under a sun umbrella, Maggie asleep by your feet, your fingertips feeling the moss and tracing the furry stem of a daisy; sounds of an English summer ease through your consciousness. A single wasp, a small plane in the distance, high up in the sun; a far-off lawnmower, a child's laugh carried softly from up in the village, the scrape of Norman's back door as he comes home for a glass of cold water. You open your eyes as the shadow of a high pigeon flicks across you, and see butterflies and milling flies under the haze of the lime tree.

The phone rings. A friend from a city.

Yes, I'm fine, yes, doing lots of writing (you lie). Work? Oh, bits and pieces, you know, paying the bills. (Again.) How are you?

It's a Tuesday afternoon. You should be sitting in a meeting. Taking notes. Instead, Maggie stirs and pads over. She sits at your feet, head up, tail wagging. C'mon on, she says, let's go for a run.

During our first disjointed summer at Lettem, harvests came and went with all our comings and goings, and fields changed from swirling coats of golden crop to stubbled, shorn patches of brown, always it seemed, on the days when we were away. This summer, we didn't move and watched the rape turn yellow to green, the grass green to hay, and the green barley golden and then gone.

At Parish Farm, it started with the cutting and the baling of the hay in the first two weeks of July. Norman was, to my amateur mind, first and foremost a stockman. Hay, then, was his most important crop for the long winter ahead with its daily distribution to the sheds and sodden, grass-gone fields. His weed-infested crops of wheat and linseed were vague concerns, and against the huge acreages of Marsham's industrialised fields, sprayed and manicured all year round, modest and irrelevant. Hay was the thing; without it, feed would have to be bought.

Despite the busyness of the season, Douglas continued to work his three-day weeks, as much because of his own wish not to work more as Norman's inability to pay more.

Norman was one of the last farmers in the area still to make small bales, and as a matter of course, and for many years, he would often bring in an entire field of small bales on his own. The field would first be cut, then the hay rowed-up, then baled. Once baled, small stacks of six to eight bales were prepared, to protect the bales from overnight rain but also to facilitate their being collected.

For the collection, Norman would enter the field with a tractor and trailer, go to a small stack, get out, then chuck the bales on to the trailer. Then he would have to climb on to the trailer, stack the bales, jump down, get back in the tractor, drive to the next stack and start all over. Once the trailer reached the height of a few bales, this job either involved considerable strength and stamina to chuck the bales to be stacked on to the top, or required the addition of another phase, the second chuck to the top of the stack after the first on to the trailer.

As a result, the haymaking that a well-staffed farmer might hope to conclude in a frenetic burst of multi-handed labour, on Parish Farm dragged on well into August. Given the vagaries of an English summer, the chances of completing this task on a fifteen-acre field, single-handed, without there at some point being rain, was low. But Norman had done it anyway.

Ideally, bringing in the hay was at least a three-man job (one to drive the tractor and trailer, a loader and a stacker), and sometimes extra hands came in the shape of Murray or Douglas, and Malcolm. And this year, me.

Malcolm was bookish, thin and bearded, his veiny legs revealed by the shorts that he liked to work in during the summer, with ankle socks and sensible shoes. He would say 'cheers' every time I passed him up a bale, and he liked to stack. Norman told me how his father was always complaining about how useless Malcolm was about the farm and how he wouldn't let him do anything.

'"You better clear off and find something else to do, because you're no good round 'ere," he used to say,' Norman told me. But despite his father's words, Malcolm frequently came back to help Norman and it meant a lot to Norman, I am sure. I thought of Norman and his brothers and tried to imagine their father, Freddy, whose influence and aura lurked in every corner of the farm and their lives, and whose reserve and suspicion had been passed on to his sons. Geoff told a story of how, one Christmas Eve, he had called on the cottage with a box of chocolates for Norman's mother.

'"*What you want?*" asked Freddy. "It's Christmas Eve, Freddy. I'm dropping off a present," I said. "*Why?*" he barked. Never a thank you, never a word, always that suspicion.'

At first Malcolm didn't trust me either, I felt. What did I want, why was I helping his brother? I'd come to the yard and ask Norman to come over for a meal and Malcolm would speak up for his brother, protecting him, and I liked him for it. As Malcolm spoke I remembered my own brother, how he used to look out for me; fending off the other kids from our hoard of sweets, gathered in the shade of a summer garden tree, sweets we had won in games at a children's party, before he ran off to win us more.

No, he can't possibly come, he's got to feed the cows now, Malcolm once said, and then went off home and left us. Norman came over anyway.

But stacking bales over the summer, Malcolm and I got there, sort of, swapping little pieces of information about each other with each load of hay. He quietly let it be known that he knew there was more out there than Parish Farm or what his brother might know, and that he knew the farm was in something of a state of disrepair. But he never criticised Norman and always defended him.

'That's a winter job, that is,' he would say as, for the umpteenth time, we went through a smashed-up wooden gate held together by baler-twine. At the yard, the hay barn whose roof had partially collapsed over the winter had still not been fixed, and the last of the old and rotting hay from last year stood uncleared on the ground. Norman, the same man who was unstressed about the future had also not prepared for its arrival. Nothing had been done to ready the barn for the harvest despite the granite certainty of its annual occurrence. Norman's farm and farming were endless days of dealing with the here and now, never with the future, with no time spent on fixing a broken gate that, within a hundred openings of it, would pay back the time taken to repair it.

Everything seemed undone, impossible, behind schedule, needing time and attention, but Norman was his normal unfazed, untroubled self.

'There just isn't the time now, is there?' Malcolm would add, and we both knew there never would be and that the whole farm was a winter job.

Murray, head shaven bald for summer, liked to work in the cooler evenings, and it suited me to join him then after a day at my desk writing or working on my rarely successful, half-hearted efforts to try and drum up a consulting project.

In the evening light, long and warm, we worked together, Murray bare-chested, white and flabby, sweat running off his shorn pate. Looking at Murray, one couldn't imagine he was as strong as he was, but nothing was too heavy or too arduous because no one had ever told him it was.

The stack of bales on the hay trailer was tall and wobbly and I said little as I chucked up the bales. Who was I to comment on Murray's stacking? Nearly done, Murray moved the trailer to one last pile and the entire load leant, hung in the air for a tantalising second and then tumbled into the field; an hour of hot, sweaty labour collapsed at our feet.

'Fuck,' said Murray quietly, unperturbed and matter-of-factly, and started to pick them up. This was going to be a long night.

Norman showed up. He stood and looked at the work we hadn't done and the pile of broken bales. I wondered what he would say. But Norman didn't get angry, not at all. Was he tired and exhausted by Murray and his stacking, or was there nothing to be angry about?

'The bottom layer doesn't come out over the edges, does it, Murray?'

Murray grunted.

'I've told you about that, Murray,' he said quietly, and then, without further words or censure, he jumped up on to the trailer, rearranged the bottom layer and began to stack as we threw the bales up. Murray and I were hot and white and sweating, hay stuck to our faces and backs. Norman was brown and lean, and swung bales effortlessly with one hand, not a drop of sweat seen on his face as we reloaded the trailer.

I drove the antique tractor and trailer home, the sun going down over Frimley Wood, Murray lying on the top of the hay bales, Maggie racing alongside and running circles around us; the heat and the smell of the engine, pigeons overhead on their dusk flight home to the canal. It didn't occur to Norman that a wholly inexperienced driver, with no instruction and no supervision, wasn't the ideal person to manoeuvre a heavily laden trailer down a hill using a tractor whose brakes didn't work, at night, with no lights, because they didn't work either.

In the Marsham field on the other side of the lane, two enormous, gleaming new combine harvesters were cutting the rape, and the contrast between the scale, equipment and staff of these two farms was laughable. With Maggie running behind me, holding up a car heading to the pub, and Norman off somewhere bringing in escaped animals, I liked to dream that my tractor and I were the true face of Cotswold farming and that the heavy-industry behemoths opposite were just impostors whose economies of scale would one day implode, collapsed under the weight of obscene subsidy and the guilt of economic rationalism that had steadily destroyed the natural world of the English countryside.

The big round bales that looked like large Swiss rolls was how most baling was now done in the Cotswolds, and Norman's battered and rusting square baler with its jams and stoppages and baler-twine and the release sleigh that dragged behind it was an ever rarer sight. William Coxley, the contractor who lived in the village, did some of Norman's baling, a whiz round a field in one of his monster tractors doing in a matter of a couple of hours what Douglas and Norman would take a day or more to do. Norman greatly admired Mr Coxley, the son of a stonemason, who had built up his contracting business as the estates and gentlemen farmers laid off their employees and sold their equipment and houses. I liked to think that Mr Coxley's rates for Norman's round bales were considerably less than he charged the richer farmers, and they probably were.

'He's a self-made man, he is,' Norman would say. 'He saw the future of farming all right.'

With Coxley's round bales, the only job then was to pick them up, one at a time; skewered on the fork of a front loader and dropped on to a trailer for the trip back to the yard. Four on the bottom row, three on the top and me or Malcolm at the wheel of one of

Norman's ancient tractors, straining to take our heavy loads home. If a cross-support bar would break on one of Norman's rotting trailers, Norman would shrug and carry on, the trailer bed resting on the bald back wheel, creating the effect of a permanent handbrake. Nothing could throw Norman; it was just part of the day. Repairs consisted of Norman lifting the trailer bed up with the front-loader fork as I jammed in a piece of spare wood grabbed from the pile in the yard to serve as an improvised support until it broke and the job would be bodged again.

Ludd-land spread further than the confines of Parish Farm and, having only some two-hundred-odd acres, finding extra ground for hay and grazing was essential to the farm's already precarious viability. There were a couple of paddocks Norman rented from Marsham, too small to be profitably used by the big machines of the Estate, along with land attached to Rathbury, and Mr Proctor's paddock in front of Lettem House. These were supplemented with some grazing in nearby villages and a few acres inherited or bought from an uncle, I wasn't sure which. He also took the hay from the fields belonging to The Weekender.

'She's a very frightening woman, she is, always shouting if you do something wrong,' I remembered Douglas once warning me as I turned my tractor and trailer down her drive.

I only ever saw her once. As we worked one afternoon in hot, hot sun to fix a broken trailer wheel, I watched her in her garden, dressed in a kaftan, staring at us; I wondered if she might bring us a glass of cold lemonade.

These precious acres were crucial to Norman, but their future was not assured. More money could be made renting these piece-meal fields to the horse owners and the hunters, the people in the big houses who scrabbled for land in an area where Marsham and one or two other big landowners seemed to control anything worth having. Most of the small paddock fields of the area were gone anyway, the drystone walls that delineated them long knocked down and their stone sold to property developers or buried under tracks. There had been two eras when most of the Cotswold walls had been built, firstly during the eighteenth-century enclosures, and then in the nineteenth-century depressions when enlightened large landowners, very likely the Marshams of that time too, had sought to provide work for the many unemployed. It was ironic that these same great landowners a century later had knocked so many down.

Norman's scattered grazing was the reason why I found myself on a hot summer's evening searching with Norman and Murray for escaped sheep in the high-sided valley that carried the canal when it left its dark, dripping tunnel the other side of Frimley Wood. Han and I had explored up here on our bikes, but Norman seemed surprised we should know this part of the county, although but a few miles away. It was different: deep and hilly and ancient.

'Come 'ere you fucking things,' Murray screamed, futilely running after the sheep down the sides of steep hills and wooded banks, energetic and enraged. When this wouldn't work, he would take to calling them like he would an errant dog, as if the sheep would now come to his gentle calls and pleas. They didn't, and back he would switch to cursing and yelling and shocking nice-looking people as we got the sheep out of their gardens.

I was tired, it was hot and now it was dark; no light, no moon and only Norman's ability to see in the dark and the sound of distressed sheep to guide us. The thick summer foliage covered the deep-cut lane, so it was cool, at least in there. Norman relentlessly plodded on at our task, knowing that given time, finally his will would prevail.

'What do you think we should do, then?' he asked quietly after the failure of yet another effort to steer the sheep through the right gate, the sheep instead pushing past Murray out into the lane he was supposed to block. I didn't know what to say. I wanted him to be in charge and confident and successful, with all his gates hanging true, his hay brought in and a wife at home who would have run him a cool bath and serve a pie she had baked.

Instead, he will go home and Sukey will have eaten the meal, long cold, left sitting on the ground at his back door by Dan or Rose, the young couple who had taken over the cottage from Stephanie and the catering deal that came with it. And I'll try and have him come and eat with us – it's past eleven and I'm hungry and he must be too – and he'll say he can't, got to check the cows, and it'll start to rain, and the hay to feed the cows, left to catch the sheep, will sit wet and heavy on the ground, and this winter when he breaks into it, it will be mouldy and spoiled.

After Norman and I finished working one day, stacking round bales high under a natural barn of beech trees up against the canal, we walked home in silence in the summer dusk.

Coming out of River Head Paddock and over the bridge by the Lambing Sheds, he said, quite suddenly, 'So how much do I have to pay you for all this?'

'You don't have to pay me anything, Norm. I enjoy it.'

He snorted and grinned sheepishly and we walked on in silence.

'I'm very grateful,' he mumbled.

'There is one thing you could do, Norm.'

'What's that then?'

'Move that caravan.'

Norman muttered something about speaking with Lewis (his other, middle brother), and the subject was dropped.

Some days later, he asked us if we liked lamb, and I knew the caravan discussion with Lewis hadn't worked out, if it had ever taken place. Norman gave us a leg of Parish Farm lamb from his freezer and we invited him to lunch. Han tried to cook it like Norman's mother would have, long and with two veggies, mint sauce and followed by an apple pie. He liked it. Dan and Rose were younger and used things like rice and pasta, and I don't think Mrs Bruce or Mother used much of that.

'It's sort of, well, slop, isn't it?' he said, grinning, knowing he was being cheeky.

Norman would pay me, in lots of ways. He tolerated my intrusiveness and my dilettante attitude to work on his farm, showing up to help when I wanted to and not when I didn't. On land where a rambler strayed from a footpath at his peril, Han and I could walk where we liked, and he let me run and play with Maggie, the ruination of any working dog but he reckoned she was wrong from the start.

Better, he told me details and showed me things I wouldn't have learnt without him, local stories and gossip, places and histories.

After rounding up some sheep one day, he asked me a real question.

'You got a bit of spare time?' he practically whispered, a little self-conscious, I think, that he might know what would please me, or self-conscious in wanting to please me. I wasn't sure.

'You know me, Norm,' I said.

'You ever seen Rathbury House?' he asked me of the place that stood invisible and cut off from the rest of the village.

Norman led me round the back, armed with the excuse of inspecting the sheep that he grazed on their fields.

It was a big, brooding, Gothic beast of a house tucked in under the screaming, towering rookeries on the site of an Iron Age hill fort; on a hot summer's day in the mid-afternoon, the air in the trees was cold and damp. I told Norman about the 1871 census I had seen, and the names of some of the families who had lived in the village, including at Rathbury House.

'What was the name then?'

'Inge.'

'That's it! Inge!' he said excitedly, the flash of a childhood memory. 'Old Mrs Bruce used to speak of them!'

The buildings that surrounded Rathbury House, the old coach houses and stables that once housed the Inges' staff, were now at least four separate homes, one lived in by the estate-agent son of the owner of the main house.

Before leaving, Norman showed me Rathbury Farm, Goonetilleke's place, originally the old farmhouse of the Rathbury property. I saw an ugly extension, expensive gardens and a tennis court, and, behind it, the private polo ground that once upon a time Norman's father ran sheep on.

The spring thieving, which at the time had offered such intrigue and excitement, looked pedestrian compared with what took place in the village that summer. 'The Poisoning' made the national newspapers and local television, and the village was full of detectives, journalists and amateur sleuths. Everyone knew who did it, or at least they thought they did. And the person who didn't know who did it, but was quite sure that we all did, was the victim.

Some time over the first summer bank holiday someone had entered the garden of Lettem Barn, the house of the Larches (the couple we had met at Miss Dibden's who edited the parish magazine), three-year residents of the village. Newcomers, one might say. There, a person (or persons) had spread what was most likely weedkiller over several hundred pounds' worth of carefully planted and tended plants and trees and a third of an acre of lawn. This much we all learnt from the 'Police Witness Appeal' published in the summer edition of the parish magazine.

Stapled to the facing page was a photocopied insertion that read:

> REWARD: *A substantial reward is being offered to anyone who provides information to the police which leads to a conviction of the person who carried out the criminal damage to the garden at Lettem Barn. The police telephone number is on the inside of the cover of this magazine.*

Everyone knew of the crime long before the parish magazine came out, not because we were such a tight, intimate community, but because Peter Larch decided that the best way to handle this nasty and bitter act of vandalism would be to launch his very own local and national media campaign. We heard about it in the local paper, and it went from there.

That the Larches' garden was in trouble was already common knowledge. One couldn't help but notice the slowly browning lawn and dying plants. But even Peter Larch at first thought it was perhaps a watering problem or some other natural phenomenon. It took him a good three weeks from the time he saw the damage to the time it dawned on him what had probably happened, and by then he was a very angry man. What hurt him most, I think, was the destruction of all the work his wife had so carefully done, taking cuttings and shrubs from their old home, even from her mother's house, which had made the garden something more than a garden, a place of memorial.

Had it happened to us, Han and I would have been upset as well. I would probably have kept it quiet. Unless it was an entirely random attack, surely it would mean that I had badly upset someone.

But that wasn't Peter's reaction. He was morally outraged; he wasn't going to be beaten by the vile little minds who would commit such a crime; he was going to fight back. Despite the fact that he was probably dealing with someone local and that the crime was so rural (killing a man's plants, not vandalising his car or breaking his windows), he decided to apply methodologies that were entirely urban: PR and the police.

In contrast the person(s) who did it hadn't publicised their crime in any way. They hadn't even spray-painted Peter's walls or set a fire. This was a more private exchange between the perpetrators and Peter, but Peter let in as much light as possible. His behaviour had the air of a sort of schoolboy morality which had pupils nobly owning up to their crimes to benefit the greater good. I think it was his belief in this world that led him to conclude that if he was open and upfront about the crime, not only could he shame the less morally enlightened into giving up one of their own, but he could also deflect the notion that the crime was in any way justified.

Peter called up the local newspapers and invited them to his house to interview him about what had happened and to take pictures of his dead garden. And the local TV news. And then even the national press were on to it.

'I've got no idea who has done this. We haven't lived in the village long enough to make any enemies,' Peter said to the local paper.

Han and I were genuinely shocked and sympathetic. Violating someone's garden in such a way was a vicious, determined and wilful act of destruction, and we wanted to show our sympathy, so we wrote a card, and the next day I went up the lane to drop it off. I also wanted an excuse to have a good look.

There was Peter in the garden, in the company of Central TV's gardening expert, the camera crew due to arrive shortly. Peter was overexcited, and I had this slight sense that there was perhaps something positive for him to be found in this horrible event, plenty of things for the retired manager to do, excitement stimulated by the drama. But equally, this was very much his wife's garden, a garden she had given so much care and love to. No wonder he was as angry as he was.

He explained his strategy.

'Somebody, SOMEBODY knows who did it, and I'm going to shame them into telling me. I'm going to make sure EVERYONE knows about it. They used a knapsack sprayer, you know, sprayed the house right up to the reach of the outdoor lights on the house, so it must have happened at night. They must be sick. SICK!'

'Terrible,' I muttered, and the gardening expert shook his head.

'*Someone* in this village knows what happened,' Peter said, so angrily and directly I felt he thought I knew who did, 'and I'm determined to get them. I will get the person and I won't stop until I have.'

Right.

'Police being helpful?' I asked casually, thinking back to the bobbies I had met.

'*VERY!* In fact, that reminds me,' he whispered conspiratorially, 'I have some information for the police that I must give them.'

I can't deny that, for a moment, the idea of a summer playing Miss Marple was appealing, and there was no shortage of gossip, hints, suggestions and outright accusations to work from. After a while, I took time to itemise every theory I had at one point or another heard, and it was a long list.

First and foremost, the ubiquitous 'youth from the village': prime candidates. The people in the big houses only had a vague idea who these people actually were because they didn't live in the houses next to these people or have anything to do with them, so it was a convenient catch-all that loosely translated as 'the working-class teenagers who live in the council houses'. For those who knew them by name and reputation, they were a possibility; but a stealthy, deliberate, midnight act like this looked like the work of an adult, not a bunch of kids breaking in and trashing the cricket club pavilion. Peter could call it vandalism as much as he liked, but weedkillering at night in one particular garden was neither random nor mindless.

A variation on this theme was one of the parents of 'the youths from the village': a more likely theory, not least because the act was entirely adult in terms of its nasty sophistication and cleverness. The theory ran that someone was just fed up with how the newcomers had, in three short years, taken over the parish magazine (with its 'youth behaviour' editorials), become churchwardens and parish councillors, and were now even hosting the next-door village's school fête. In short, was this an attempt to put the Larches back in their place and remind them of deeper and more ancient village hierarchies?

Moving on: the rival gardener theory. Jealous of the fact that the garden under his care was being ever more eclipsed by the relentlessly fine horticulture of the newcomers at Lettem Barn, and concerned they might win 'Village Garden of the Year' again, he or she struck. Supporting evidence included 'the weedkiller-on-sole-of-shoe-footprints' in the grass leading from the gateway of Lettem Barn towards the house of the rival gardener.

'Random someone' was another idea I heard proposed. Someone from somewhere who picked the Larches' garden for this prank entirely at random, wanting to get the same buzz as aliens who come down from outer space and make crop circles.

Then there was the bloke who Spider was sure had done it but wouldn't name, however hard I tried to wangle it out of him, who was I think the same bloke who Norman was sure had done it but wouldn't tell me either, however hard I tried to wangle it out of him.

'You mean ...?' said Norman to Spider in front of me, nodding his head without saying the name. Spider nodded back, and I was sure that everyone in the village knew who did it except me, Peter Larch and his friends and the police.

Knoxey, of course, had to be on the list, if only because he had sort of incriminated himself one night in the pub by telling me how he had once sprayed in weedkiller the word 'c—t' on the eighteenth green of a golf club that had banned him, so there was at least some methodological precedent.

My favourite theory of all was the very least likely. It was Norm what done it. Norman was odd, he frightened people and was capable of anything. At least, this was the received wisdom. Norman and I regularly laughed about this one during the summer and took pleasure in accusing each other.

One thing was clear. There were two broad schools of thought. Peter and his friends found it much more digestible to think of the crime as a mindless act of vandalism. That made them potentially more vulnerable, but it meant at the same time that it wasn't, to be blunt, an act of class war against people who lived in big houses, sent their kids to boarding schools and hosted their noisy twenty-first-birthday parties in marquees in the garden. It also meant that Peter hadn't done anything to warrant it.

The other more local school of thought was that Peter Larch had badly upset someone and, around here, if you do that, despite all the steady gentrification and class cleansing and barn conversions, this is still deep rural England, full of Gloucestershire men who'll 'ave you.

Peter wouldn't let it go, and when his first PR campaign failed to produce any names that reached his ears, although the village and the pub were buzzing with them, he pressed on. To everyone's amazement, he recontacted the newspapers.

'Have you seen this?' Norman said, passing me an article in the local paper.

This time, I'm afraid, it read as if Peter had accidentally managed to simultaneously insult and appeal to those he referred to as his 'so-called respectable neighbours', who he said had failed to tell who had done it.

'I've had plenty of letters of sympathy,' he said, 'but so far no action.'

It was clear that he was convinced everyone knew who was guilty, but was refusing to give them up. He equated people 'not knowing' with people who knew but wouldn't tell, and I wondered if this article would pretty much see the end to any possible collaboration some of the village might have eventually given him.

It had been a strange summer of chilly days popping up in July and misty, cold autumnal colours and smells stopping by in August, and then back to summer and dry heat. I had to go away before the month was out, and the leaves were already turning. My relationships had changed that summer, and each week had seen little milestones of knowledge and confidences. I had even got to know Tom, the mysterious man from the pub, who for twelve months had not said a word to me.

Tom was difficult to place, and therein perhaps lay the reason I warmed to him. He had the manner and bearing of a man of authority and knowledge, and yet at the same time was modest and charming. He was about my age, probably a little older. He was tall and lean and he always wore the same type of clothes: heavy cotton white or brown shirts, well-worn green moleskin trousers, and boots. He wore a leather belt, not, I think, to hold up his trousers, but to carry a small leather pouch, in which I assumed there was a knife, which he was never without. He had a particular way of walking, straight-backed and quick, that disguised what was in fact a gentle limp. Round his wrist he wore a copper bracelet, and he steadily smoked rolled-up cigarettes, but without the urgency of a heavy smoker.

He seemed known to everyone in the pub. He spoke with the phrasing and the ordered grammar of someone well educated but without any of the edge or annoying phraseology that sometimes comes with a public school accent. Instead, his English was spoken with a delicate Gloucestershire accent, sometimes so faint as to be almost undetectable, sometimes stronger, given the beer or the company.

What was strange was that he and I must have both been in that pub at the same time on dozens of occasions, and yet we had never spoken, despite speaking to many of the same people. At some time that summer, at a moment of his choosing, he must have decided that I was all right, because suddenly we were speaking, and the next time I saw him we were drinking and laughing, and when the pub closed, he invited me, among others, back to his house the other side of the village for a drink. Whereas Knoxey and Spider and others had been open and trusting of this newcomer many months ago, Tom had studied and bided and sounded it out and finally thought he might give me a go.

'John had said you were all right,' he told me later, 'but I wasn't sure.'

Tom's remote house was that of a countryman from top to bottom. Everything was neat and tidy and just so but, like him, not in a precious way. It was the house of an organised man, independent and busy. But busy with what? There were no clues as to his profession, unless this was a man who was a professional countryman. There were stuffed animals and birds, some antique clay pigeons, foxes' brushes, wildlife photos and paintings, a cup won at a country fair for shooting, books on birds and poaching and trapping and angling, fly boxes, rods, nets, gun cupboards; and two large black Labradors, one old and grey, and one younger, barking and loud and banished to the kennel in the back garden. The back porch, which led off the kitchen into the garden, was bulging with boots and green outdoor clothes for every occasion, all of which, like his house and his clothes, looked frequently used but were equally neat and tidy.

The garden contained a shed and a large pen holding ornamental pheasants, which he bred. The pheasants were sitting up on a pole that ran across the width of the pen, which he had made himself. The birds had long, exotic tail feathers closer to a peacock than any pheasants I had seen.

'The pheasants like to sit up on something off the ground,' he said, 'they like to roost on something, up out of harm's way.'

He passed me a beer and we drank standing out under the stars. That was the first piece of practical information he told me, and I remember it well.

This Lettem summer was too good to leave, but I had been offered a media project in the Balkans that I much wanted to do, and had to spend a few weeks travelling there. With the last few months of the pregnancy, Han was stopping work. Even though I planned to keep writing and not go back to full-time work, I did need to take on something that I hoped might develop into some better-paid consulting, despite my reluctance to search it out. In the snug bar, my destination was now conclusive evidence that I was a spy.

I had stopped round to say goodbye to Norman, when he told me that he had reached an agreement with Lewis and Malcolm over the farm. It wasn't to be sold, but instead his tenancy of the farm from the brothers was secured, and there was nothing they could do to sell it out from under him. Other than Han's pregnancy, this was the best piece of news we had heard in our time at Lettem, and I think Norman was perhaps a little surprised at how pleased we were.

At the pub, Han and I spent an evening drinking with Knoxey. It was difficult to say, as someone who couldn't presume to know him well, but that summer he had seemed a little different from the man I had got to know the past year. He had more or less forgiven me for a disastrously drunken party I had organised at The Leggers' at the beginning of the summer for my friend Scott as part of my best-man duties. It had only been salvaged by Peg's gentle forbearance, May's good humour and the amused tolerance of Liz, Spider, Liam and Lennie who were there to witness it; but I didn't think it was that I was picking up on.

At times he would strike me as somehow a little absent, pre-occupied with memories or worries, or secret ambitions for a happy future that didn't include endlessly entertaining and listening to us and all our nonsense. Spider said something that made me wonder if Knoxey hadn't even been short with him, and Knoxey cared for Spider, I think, in a way neither would ever admit.

It was a warm, late summer's night. There was a full moon, Han and I the last to leave the pub. Knoxey walked out with us and we stood in silence and looked at the light in the sky and how the moon haunted the high beeches over the canal. He pushed his chest out and breathed in that smell of summer night, and we said nothing.

'Good night then,' he said finally. He was taciturn but seemed laden with thoughts. He had been lucky, blessed; to be here, to have this, and he knew it.

# CHAPTER 8
# HUNTER'S MOON

Hotel Moskva, Belgrade. Sunset. Lying on a bed in the late-summer heat of a room that overlooks the Sava. In the distance the burnt-out shell of a government building destroyed by cruise missiles. The bloody sky is filled with a steady high stream of black crows coming in to roost in the city above the rivers. I see German bombers over Belgrade; black rooks coming in over Parish Farm, to settle in the high Rathbury trees above the Lambing Sheds. I see Han, pregnant, gardening in the cool dusk, Maggie for company and Norman out in the fields.

In Skopje, with helicopters overhead at the airport and trucks at the gate of the British base selling boxes of DVD porn, I arrive on the heels of the Parachute Regiment, men routed out there via a base near Cirencester. I hear of the bombs that go off each night. I want to be home.

I was away for five weeks and when I returned, the world, they said, had changed. I was in Sarajevo on 9/11. The Bosnians remembered their long agony and we drank whisky in the afternoon as we watched CNN in an office a hundred metres from the zeroed ground of their own: the market and the site of the first mortar attack on the city, remembered in a splash of blood-red paint on the pavement. My Bosnian companion told me that if his war had taught him one thing, it was not to think of history in terms of the morrow, but to understand that today's events will have repercussions we can only begin to imagine. One should prepare oneself for the long run, he said, and one's tiny, helpless part in it.

Back at Lettem everything had changed, but it was only the

season, the weather and the tint of the land: the falling leaves, the return of the rain, logs burning in the open hearth of the autumn's first fire and the smell of heavy soil, ploughed already for a certain future. The cottage stood solid, warm, thick-stoned; there wasn't even a mention of the Twin Towers in the rector's letter. I don't think Norman would have known what the World Trade Center looked like before, during or after the attack, and I wished I hadn't either.

Marsham were well along with their ploughing and drilling. On the far side of the canal valley their fields were tidy sheets of rusty browns and reds, golden and burnt as the sun picked out the soil's shades and moistures between the dappled shadows of autumn clouds high overhead. At Parish Farm, Norman's maize stood tall and unharvested, and in Railway Piece his linseed crop lay battered, weed-infested and beyond use (or so it seemed to me). His wheat in Scot's Plantation remained uncut, combine harvester left out there with it, lonely and exposed, seemingly abandoned.

Lettem now smelt of nature's steady death, of turned earth, mulch and mast. The leaves of the beech trees on the track to The Leggers' were turning, and in the hedges blackberries were ripening thick. We picked and picked and came home and made huge pots of jam on the Aga, the sweet smell steaming up into the house, laughing at our newly discovered selves, the jam-makers. Han showed me her chutneys and jams made from the plums and the apples harvested from the garden trees in my absence, and I wished I had been here to feel the fine late summer that everyone spoke of and only I had missed.

Norman and Douglas and even Malcolm seemed happy enough to have me back, Malcolm singular in being much interested in where I had been or why. Douglas did tell me he'd like to travel but that he'd want to do it with someone who spoke the languages and with experience, and all that; then, remembering the very important thing that had happened while I had been away, he showed me the new light on his bike.

'Know what that's like, Ian?'

'No, what?'

'Battlestar Galactica.'

'Isn't it five o'clock yet?' joked Norman.

I got my bike and cycled down to the paddocks next to the canal where Norman had taken the sheep. It was an autumn dusk, quiet and crisp.

For a long time I stood silent and immobile next to Norman, staring at the sheep.

'It's good to be back,' I said.

'Is it?' he chuckled.

'Yes.' I wanted to say more but instead I stretched and stretched a silence and I hoped it spoke for me.

'I'm counting sheep,' he said finally, his voice as quiet and calm as ever. 'Got up to twenty-eight.' Before you interrupted me.

'Ninety-six?' I eventually ventured.

'That's about right,' he said. Close enough.

Douglas came and joined us on his way home, his Battleship Galactica headlight on full in the dusk light.

'Hello there then, bootiful evening it is. Bootiful.'

'They look well,' I said of the sheep.

Norman snorted.

'They won't fatten, they won't. I keep worming them, but they don't.'

A car went down the lane.

'Opel Astra,' said Douglas.

We stood all three in silence, doing nothing much. Another car.

'Audi TT.'

A long pause.

'Top of the range, it is, this light, Ian. Halogen. Super-bright light.'

Norman looked at me and we had the tiniest smile, and he knew why it was good to be back, better never to have gone.

The sun when it came was weak and watery, and evening mist filled the fields for the last weeks before the clocks would change. With the harvest on hold and the heavy work of winter cattle feeding still to come, we worked on the walls.

Norman even had time to pick mushrooms, which grew somewhere on the farm and which he would leave for us in a basket on our outside table. The first early morning that we went outside and saw them, I realised it was the gift of a secret: delicious fat mushrooms on land that no one walked or ever saw and that only Norman knew about. We asked him where he found them and he just grinned. Han took him her blackberry jam and chutney.

Harvest was supposed to be over, and so it was time again for the festival. Parish Farm ran on a slightly slower calendar, but Norman came nevertheless. He had little to do with the village but he did go to church one Sunday each month to ring the bell. It was a misty, close morning and we walked to church to the sound of Norman's single bell calling us in.

Compared with his usual attire, Norman looked fantastically well-groomed and prosperous, dressed in a brown jacket, shirt and tie, smart trousers and clean shoes. But it hadn't been a good year for Norman; only the maize crop in Upper Rathbury Field still held any promise.

The rector gave one of his popular, child-friendly family Communions and spoke to us from his pulpit ringed with a row of conkers, brown and shiny. The church had been carefully decorated with old man's beard and hedge clippings, gathered by the children of the farm club and the Sunday school, in the procession always organised by Mrs Stanton that once again I had managed to miss. He asked the children if they could think of any stories told by Jesus, and a little boy put up his arm and said, 'Joseph.' The rector said, kindly, that Joseph was a Bible story but not one told by Jesus, and then told his own story, the parable of the sown wheat. This year it was to be an action sermon.

The north aisle, in which we sat, was to act out the seed sown on the stony ground. We stood as we grew but then wilted back into our pews. At the very back of the central aisle was Norman, arms raised hesitantly over his head, supposedly starring as a tall stalk of very strong wheat.

After the sermon, the children paraded round the church pretending to cast the imaginary seed as we all sang a hymn, and then the rector led us in prayers. We prayed for farmers and retailers. I was just getting used to praying for the Queen, and now we had to pray for supermarkets. 'Let us pray for food distributors and retailers that they do it cleanly and offer fair prices to customers and farmers alike.' I agreed with his sentiment, but wondered what Norman made of praying for supermarkets and the notion that they might pay him a fair price.

As we celebrated this festival and prayed for Tesco's, Norman's crop stood in Scot's Plantation, awaiting the impossible: warm dry weather in October that would let him bring it in for a price that would make him bother.

I had seen the old pheasant-release pens in the two coverts on the farm, long deserted, with collapsed fencing and broken feeders. I asked Norman who had done the shoot on the farm and when it had stopped. A solicitor had had the rights to shooting on Parish Farm, he told me. They had been given to him free of charge for ten years in return for the legal work he did for Norman's father when Freddy had bought the farm from Lettem House. Whether the ten years were simply over, or the solicitor had become too old, or he hadn't wanted to continue, it wasn't clear; but no one had shot pheasants on Parish Farm for several years.

The little I knew about shooting I had learnt not from people who owned 'shoots' or from their 'guns' (people who paid to go shooting or were invited to do so), but from the people who worked for them. These were either gamekeepers, full- or part-time, past or present, like Tom, Spider and John; or 'beaters' like Murray and Liz who managed the local horse yard, the people who on shoot days would be paid to walk in front of the guns and flush the pheasants from cover to make them fly towards the guns.

The popularity of pheasant shooting had exploded in England during the 1980s and '90s, and was no longer the preserve of land-owners and their friends. The corporate entertainment industry had seized on the idea of taking clients and employees pheasant shooting. The estates also realised that there was a large market of people who might not have had the social connections to receive free invitations to shoot, but who were quite willing to pay hundreds or even thousands of pounds per day to do so.

Many estates in England quickly grasped the potential of expand-ing their shooting from a limited number of 'family' and some paid days during the shooting season (which ran from October through until the end of January) to shooting up to two or even more times per week, and selling those days on an open market.

However, more guns and more days demanded more birds, as 'driven shooting' turned from gentlemanly pursuit to full-fledged agribusiness. Few shoots in England, especially those with paying guns, could rely on wild pheasants. Instead they would artificially incubate their own eggs purchased from game farms and hand-rear them before releasing them into the open, often not more than a few weeks before the season started. In addition, or as an alternative, many would buy in eggs, day-olds or poults. Little of this was new, but what was new was the sheer scale of the endeavour and the extraordinary quantities of birds now shot each year. Depending on the time of year and the price, many of the shot birds would be buried in holes in the ground at the end of the shooting day, once the guns and beaters had departed, taking a few with them. Oversupply in the market could make the prices offered by game dealers so low that it wasn't worthwhile to pluck and prepare pheasants to be sold.

Many people who took part in shooting were adamantly against the type of shoots conducted by the principles of commerce and not of the countryside. I met gamekeepers and ex-gamekeepers who found these shoots totally disrespectful to their way of life, let alone to the birds; but the managers of these large shoots, almost always large farming landowners and estates, would argue their need to diversify, to survive; to follow the money.

In the Cotswolds there were pheasants on every lane and field, it seemed, and I suggested to Norman that perhaps he should sell the shooting rights to Parish Farm again. It would pay more than his wheat would this winter. He had sold a cow that week for only a hundred pounds.

Returning from a run with Maggie one evening a few days later, I found Norman shovelling cow shit from the sheds in the yard. He'd been thinking.

'You know that shoot?' he said. 'I'm going to put an advert in the paper.'

On the spur of the moment, I told him I could save him the price of an advert. I would take on the shoot, find the guns, get him his money. Spider had been filling me with tales of the shoot he was the gamekeeper for over on his boss's farm, and it sounded fun, what people did, something for winter.

'What do you want out of it, then?'

'Nothing, just the pleasure of doing it. What I get, you'll have.'

'Are you sure?'

'Yes, I'm sure.'

'You reckon you can find guns then?'

'Not a problem.'

Actually, I had no idea. I didn't know what I was doing, had never shot, had only ever beaten a couple of times as a boy. I didn't even own any green clothing. But I knew people who did. And so was born the Parish Farm Shoot, and I stumbled into the world where people killed animals for pleasure.

The plan for our shoot was a little different from the syndicated shoots that surrounded us. Norman reckoned that with just relying on wild birds, the farm could support three half-days of shooting during a season, with six guns on each shoot. I would be one and could borrow Norman's shotgun, leaving me to find the remaining five guns.

We called them 'wild birds', but actually few people these days had any idea which birds were wild and which were released. It was said that reared pheasants tended to be more susceptible to disease, and this, combined with being released directly into a killing zone, meant that released birds might have a life expectancy of little more than twenty weeks, when in the wild they could live several years, in the unlikely event that they lived somewhere with neither shooting nor too many foxes, stoats, weasels or magpies. What we called wild birds were in fact most likely to be released birds from neighbouring shoots which had sought refuge on Parish Farm.

Norman wouldn't shoot, he said.

'I know the birds too well, I do, by November. I don't like to kill them. Happy to shoot a fox if we see one. Funny how these shooting types don't want to shoot foxes.'

He, Douglas and Murray would beat, along with any friends or family the guns and I could muster.

I thought it best to check with Norman if he'd mind Knoxey coming on the shoot. There was the history of the burnt tractor and who knew what else. To my surprise Norman missed not a beat when I mentioned Geoff coming. Then I mentioned Spider too. I wanted very much for him to come; the shoot would not be right without him.

'I'd rather not.'

'Why not?' I asked. Norman and Spider had always seemed fine in my company, and Spider said never a bad word about him, nor Norman of Spider. Norman shifted slightly and gave me one of his wide-eyed 'I've been a bit naughty and I'm surprised you don't know' looks. There was a long pause, but I let it hang and Norman grinned and shifted on to the other foot, patted Maggie and hoped I'd move on, but I didn't. Finally, he relented.

'His father and I don't get on actually.'

'Why's that, then?' It wasn't like me to be so direct, but this time I couldn't not press on.

'Haven't you heard then?'

'No, what?'

Spider's dad and Norman had had a falling-out over something long ago and were not on speaking terms. Although it had had nothing to do with Spider, Norman had his reservations. This posed a big problem; how could I not ask Spider?

Han and I chewed over the problem and I conferred with Knoxey. He'd be the man to ask. Knoxey understood the problem and knew the cause of the feud that Spider was now the victim of. Sheep were being moved along a road, someone was there in their car, words (and some say blows) were exchanged and it ended up in court. Knoxey advised me to ask Spider to come anyway. He'd be sure to be busy with his own shoot that day; he'd decline, problem solved.

I asked Spider and he said yes, free that day, thanks very much. Good plan, I told Knoxey, what the hell do I do now? and Knoxey laughed.

With the shoot now on and the guns arranged (friends and friends of friends) it was time to check that there were indeed some birds to be shot. Maggie and I headed out on long rambling patrols to see what pheasants were about, enjoying the last half-dry days and autumn ground before we would have to return to the roads and lane for winter running. Norman, who was worried that we wouldn't have any birds on the day and about the expectations I may have created with the guns, announced he would put down feed some ten days before the first shoot in November. Our season was to start as early as possible, as pheasants didn't winter well on Parish Farm. There was too little cover for warmth, he said, and too many foxes.

Too many foxes were the result of the Marshams not allowing the shooting of foxes on their land, staunch supporters of the local hunt as they were. No one much minded that there were foxes after

Norman's lambs every spring because few people either knew about it or kept sheep locally themselves. As the hunt hardly ever caught a fox, and with no gamekeeper or shepherd to shoot them to curb their numbers, Parish Farm was swarming with foxes; bad for both Norman's lambs and the rector's chickens. Occasionally, the rector would complain of a particular night raider and Norman would sit up and shoot the offender and hang the brush on the rector's gate to show him and the foxes he'd been about. But fox-shooting, as I was to learn, is a night-time job, and Norman needed to sleep.

Our birds would be wild ones plus those put down by the shoot on the Marsham ground around Tidcombe. Marsham let out the shooting rights on this land (which bordered Norman's farm) to a man who lived in London, I think, and came down with his friends in the season to shoot. This man employed a part-time gamekeeper who bought in young pheasant poults in the summer, fed them and released them, and ran the shoot days. The gamekeeper was up against it; the Marsham land there, with its high cold acres of exposed fields with few walls, and small, scattered, spartan woods without the necessary short under-storey, was hardly the ideal ground for holding pheasants. And nor was the gamekeeper allowed to control the foxes. Hence they strayed, often encouraged by the hunt's regular practice of riding down the feed drives. Many of the pheasants would show up at Parish Farm to sit out the shooting season.

'We better not shoot too many of Marsham's birds. Most of them are up by Field Barn by the railway,' Norman said.

'If they're on your land, they're your birds, aren't they?' I teased.

'Not a very sporting attitude, that,' he chuckled, all gap teeth and naughtiness. It might even be called poaching if a man were to put some feed down up there to attract them over the railway to Parish Farm. 'You have to be careful, you know, round 'ere. Last time we had a shoot here, old Edward Marsham – Lord Marsham's younger brother – he phoned up, he did, that night. He'd heard there'd been a gun on his land, one of our guns had gone to pick up a bird on his side of the railway. You wouldn't think an old boy like that would know, but he did. "What you doing on my land?" Edward said.'

I didn't tell Norman, and I wouldn't do it now, but the next day I was up there fast, feeding corn from Norman's silo all down his side of the railway. It was not the right thing to do, not 'done', but I still had much to learn.

The first gun I had signed up was Knoxey. He'd suggested a shoot lunch afterwards in the snug, and for the shoot at Christmas time he'd do the full works, a Christmas dinner and everything.

From the summer and into autumn Geoff had carried with him the combined air of someone distracted and someone wanting to share memories and secrets. That autumn, unprompted, Geoff told me the first part of his story. Perhaps he told everyone his story, perhaps everyone who had ever been a local at The Leggers' knew it. He sounded reflective and I listened in silence.

Geoff had been a footman at Mayford House in Little Mayford. A footman was a junior butler whose everyday tasks included setting tables and sideboards and waiting at table, cleaning plate, glass and furniture and clothes. At the age of sixteen, he got the seventeen-year-old Austrian au pair of the house pregnant. She had had the baby, a girl. That meant he now had a forty-two-something-year-old Austrian daughter somewhere. He'd only recently told Peg this, he said, and again I wondered why he was telling these things; why now?

For this extravagant overreach of his duties he was dismissed, and he received lengthy lectures, threats and warnings from everyone from the vicar to his mother. No doubt the entire village told him he'd ruined his life and possibilities. I pictured the scandal. It is 1959 and the local aristocrat, responsible for the welfare of a young Austrian girl, has had to send her home to her alpine village or bourgeois town house, pregnant by a young Gloucestershire boy. What was said?

Geoff listened to the lectures and the dire warnings and then went and got another girl pregnant, a Cirencester girl named Carol. Knowing that the heat would be unbearable in the wake of the Austrian affair, he decided they should elope. That morning he chucked his clothes out of his bedroom window so his mother wouldn't suspect he was leaving, but when he came downstairs, there was his mother, looking at the pile of clothes in the garden.

'Oh, they must have fallen out of the window, Mum,' he said, and with that he went north to Gretna Green with only the clothes on his back, picking up Carol after she left her work that evening. She must have left a note for her parents; he didn't say.

They drove overnight to Gretna in Geoff's little car (a tiny old Austin) but found on arrival that the law of the day was not as simple as he had imagined. You had to live in the village for three weeks before you could get married. He had thirty pounds to his name, Carol savings of a hundred. They had to get jobs.

Being near Christmas, Carol got a job in Woollies in Carlisle and Geoff found work on the railway, laying track. Lots of people wanted that work. Jobs were short, but when it was discovered that Geoff, at the back of a long line of applicants, was a runaway, there was sympathy in the office and he was in. He was taken into the shelter of an army of big, aggressive, dodgy types who treated him as a son, who looked after him and whom he didn't forget.

It wasn't long before Carol's parents showed up, looking for their pregnant daughter. They spotted Geoff's car parked by the road, and that's how they found him.

'We're taking her home,' they said.

Carol turned up at the showdown, back from her work at Woollies.

'Mother!' shouted Carol's father. 'Put her in the car.'

'You're not taking her,' Geoff said.

'Mother, put her in the car!'

And so Geoff punched Carol's father.

'I'll never forget his shocked face, sitting on the ground.'

Her parents drove the long way back south, and Geoff and Carol were married.

That Easter they decided to come home for a visit. Geoff, being Geoff, headed directly for the point-to-point at Siddington, the steeplechase horse race organised every year by the hunt. There he met a man who knew the butler at the family seat of a Wiltshire earl. The man told Geoff the butler was leaving and that there would be an opening.

Geoff rang up the house from a phone box and spoke with the lady of the house.

'I can't believe I did it. I wouldn't do it today,' Geoff said.

Impressed by his nerve, she invited him to an interview.

A few weeks later he received a telegram. He'd got the job. He couldn't believe it.

He and Carol and their baby left behind Woollies and the railway gangs and the cold north, and began life in the service of an earl and his countess.

The last day of October, Coxleys the contractors come with one of their huge machines and cut what must have been the last crop of maize in the county. It was harvested late because it was planted late, but this time Parish Farm time had worked in Norman's favour and the contractors reckoned that for whatever reason it was one of the best crops of maize in the county. They used a machine that cut eight rows at a time and chewed stem and cob into one mushy green mess that was to be dumped in the clamp, a large hole in the ground, walled by the dug-out earth.

The clamp had been dug by Kennie. Kennie was a local bloke known for his fast cars and faster driving. When we had first seen him racing across the Humpty Dumps in a huge yellow JCB digger it was peculiarly impressive; speed was something we didn't see often on Parish Farm. But when he started to dig a very large hole we had been horrified. This being Kennie, there was a frightening range of possibilities as to what might happen next. Maybe Kennie was building a trail bike course or wanted to dump something large and metal up there.

Kennie was in his early twenties and worked for a contractor. What Kennie actually wanted was to be a mechanic and have his own garage. He was a local man, but he couldn't find a house in this village, not with people like me buying up the cottages and making the place ever more expensive. Instead he had to live in a shed at the back of his boss's yard. Kennie would always wave at me when he drove past in his big blue truck, which he would drive at ridiculous speeds down the lanes, and nod at me in the pub or stop for a few words. I liked Kennie, even though he had once paid Norman five pounds for permission to race an old wreck of unknown provenance around River Head Paddock before leaving it there, smashed to pieces, in a dip in the ground. In winter it would flood, and only the very top of the roof could be seen, but in the summer it sat there ugly and rusting.

'I'm having a swimming pool put in,' Norman had joked about the clamp. 'I put it behind the covert so you can't see it from the house,' he added apologetically. It was his land and he could do what he liked, but he knew all about the visual sensibilities of the newcomers who like to see the countryside clean and tidy, without any mess. 'They don't like barbed wire you know.'

I walked over with Maggie to watch the harvester at work before helping Norman to shovel in any of the loads spilled over the lip of the clamp. The field was full of strange walls and avenues of half-harvested maize, straight lines and tractor trails in the damp autumn mud. Above there was crystal blue and it was cold. Too cold for harvesting, but not for Norman.

Norman and I spread salt over the crop, pulled the plastic sheet over it and weighed it down with heavy stones. As we worked, Norman told me about the harvest moon, the full moon closest to the autumn equinox, and how it usually came in September. The hunter's moon was the next full moon.

As we finished working, up she came over the village, huge, heavy and golden, and hung low in the sky and lit our dusky autumn work. We stood on the top of the clamp and admired the moonlit view down over Valley Ground and up to Tidcombe, house lights coming on and cars going home in the far distance. It was the exact moment when the fading sunlight over the far side of Frimley Wood briefly met the moonlight behind us, those short minutes of ethereal time that feel as if the world might remain like this for ever.

We stood in a long silence.

Does Norman think in these moon moments that he is the luckiest man on earth to own this, for this to have been his entire life?

He said nothing, but then started picking out the calls of owls, like Douglas absent-mindedly calling out the names of passing cars. We laughed when we realised the call of one owl was actually a firework going off behind us in the village, signalling that the annual Guy Fawkes Night was coming again to the village for the 396th time. It would be my second in the village. The firework exploded and splashed colours against the moon.

'The crop's a good one, the Coxleys say,' I related to Norman. 'One of the best in the county they've seen this year.'

'Oh?'

'Yes.' He seemed tired and I wanted to encourage him. 'The shoot will be good too. Good money. That's what you farmers have to do these days, isn't it? Stuff like that?'

'It's not farming, is it?'

There was a long silence and we watched another firework go up.

Eventually, he spoke. 'A few years ago, I sold a Friesian for dairy for sixteen hundred pound. Sold beef cattle for six hundred pound a beast. You know what I had for them two cows last week? Less than five hundred pound. It's the Common Market, isn't it? That's what's done it.'

We were staring down at the linseed crop, grown for the subsidy and unharvested on the eve of winter. I could smell the smoke from the fire Han would have lit up at the cottage. Norman, Maggie and I would soon walk home in the moonlight. We'd climb the stone wall using as a step the 'througher' stone placed there by Norman's father fifty years ago as a stile. Before the next month was over, I would be a father.

I didn't know who was to blame for the prices and the linseed and the fact that Spider had to live with his parents if he wanted to live in the village of his childhood. I didn't know who was to blame for 9/11 and the fact that the trains didn't work. I didn't care that the wall to the goat barn had fallen down next to our oil tank and there was little chance Norman would rebuild it and that the brothers wouldn't move their caravan. It didn't matter that Maggie had become a stick bore and preferred to run after pieces of wood rather than sheep, and that Kennie drove his truck so fast past the cottage that the windows rattled. It didn't matter that the only partridge I had ever seen in the fields around the village were on Norman's farm because every other field was so farmed and sprayed there was nowhere else they liked to settle (although Alan told me he would still hear the rasping, creaking call of a cock partridge up on the Marsham ground behind Tidcombe). Right now there was nothing wrong and no one to be blamed. A hunter's moon hung over Lettem.

## CHAPTER 9

# WINTER

Sometimes the seasons merge, sometimes they arrive exactly on the day. This November first, a hard white covers the farm and the ground freezes. I stand at the garden wall this first frosted morning, misted breath and coffee steam before me, and watch for it; it's nearly time. The train heading to London. I wish my father had taken the train, but he liked to drive, fast.

With fog hiding the Humpty Dumps, a November harvest was announced by the sound of Norman's invisible tractor as it stuttered and lurched down from the yard. It headed for the linseed hay in Railway Piece, cut the day before, and started to turn it. There the hay would dry beneath azure skies when the weak winter sun finally arrived, and by dusk there were bales to stack with a full moon rising.

These early winter moons were astounding, how low and yellow they sat above Bee Copse. From behind the trees that shielded the new clamp came the voice of Douglas singing and talking to himself and the slow ring of his sledgehammer on a metal post; from the covert surrounded by cut hay, the snap of breaking undergrowth clear and sharp across the field as Maggie chased up a fox.

The linseed was cut low, the earth beneath it rich and moist, all browns and the hues of wood. The sleigh that dragged behind the baler was supposed to catch the bales, then release them in groups of eight or so, but the release lever was broken, and it dropped solitary bales as they were made. It was heavy work picking up and carrying the isolated bales to the small stacks I built. They were wet and dense and scattered far. As I worked I had the last of the crimson, sun-stained sky to the west, but after a while I struggled to make out the bales in the fading light.

Somewhere down the field I heard the tractor being switched off. The baler had jammed again or the hay had become too damp with the evening dew. I sat with my back to a twiggy, weed-woven bale. An owl close off was answered by another near the railway. Then a flap from the covert. The owl flew low, loping and heavy, passing a few feet above me as it moved to the hedge, where it settled.

'I've worked like this all my life, I have,' said Douglas, who had arrived to lift a last bale on to a stack. 'You should do that, Ian, carry on working like this.' Norman emerged out of nowhere, grinning at Douglas's suggestion. I wanted to, but I wasn't sure how long my money would last, and with the coming baby, Han was stopping work. But I'd pick something up, wouldn't I?

We stood in silence, looking at the moon.

'We'll all be living on the moon one day,' said Douglas after a long while.

'Did I ever tell you that before I came and lived at Lettem I couldn't see a low rising moon?' I said.

'Why's that, then?' said Norman eventually.

'Too many tall buildings to ever see its early rise, inside offices at the wrong time, I don't know.'

'Cities that is, Ian. Terrible places. Wouldn't want to live there. I've lived round here thirty-five years I have.'

'I've lived here all my life,' said Norman. The first time he'd told me this was the very first time we met. It seemed like another life. 'I was born on the kitchen table over there,' he added, pointing towards his cottage.

'Have you ever been to a city, Norm?'

'Yes.'

'London?'

'Yes. Twice. Smithfield show and that countryside march. And Nottingham.'

Long, silent pause.

'And Lincoln.'

Nobody said anything until by accident someone said out loud what was on their mind. I realised it was me.

'To think, the moon is as big as the earth.'

'Nope, it's smaller,' said Douglas. He pulled himself up, placed his feet apart, prepared his hands for pointing and emphasising and told us all that he knew.

'That great red spot you got on Jupiter? That's about three times the size of earth, that is.'

'Yeah?'

'Pluto, that would be your coldest planet. You'd die there. Just like that,' he said, holding up his thumb and forefinger but making no effort to snap them. '3,666 million miles away from the sun. Know how far we are from it? 92.9 million miles.'

'You know a lot about the planets, Douglas.'

'It's because he never goes out,' Norman teased. 'He just goes home and watches TV and reads books. That's how he knows so much.'

Douglas took the tractor back to the yard and Norman and I walked home in the moonlight. We talked about the summer and how I'd wanted one of Laurie Lee's Augusts but was happy with baling in November. Later, as we climbed the garden wall into our cottage gardens, he asked me if I knew him.

'Did I know who?' I replied.

'Laurie Lee.'

'No.'

'I did. Used to rent a field off him over near where he lived. Near Stroud.'

'In Slad?'

'That's right.' Norman seemed quietly surprised I knew of such an obscure place, which was in fact not so far away.

'What was he like?'

'He used to speak in descriptions. He'd describe things, things you'd just take for granted. Like a leaf.'

We stood at the wall in silence and thought that over.

'I'd see him once a year. Every year he'd say the same. "I remember you," he'd say.'

More silence.

'He left his field to Sheepscombe cricket club, he did.'

We didn't move. Parish Farm was ready to bed. A vixen called and we heard the whir of Douglas's bike and saw the flash of his Battlestar Galactica light.

'My father wanted them to sell, you know,' Norman said. He was talking absent-mindedly to the moon about his brothers, only by accident to me. 'But my mother'd say, "Don't you let them! If you want to stop here, you stop here!" My father fought forty-two years of his life to get this place.'

Walking back from another evening's baling, the sky was full of fireworks and their reflections bounced off the low cloud. The distant noises and flashes in the clouds behind Tidcombe were eerie and warlike in that post 9/11 early November. At the cottage, Han was waiting with fireworks of our own and told Douglas we planned to light them. Han offered Norman a beer.

'Oh, no thank you, better not,' muttered Norman, as he would at any offer.

'Go on, Norman! Treat yourself!' boomed Douglas, like a son talking fondly to his old father. So he joined us for a beer and Douglas had a Coke; he had to bicycle home still, he said.

At The Leggers' the next night, the display was extravagant and drunken. Knoxey, who loved his fireworks, had his usual generous supply. The display went on and on, better than the one in town probably, and just twenty-five-odd people to watch. If Knoxey had put on the show to drum up business, it hadn't worked. We preferred to think he put it on for himself, and May's kids and the teenage 'crèche' from the village, as Laura would affectionately call them. Peg, shivering and smoking, smiled and put her arm round me, perhaps thinking of the time when her kids were young and Knoxey would do fireworks for them.

'Magic,' Geoff said with a broad grin as the last fireworks smashed into the pitch-black sky and then blasted the tall leafless beeches into daylight. 'Love it.'

I try to remember a Guy Fawkes night with my father, but there is nothing. Then this: the field behind the swimming pool; it's raining. He has built a huge bonfire but it won't light. Is he angry, is he joking, does he give up, does he get petrol? I can't remember. I can't remember who he was.

The Lettem Cottage fireworks display was sixteen single white rockets, launched from Home Paddock with an audience of four. Han held the torch while Douglas, dressed in his bike helmet, lit them, then leapt back to guzzle his Coke. Norman and I drank beer and laughed, especially at the first rocket. It was stuck directly into the ground, no bottle or tube for a launcher, and it exploded loudly directly in front of us.

'Put them in a bottle!' Han laughed.

'Right then!' said Douglas.

A rocket climbed high into the sky and burst over Bee Copse, loud and brilliant. As the embers tumbled to the ground we saw the shadows of the trees and the tractor in the Humpty Dumps, and then darkness and calm until the next.

Murray came home for winter. He showed up at the yard as Norman and I were setting out to load the hay cart and bring in the linseed bales. We hadn't seen Murray in a while. He told us he had been off working with his mum at Luton airport. He'd been washing up in the kitchens. He'd earned five hundred pounds in a month, a fortune.

'What sort of hours did you work?' I asked.

'Long, long hours. Hard hours, they were.'

'Wow.'

'I'm on my way to town, get the paper for grandad. Gotta keep up with the gossip, 'aven't yer?'

'Which papers are they then?' teased Norman. 'The *Sun*?'

'Yeah, and the *Mirror*. And that one,' he added, thrusting a scrap of paper at me given him by his grandad.

'Western,' I read.

'*Western Daily Press*,' said Norman. 'That's a good one.'

Murray lived with his grandad who was about eighty. Norman told me that when he died, Murray's mother thought 'the social' would rehouse Murray.

'I don't know if you're a socialist, but I'm not,' said Norman. 'I think it's wrong.' I passed up a bale and he stacked it on the trailer. 'You take Steph who used to live up in the yard. It was rent-free but she cooked and cleaned for me, she was doing something. Now she doesn't do anything, everything is paid for. That's not right, is it?'

Murray had told me he read the papers, but according to Norman he never went to school and couldn't read or write. 'How he finds out about all them farm sales he's always going to, I don't know.' Murray travelled all over to these auctions on his moped, some-times to work at them, sometimes just to look. His knowledge of machinery and prices paid was as exhaustive as Douglas's knowledge of bikes and planets. Murray would pull up beside us at a stack to be loaded on to the trailer and regale us with tales of this bargain or that at this auction here or there. When he remembered a particularly good deal, his normally loud voice rose to an even greater volume of excitement, shouting out the memory and nearly jigging with the pleasure of it.

'SOLDTHEFUCKIN'THIN'FORFIVEPOUNDTHEY DID!!!'

I asked Murray if he would beat on our shoot.

'You don't want to do that,' Norman told me as Murray drove us to the next stack. 'He got thrown off the shoot at Breesley House for hitting one of the other beaters with a stick.'

'Yeah, all right, I'll do that,' shouted Murray when we arrived at the next stack.

'Even if Douglas is there?' I asked.

'Yeah, s'pose so.'

'You'll have to be well behaved. This is a shoot with affluent people,' said Norman, teasing him and me. 'You can't muck around with affluent people.'

We finished loading the pile and Murray started to pull off but then suddenly stopped. Norman was thrown off balance and nearly off the trailer. The load wobbled, threatening to collapse.

'He's hopeless. Hasn't got any respect for anyone,' Norman grinned despairingly from the top of the pile. 'Go on, Murray, move on there and easy.'

I asked Norman if there had ever been horses on the farm. Maybe I was of a mind that horses would be safer than Murray and a tractor.

'We had four, Father did.'

The last horse was on old mare called Flower, who left the farm in about 1966, Norman reckoned. The tree that stood by the wall that divided the two Home Paddocks had been her shelter, and if you looked you could still see where the ground dipped down from all those years of her standing there.

'She was white,' Norman went on. 'Father used to have her pull a cart with feed for the cattle. Every morning we had a man working for us who'd come and fetch her up to the yard.

'Mother wouldn't let Father take her away. She just stood in front of the dealer's car and wouldn't let him go. Father had to get the dealer to come back a few weeks later when Mother wasn't there.

'That's a bit rough, isn't it?' Norman added after some thought. 'Horse, working a farm all its life, going off to the knackers like that.'

'Your father wasn't a very sentimental man, then?'

'No,' said Norman, smiling at that adjective and 'Father' in the same sentence.

'You wouldn't have lasted long, would you, Maggie?' I asked her, as she sat, as always, head forward, tongue panting, hoping I'd throw her a stick. You shouldn't really play with a sheepdog but we couldn't resist. We laughed and Norman leant down and stroked her head and tossed out a twig.

I asked him if he would have got rid of Flower.

He grinned, trying to pretend he would. He wouldn't. I thought of Sukey, and he must have too.

'I've got to shoot that old dog some time.'

'Sukey's all right, isn't she?' I asked plaintively.

'I don't know,' Norman mumbled, his eyes down, shaking his head. He tried to laugh off his thoughts and his sentiments. He wouldn't let himself be too soft.

Walking down from the yard in the dark we saw Sukey, thinner and greyer, scraping along behind us. She couldn't follow us out of the yard as the gate closed behind us. I wondered if Norman would walk back to let her through, and I had to fight the urge to do so. He didn't.

'She'll come round,' he said. But later, when he didn't know I was looking, he held her and whispered to her, and stroked her tired back.

The week before the first shoot, Han and I went and fed the pheasants. I'd bought expensive bags of pheasant feed from a farm shop in Northleach. When Norman saw this, he told me I could take grain from his silo, unsold from last year because the grain merchants wouldn't come to the yard and pick it up. Their trucks now were designed for the custom-made drying and storage yards of the big farms.

Marsham had built a vast new plant on the edge of Frimley Wood up by the sawmill. Marsham's thousands of acres of prairie farming got the planning permissions it needed to build the new dryers despite opposition from local residents, many of them newcomers and unfamiliar with the needs of a farmer, be it Norman or Marsham. The plant tried to tuck itself up against Frimley Wood, but for all the efforts to hide it, it stood there brutal, ugly and shameless, with a huge expanse of concrete in front of it for the trucks to turn on. The grain trucks needed large gates and larger turning circles and wanted to be loaded and gone within minutes. The gate to Norman's yard was too small, not enough space to turn. They wouldn't come any more for his few tons of grain; not economic, apparently.

Han and I rattled and bounced around the farm in Norman's ancient Land Rover. She was heavily pregnant and I had visions of a bump in the track over the Humpty Dumps bringing on her labour and Norman delivering the baby in the back of his filthy Land Rover, like one of his calves.

'IAN!! GETOVER'ERE, GETOVER'ERE!' screamed Murray, very overexcited. There was a job to be done.

Two cows, three years old and cared for by Norman since they were calves, had to be cut out from the herd. Their fate was to be a 4 a.m. trip to Cheltenham on Monday. There they would be shot and shipped to Yorkshire to be burnt. No cattle over thirty months old could be eaten, a law that had come into effect because of mad cow disease and the fears of transfer to humans. These two cows had missed that deadline because of foot-and-mouth restrictions. Norman would be paid two hundred pounds a head. Fit animals designated diseased because of delays caused by another disease.

It was a miserable task, cutting cows out from the herd and moving them to the yard. I felt cruel and unpardonable watching them walk their final journey over the tranquil fields of Parish Farm. We left behind their mothers and brothers and sisters mooing crazily in the dusk light, deeply disturbed by all the running, shouting and swearing that was Murray moving livestock. Sneaky, of course, was nowhere in sight.

The crowning sadness: the dark, dirty shed, deep in shit, where they would spend their last hours on the farm.

Putting meat on people's plates is tough work. Delivering animals on a cold March night, arms covered in blood as you try and pull an animal from her distressed mother's womb; feeding, watering, worming, dipping, injecting, shearing, clipping, impregnating, finding, enclosing. Endlessly, no matter your mood or your health or the weather. And then the choosing and selecting and capturing and sending to be killed; animals you have spent every day with, as familiar as office colleagues. It's about killing, killing to make meat.

It takes a damp November afternoon rounding up a sentient animal for its execution – an animal you have seen every day and which has leant its head over your garden wall to sniff your hand in the summer – to think that all through. At least it did for me. Knowing you are doing this so that he can be tossed on the back of a lorry in a pile of corpses to be burnt doesn't make it easier.

Our two victims locked in their shed, Norman, Murray and I drove a lone cow that had followed her sorry companions to the yard back to the field with the rest. We found the herd standing on the Canal Bridge.

'GET ON THERE!!' Murray screamed. Like most animals when they saw Murray approaching, the cows turned tail and ran away into the canal, heading for the gardens of Rathbury House. Then, like the evening of our sheep-gathering in valleys beyond Frimley Wood, we spent an hour in the thickening dark chasing these animals.

'IAN!! WHERE ARE YOU?!! GETOVER'ERE!!'

Norman didn't comment on the debacle.

'How much does a new gate cost then, Norman?' I asked.

'I don't know. I haven't bought one recently,' he replied deadpan. A slight pause. 'As you can probably see.'

In the dark, Murray panting and huffing up the hill behind us to catch up, I could make out that Norman was grinning, and we laughed.

It can't be denied that the Parish Farm Shoot was also to be about killing, but I had romantic visions of roast pheasant, more fun in the gathering than a trip to Tesco's, hopefully more fun in the living for the pheasants than for a fenced-in, abattoir-killed chicken. I had by now heard a lot about organised pheasant shooting and any idea of killing purely for pleasure did not appeal. A day after which hundreds of dead birds would end up uneaten rather than on someone's table was not something I wanted to organise.

I had heard, too, the gamekeepers' complaints of 'City' guns, often quite unable to shoot, despite investments in shooting classes over the summer.

'Come November, they soon learn that a high bird on a windy winter's day is a lot more tricky than a round piece of baked clay fired on command in a field just off the M25 one evening after work,' said one.

'They all take a brace home, but I reckon they just chuck 'em in a bin I do, at Membury on the way back up to London. They don't know what to do with a feathered bird, half of 'em.'

When the guns took armfuls of birds home, forgetting to tip the gamekeeper, oblivious to the extraordinary amount of work and long, hard days that had gone into preparing the one they had just enjoyed, all for a pitiful salary and mostly for a love of their craft; unaware that he might otherwise have tried to sell the pheasants to boost his modest salary, the complaints were more serious. Much discussed were guns who had shot the birds so closely (low) that there was little left to sell, or who allowed them to be mauled by their hard-mouthed 'joke of a gun dog' animals that didn't know not to bite into the flesh of the dead bird. Guns who arrived with their own Labradors, so under-trained that their masters still carried corkscrew-like pegs to lash them to during drives, were particularly suspect to a keen-eyed keeper.

The beaters we knew and heard of did it for the extra cash (fifteen to twenty pounds for five or six hours' work, an extra fiver if you brought a working dog) and the pleasure of a walk over ground that they might not otherwise get to see (which could be handy if you were planning on going back in the dark to poach). From what I could pick up, it seemed that on most of the shoots in the area social contact between beaters and guns was pretty minimal, any refreshments or meals served or brought during the day generally being eaten by the two groups separately or at least at opposite ends of a barn or bar.

For the Parish Farm Shoot things were different.

For beaters, we had just Norman, Douglas, Murray (in principle, there being little guarantee he would show up) and Tom. Han

and I had seen Tom out walking his two black Labradors and had
stopped to ask him if he would like to shoot. He thanked me for the
invitation but told me he was 'a bit skint' at the moment. One of
us brought up beating and he agreed to come; he'd bring Teal, one
of his dogs.

Although Tom had lived in the village for several years, he, like
most people, knew Norman only by sight and reputation. When
he was new to the village, one of Tom's dogs had strayed on to
Norman's land. Used to working on some of the smarter estates
in the country, to Tom's neat and tidy eye the rampant weeds
and the stubby traces of wheat, all blown and tangled into one
soggy late-summer mess, could only mean that the field was 'set-
aside'.

Over the hill comes a man, standing in the seat of his prehistoric
tractor, hair flying, as it races, as best it can, towards him. 'Get your
fucking dog out of my fucking field, you fucking bastard' would
capture the general thread. Tom decides to calm the situation by
apologising and pointing out that it is only a field of set-aside after
all.

'Set-aside??!! That's my best crop, that is!' says Norman. 'If I see
your fucking dog on my fucking land again, I'll fuckin' shoot it.'

'You better make sure you've got both barrels loaded then, and
use the second one on me, because if you do that I'll be shooting
you!'

'Fuck off, you bastard!'

'Fuck off!'

'I'm not sure how welcome I'll be as a beater on his land,' Tom
smiled.

I had never heard Norman swear. He was a very soft-spoken
man, even in the most trying of circumstances, but it was true:
people who stuck to public footpaths were simply ignored, but woe
betide someone who trespassed on the farm.

I hoped Tom's run-in with Norman wouldn't be a problem,
because although I still didn't know what Tom did, he exuded the
steady, informed calm of a man who had been on many shoots as
gun, beater or gamekeeper. He had dogs, carried a thumbstick, spoke
of 'the ground' and 'working his dog' and where all the pheasants on
the farm were; he was, I thought, just the sort of man we would
need. What a bumbling amateur shoot captain I must have struck

him as, but he didn't show it. Probably he was just curious to walk Parish Farm and see its inner workings.

'Don't worry, they're there all right,' he said kindly when I spoke of my fears that we wouldn't see a bird all day. He didn't even correct me when I spoke of pheasants in the plural as pheasant. That would come later.

The guns were led by Scott (whom I had travelled to Istanbul with earlier that year for his stag trip) and another childhood friend from Wiltshire, Adrian, who now lived the other side of Tetbury, and whom with my mother's helpful prodding I had made contact with again after nearly twenty years. Despite both being slightly temporarily impoverished, they certainly looked the part with their expensive if second-hand four-wheel drives. They were experienced guns with all the right clothing (well worn and seasoned), dogs and whistles. Very much the gentlemen sportsmen, they joked that I wasn't wearing a tie. I was dressed in jeans, black wellington boots and a quilted blue lumberjack-type shirt.

Adrian came with his wife Ally, who was going to join my sister Frances, down from London to stay nearby with my mother, in the beating line; he had also invited a guest who arrived on a large BMW motorbike, his gun-slip slung over his back like a renegade outrider from *Mad Max*. He pulled into the yard, removed his helmet and took in his surroundings. He'd found himself standing in a junk-yard, probably not what the City gun expects of a day's shooting in the Cotswolds.

'HELLO! I'm Douglas, Douglas Hart. Very nice to meet you, and all that. Now that is a bootiful machine, bootiful, that is,' Douglas said to the biker, who was immediately marched off to inspect Douglas's mountain bike.

Next came an ex-colleague from the newspaper. The last time he had seen me I had been face-down in a Soho media bar. Today he looked quite the part, even if by the evening's end he was going to find himself in a similar situation at The Leggers', the post-shoot lunch pace proving a little too much for him to keep up with. His wife was also going to beat.

A Dutch friend from my Amsterdam days was the sixth gun. He had no idea about rural England, what a shoot was or what one would wear; he was completely and delightfully oblivious. He wore green combat trousers, high-ankled black parachute jump boots, a light tan safari jacket, an Australian bush hat and a scarf. He looked like a German parachutist on holiday dropped on to the set of a 1970s Australian drama about stylishly camp bush pilots.

Norman was nowhere in sight and nor was Murray. So I had one beater, a borrowed shotgun and little to no idea what should happen next. Thankfully, Tom arrived and I hoped he might take matters in hand.

However, after politely introducing himself, he stood back, straight-faced, earnest and silent. These people are idiots, I sense him thinking somewhere behind his composed façade.

Murray showed up next. He was wearing a thin round-neck jumper, a bomber jacket and jeans. He looked as if he had come for a stroll round a shopping centre that he was considering vandalising.

'ALLRIGHTTHEN E'!' he shouted by way of saying hello. He and Douglas kept a wary distance between them.

Finally, Norman arrived. He was as transformed as he had been when we had seen him in church, this time wearing walking boots, green trousers and an old Barbour coat. By his standards he looked extremely neat and tidy. He was a little nervous at the crowd, but curious. I introduced him to everyone, and he muttered hello.

'Are you what they call a "weekend biker"? he said to the biker, grinning at his own cheekiness.

Norman spotted Tom.

'Norm, you know Tom, don't you?' I said innocently.

'Hello, Norman,' said Tom.

'Hello,' Norman replied non-committally. If he remembered Tom (which surely he did) he didn't say anything, and it appeared we were over that little moment. We were all ready to go and I wasn't expecting Norman's speech.

'I'd just like to say a few words,' he said, so quietly that it was surprising when conversation stopped immediately. We were all ears. He produced a piece of paper from his pocket, steadying the hand that he held it with by resting his forearm on a stick. I sensed some of the guns were awaiting some niceties: a word of welcome perhaps; an 'I hope you enjoy your day'; the little rituals that expectations would call for. Perhaps he might have a word or two to say on safety.

'Today,' he said, reading slowly from the piece of paper, 'you can shoot pheasants, pigeons, any corvids, snipe, partridge if we see any, rabbits and foxes.' Norman slowly looked up at us all. 'But no hares, please.' Pause. 'Or beaters.'

The welcome speech was over. Tom coughed, discreetly reminding me that he had asked me to say a few words about 'ground game', and I added the warning.

'Please remember that there are dogs working today, and so if you do see any ground game, please be very careful that one of the dogs isn't right on its tail if you go to shoot. Anything else I need to add?' I asked.

'YES! I'll be counting your shots with my clicker!' Douglas added. I'd bought Douglas a shot counter as a present, and he'd proudly tied it round his neck on a long piece of string. He held it up so all could see, slowly turning round to face everyone like a magician's assistant portentously showing the crowd that the knife is real.

'Thank you, Douglas. Oh, and if we see any ramblers coming along, I will blow this, which means stop shooting,' I added.

I blew a whistle that made the sound of a duck, given to me by someone as a joke. It added a nice Benny Hill touch to our odd assortment of guns and beaters.

'RIGHT, THEN. LET'S BE GOING, THEN!' said Douglas, and off we headed, excited and purposeful, waved off by a heavily pregnant and rather anxious Han.

The day was mild and mostly dry, our pace ambling and relaxed. Norman and Tom, it must be said, did most of the beating; they were experienced and thorough and alert to where the birds would most likely be. The guest beaters did a pretty good job, but were too gripped by the relentless chatter of Douglas and Murray to focus on the job in hand. Murray liked mostly to walk in the fields with the guns; good company but not too helpful for beating. Douglas concentrated thoroughly on counting the shots, a job of such critical importance that it was problematical for him to do too much banging or beating either.

We started by surrounding the cover in Railway Piece. The beaters came through it, drew a blank and we headed to drive the canal. The guns walked either side of the canal as the beaters walked it. A pheasant suddenly lifted off in front of us out of the uncut wheat and flew away down the canal. I failed to even get a shot off.

'Wake up there!' Adrian laughed from the other side of the canal.

I worried it would be the only pheasant we saw all day, but it wasn't. Two of the guns took shots at birds on their side of the canal, and to my delight they shot one.

'THAT'D BE YOUR FOUR SHOTS, THAT WOULD BE!' came Douglas's voice from the canal path.

At Rathbury Woods, the beaters disappeared into the trees and the guns ranged out along the hillside that sloped down to the wood's edge.

From inside the woods, we could hear the whooping and shouting of Murray, the banging of sticks against trees and the noise of the dogs working the undergrowth. Three pheasants rose and flew away from us, towards Rathbury, but a cock bird broke cover from the trees and flew right down the line of four guns. Each of us fired twice and the pheasant flew serenely on. I could believe it, but my better guns couldn't.

'GET UP! GET UP!' screamed Murray at the birds, panting and beating.

Scott spotted ramblers; a family, a mum and dad, two children and the grandparents. I blew my duck whistle and shouted out to stop.

'Ramblers coming! Hold up!'

The noise from the wood dropped, save the lumbering, crashing and cursing of Murray from deep within the woods.

'Hold up there, Murray!' laughed Tom, who couldn't quite believe the extraordinary day he was having. Tom had been a gamekeeper and was used to beaters doing as they were told, used to there even being some birds to shoot at.

The ramblers were now parallel with Murray, who remained invisible to them inside the wood. The guns on the hillside tried not to look dangerous, but then there was the lumberjack-quilted bloke with the duck whistle and a German parachutist in safari jacket saying, 'Gud mornING' in his accented English. The ramblers looked very uncomfortable, and paused, as if not sure whether to keep going or turn back. Then from the woods, the voice of Murray.

'WHAT WE FUCKIN' STOPPED FOR??!!' he screamed.

'Er, ramblers, Murray.'

'WELL GET 'EM, THEN!!' he yelled at the top of his voice, not sounding like he was joking.

The morning done, we had lunch in the snug bar. Our bag was two pheasants and two pigeons for fifty-two shots, most, I think, fired by me, too excited and inexperienced to know when not to.

'Hello, Norman,' Peg said, trying to sound casual as she put down his meal in front of him. It was the first time Peg could remember ever seeing him in the pub, but she acted as if having him there was a regular occurrence and he was her closest and oldest local.

Seasoned guns, novices and no-hopers, wives and beaters, we all squeezed in. Douglas cornered Scott on bikes, Murray cursed ramblers and Adrian blithely lectured Tom on how the shoot might produce a few more birds.

'Norman, I've got a bit of a favour to ask,' I said. 'It's about Spider.'

Norman carried on eating.

'Look, the thing is, I really would like to invite him and, well, you know, it's a bit embarrassing and he's my friend and, well, you know.'

Long pause.

'You can ask who you like, I suppose.'

'Thanks, Norm.'

I looked down the long, laughing table, the small room muggy with the smell of damp clothes and woodsmoke, cigarettes and beer. I couldn't shoot, we'd only got a brace of pheasants all morning, we didn't have enough beaters; but the Parish Farm Shoot had been born and Norman was in the pub.

The following week, we relived the day and discussed the lessons learnt. Douglas came round and we sat at the table on the terrace, Han cross-legged and expectant on an old fertiliser bag spreading leaf mulch from the compost on to the flower beds.

'I'm very pleased with my counter,' he said. 'I was very accurate, I was. I'm going to buy a proper strap this week.'

Douglas had loved the day, especially the clay pigeon trap that we had used in the afternoon. We had stood in the bottom of Tynings as Douglas launched clays out over our heads and down to the canal. Norman had never shot clays before and, except for the odd pop at a crow, I had never seen him shoot. His shooting style was rugged and inelegant, with none of the poised lifting and swinging of the properly trained. He was by far the best shot, and there were a couple of good shots there. He dusted the black clays with casual calm.

'You know, Ian, if anything ever happens to the farm, I could get a new job doing that, clay traps, and all that,' Douglas pondered before leaning over me to show me a picture of a new type of pedal.

Norman had enjoyed the day, too. His afternoon with us shooting clays was the first time I had ever seen Norman take some time off from the farm. Our bag from the shoot, two pheasants, hung by their necks from a hazel stick wedged into the eaves of the porch roof. When I asked Norman if he would come and show me how to pluck and prepare the birds, he laughed.

'Han can do that, can't she?' he joked, his grin all toothless and cheeky. (He later admitted that his own mother refused to have anything to do with plucking birds – 'You shot 'em, you pluck 'em!' He'd come on Sunday morning and do them and we would eat them together for lunch.

In Railway Piece, now baled and ploughed, it was time to plant some winter barley. Norman had an ancient drilling machine, a red rusty Massey. It was over forty years old and would have been his father's pride and joy; very cutting-edge in 1960.

'No one has a thing like this any more,' he said a little sadly. 'All big farms, big machines now.'

There was a running-board you could stand on as the drill was pulled along, a 'tilt' it's called, Norman told me. I stood on the tilt and lifted up the lid to fill the container with the seed Norman had dressed himself. Norman had stood on this tilt as a boy as his father drove. A field mouse had set up home there for winter and I disturbed her. She thought this abandoned antique couldn't possibly be used again, let alone in late November.

'Everyone else round here's done this four, five weeks ago. I'm late, like everything,' he said as we set off to drill in the milky and misty late-afternoon winter light. I stood on the tilt, Maggie running alongside, hoping for a stick. The sun, not clearly visible, was a stain of streaked red in the sky and a waning crescent moon hung high; from the covert came the cry of the pheasants who weren't there on Saturday, taunting us.

The next day the sky turned bruised black and red. Murray and

I were out feeding the pheasants and we ran heavy-footed across ploughed fields racing the clouds that threatened to explode. We chucked straw on the ground in the covers and spread the feed over it. I suppose Tom must have told me about using straw; it holds them on the ground longer, they have to scratch around for their feed.

On our return we found Norman cutting blackthorn bushes that grew along the track that led down to the Lambing Sheds. On Saturday, we'd driven along it in Scott's Range Rover and Norman's battered Land Rover, the clay trap, cartridges and guns in the back. This was not the type of careful estate management Norman did and I asked him why he was doing it now.

'So your gentry friends can get by in their big cars,' he said, grinning.

Annie was born at 6 a.m. on 25 November 2001, at Cheltenham hospital.

I got back to Lettem late that night and went round to see Norman, carrying a bottle of brandy and two glasses. He was asleep in his chair, Sukey lying on his feet, and I woke them up.

'She's calved, has she?' he said. He pushed aside a pile of unopened bills and unwashed plates and we sat at his table. I poured drinks.

'Cheers.'

'Cheers.'

I told him what had happened, it had not been an easy birth.

'I don't suppose you've seen anything like that,' he said. It all sounded familiar and pretty normal to Norman.

It was some days before we were all home from the hospital. When we had gone in, it had been frosty with clear, sunny days, the gentle cold of early winter. But now it was December. All the leaves were gone and the wind blew bitter. We cocooned in Lettem Cottage; it was made for a winter baby.

Douglas came round with a knitted baby jumper which his mum had made and Malcolm dropped off a present too, but didn't come in. The rector thoughtfully came with a card and asked if Annie would like to be the baby Jesus in the nativity play at the carol service.

That weekend, Geoff and Laura called in. They were picking me up to take me to a demonstration in the marketplace, protesting about the planned closure of the local accident and emergency ward. They looked brown and sun-smiled, just returned from a holiday in South Africa. Knoxey was beaming with pleasure at seeing little Annie.

'Magic,' he said. 'Magic. I'm so happy for you, I always felt a bit of a special part of this, what with Han and me and our day at Ascot, her not knowing she was pregnant, getting pissed.'

Being in town with Knoxey was like going for a walk in the company of a celebrity. It seemed everyone knew him, stopping us on the street and coming up to us in the bar at a pub where we drank brandy and waited for the demonstration to start. I'd not seen him this relaxed and content in a while. They confessed they'd bought an apartment in South Africa, on the spur of the moment. Right by the golf course for Geoff, winter sun and not expensive. I wondered if this wasn't preparation for a retirement they were not yet ready to speak of. The Leggers' without Geoff and Laura wouldn't be right, but next year was to be their twentieth anniversary at the pub. They planned to celebrate it hard, but then what?

The crowd in the marketplace was a good one. First to speak was Lord Rodley, full-faced, round-tummied, face flushed, a pleasant, inoffensive-looking man in his forties. He wore the country gent's uniform of cords, a tattersall check shirt and tie, a V-neck jersey and a tweed jacket. He was, on this occasion at least, a poor speaker, nervous and uninspiring. The highlight was a speech by a highly energetic and apparently genuinely angry retired Conservative MP. His arguments were well constructed and made with conviction.

Lastly came our local MP, whom Knoxey never missed an opportunity to call by his nickname.

'Oh look, it's Clitoris Brown!' said Geoff loudly.

'Let me hear you if you're angry!' he shouted weakly, in a Tim Henman-like effort to show some passion. His speech was mostly about 'spin' and 'Labour'. Knoxey mildly heckled him as we listened; a Tory giving us a lecture on the way this government had neglected the NHS. It didn't much wash.

A poem by Laurie Lee, I remember a fragment.

*Tonight there is no moon,*
*but a new star opens*
*like a silver trumpet over the dead.*
*Tonight in a rest of ruins*
*the blessèd babe is laid.*

The rector and his wife did the nativity in a big way. Tradition had it that the youngest child in the village would play the baby Jesus, and so Annie's moment had come.

As Han and I came into the church on a cold Sunday afternoon, we were greeted by the rector, who steered us past the packed congregation and to specially reserved seats. I held Annie in my arms, tightly swaddled in thick wool blankets.

'I'll give you a little nod when it's time,' he said quietly. At the arrival of Mary and Joseph, we were to put Annie in the wooden sheep's crib lined with straw.

For the shepherd scene, they had all the children dressed in tea towels and robes, as you would expect, but they were accompanied by sheep, led into the church from the Farm Club stables that Jill Stanton ran at the rectory. Animals, children and costumes arrived thick and fast, with chickens, guinea pigs and rabbits making up the supporting cast. Mary, played by a little girl taking her role with pious and enchanting seriousness, arrived sitting on a small placid donkey led by Joseph. When the three wise men arrived, they too were sitting on ponies, which were then tethered in a makeshift stable built inside the church.

There were readings and carols, and the pleasure and the excitement of the earnest child performers mixed with the teary pride and joyful sentiment flowing from parents, grandparents, old and young. When I placed our tiny little girl in the crib and we sang, it was all too much.

The service ended, the children were arrayed round the crib, animals next to them, and a wall of cooing parents and relatives crowded to the front (my smiling and happy mother and Annie's Aunt Frances nigh stampeding to get a good spot), cameras in hand. The mood was serene and delightful, but there was a sense that complete collective emotional hysteria could break out at any moment. The children stood stock-still round Annie in their living portrait, neither fooling nor joking, completely in character and far off in Bethlehem.

A little boy came up and leant over the crib and touched Annie gently on her cheek. Mary, who couldn't have been more than seven, sat there watching Annie protectively with a serenity that made even me wonder what the answer was to the boy's question.

'Is that really the baby Jesus?' he asked, looking up at his mother, and nobody had the heart to say no.

I wish I could remember something my father said to me. Anything, just one sentence; not even the sound of his voice, just some words.

The Tuesday before the next shoot. I am out running. The canal path is wet and the fields too. Back to winter running on the lanes.

Just after the turn to The Leggers' I hear a car slowing behind me. I turn and stop, happy for the excuse. It's Knoxey on his way to the bank, his takings on the passenger seat beside him, Pinto his Alsatian in the back. He lowers his electric window and stops the car. Short of breath, I crouch down at the open window, resting my arms on the door. Geoff strikes me as being strangely serene. He looks not tired but at ease.

'Good to see you, Geoff. How are you?'

'Not too bad. Everything all right?'

'Yes, girls are doing great. Bit out of breath. Just getting back into the running again.'

Geoff smiles at me and there is a pause.

Then, with a greater warmth than I have ever heard him use when he speaks to me, he says, 'You're a good boy, Ian, a good boy.'

I smile and for a moment we are there in the lane in silence.

'I'll see you later in the week then,' I say. 'Sorry I haven't been down much, just, you know.'

'I know. Give Han and Annie a kiss from me.'

'I will.'

And with that he drives off.

Magic.

Geoff died two days later on 20 December 2001. That morning he had a stroke, a cerebral haemorrhage, and he died that evening in Cheltenham hospital.

# CHAPTER 10

# CHRISTMAS LANDSCAPE

The funeral was at Little Mayford, the village at the end of the brothers' footprints in the snow. The morning was bitter, the ground cracked frozen firm, with the churchyard dressed in mourning clothes of starched white frost. The small thirteenth-century Cotswold-stone church, cupped in a gentle dip on the side of the May valley, stood shoulder-squeezed to celebrate this man.

There were hundreds of people present and we recognised only a few. Han and I were newcomers to Geoff's long life and knew almost nothing of it or of the many lives he had led within it. For Laura, Peg, May and Spider, the day laid memory after memory thick upon each other, and the weight of their heartbreak was hard to bear.

The service was led by a triumvirate of vicars: Russell from Storeton who knew Geoff best, the vicar from Little Mayford who knew Geoff not at all and Charles Stanton from the village. Though they had been the first to arrive at the pub the morning after Geoff had died, the church was full by the time Lord and Lady Rodley arrived. Liam, rather to his own surprise he later admitted, deferentially gave up his seat for them.

The eulogy was given by Cameron, a kilted Scotsman who had become Geoff's friend some years ago when studying at the agricultural college. Geoff was his drinking companion, mentor, father and friend. He spoke of Geoff as being non-judgemental, generous and welcoming. These, I thought, were the characteristics of a man so deeply grounded in who he was and where he came from that you couldn't imagine he could ever fall.

Geoff was born in this village, christened in this church, buried in this church. I recognised the graveyard from an old black-and-white photo Geoff had shown me of him as a choirboy, following his vicar through the tombstones. Near the church, I saw the house where he had worked as a footman and had made love with the young Austrian au pair; in the valley below, the pub he had come home to run and once again to leave behind.

Geoff had had a place, a centre. His roots had been deep and they had held him strong and tall, with huge branches held out wide that the leaves of thinner trees could blow up against and be held fast. He'd offered a fixed point of reference, standing behind the bar at The Leggers' for nearly twenty years. Permanence.

I wondered what would happen to the pub, if the new owners would be Gloucestershire men, if they would stand behind the bar for twenty years. Would they offer anything beyond product, or were we burying the last of the givers, and ahead would there only be the takers?

It was an English funeral of an Englishman, a Gloucestershire man, and so we sang 'I vow to thee, my country' and concluded with 'Jerusalem'. At my father's funeral I could remember singing 'For those in peril on the sea', but I couldn't remember who was there.

He died when I was ten, in a car crash. He drove into a fallen tree one dark October morning, rushing to London. The drought of '76 had been to blame, ancient roots loosened in parched soil and waiting only for the first storm of autumn for their trees to fall.

At the time of his funeral I knew only that it had been a car crash, nobody told me where it happened. Or about the tree in the road; that I learnt about much later. I can't remember crying, but how could that have been; how could my mother have withstood his loss?

Now in Geoff's church I did cry. I had come to Lettem unable to feel, uncertain why; but now, just as at Annie's birth, I cried and I couldn't stop. I wasn't sure exactly for whom or what my tears were falling, stood in this ancient church, in this ancient line of English birth and death.

The wake was at The Leggers', where a large marquee had been added to the barn to accommodate all the mourners. It was a wake of reunited friends and unfolded memories, little secrets and quiet sadnesses. The mood was upbeat, for no one could conceive of

Knoxey's final party as being anything other than fun. Laura was composed and dignified, Peg focused and hospitable, leaning on her work and her introductions and mingling. Sometimes they would falter, but then they would wipe their eyes and carry on. 'I'm so *angry* with him,' Peg said to Han and me, her body slightly shaking as she tried to smile, 'the old bugger, leaving us like this.' Geoff had been a partner, not just to Laura, but in many ways to Peg and May too, and in his absence it was all the clearer to see.

May and her husband Bob sat and drank and tried to be cheery, with their red eyes and wet cheeks. Kelly looked stunned, and then someone would make her smile and she was Kelly again. Han and I were there with Annie; she was scooped up and celebrated and her tiny young life and energy reminded us that this day stood as an endless continuation of everything.

'Geoff felt very connected to Annie's birth,' said Laura, reminding us of his day at Ascot with Han, when she didn't know she was pregnant, and then the secret we had shared with him which he couldn't keep.

Peg introduced me to a woman who had lived in Lettem Cottage. She was the wife of the airline steward, and they had left Lettem Cottage when he took over the lease of The Marsham Arms in Little Mayford from Geoff and Laura. We spoke of the garden and some lawn she had replaced with the kitchen vegetable patch and the three fruit trees that she had planted. I told her about our jam and chutney and the pleasure it gave us to smell the blossom in spring and pick the fruit in the early autumn. To plant a tree is such a generous, forward-thinking thing.

'I'm glad you didn't chop them down and build a garage or something,' she said.

She had bought the Aga we made our jams on for twenty pounds from a house in London and had it delivered. To her surprise it had arrived in pieces and ran on wood.

'Your successors tried to sell it to me for over a thousand pounds!' I told her. We laughed.

After some hours the crowd thinned and we moved from the barn and the marquee to the pub, still crammed with people, the hardcore of days past and present. Spider and I wore matching three-piece suits and sat on the bench near the bar, watching the crowd.

When Peg had rung us with the news that Geoff had died I had gone to see Spider. I had found him in the yard, listlessly going through the motions of tidying up a shed. I pulled up outside and he walked over, slow and sad. We didn't say much.

'Hey, Spider.'

''Ello, mate.'

'All right, then?'

'Not really.'

'Yeah.'

'Fuck.'

'Yeah.'

We stood in silence.

'I can't believe it. He was going to shoot with us tomorrow.'

'I'm going to feed the pheasants,' he said. 'Do you want to come along, show you the place?'

'Sure. That'd be good.'

And so we had climbed into Spider's tractor and spent a couple of hours going round the farm he worked on, he showing me the pens and the drives and the boundaries of the land that made up his life. He talked a little about Knoxey, the time he had gone with him to Dublin to watch the rugby.

'You going to be OK?' I said when we came back to the yard.

'I'm going to go home, get a bottle of whisky and get bloody drunk.'

I don't know if that's what he did that day but at the funeral that's what happened. There was much drinking. I fear I failed myself and the occasion and ended up drinking shots long into the afternoon with Spider, Tom and Peg's son-in-law.

At the urinal, I stood next to one of Geoff's sons. I was drunk and thought I should say something as I pissed. 'Your father was a very special man.'

He nodded, finished and left. I asked myself what Knoxey would have made of me: drunk, cock in hand, dizzy with tequila and death, trying to console his son.

In the crowded pub there was a tall young man, handsome and fragile, a little overwhelmed, standing near the door. As I teetered towards the bar, Peg asked me if I knew who the young man was.

'I think I do, yes.'

Norman had told me the story soon after Geoff had died; perhaps he had felt that now he could. 'There was this woman, married to a man who lived in Little Mayford she was. You heard about her then?'

'No,' Han and I had said in unison.

'About eighteen years ago, she asks my brothers if she can live in the cottage in the yard. They said no, like, but then she made them an offer they couldn't say no to. She moved in, she did. With a small child. And her boyfriend. The father of this child was already here down at The Leggers' – Geoff Knox. That's why she moved here I reckon.'

'How long did she stay?'

'A few months.'

Back at the bar Peg continued to speak of this son of Knoxey. 'It's very sad. The vicar forgot to say his name when he spoke of Geoff's children.' The vicar hadn't mentioned the Austrian au pair's daughter either.

In the snug bar I stumbled into snippets of speculation and gossip that entered my befuddled brain and turned into a history I had never heard before. It seemed Geoff's death opened a door for people to share what they knew, or thought they knew, with those who didn't, or thought they didn't. What was true and what was not, I was too drunk and emotional to follow.

'Laura was the partner of a big London financier and Geoff was his butler when they went off together. Geoff left his wife and the kids and they've never forgiven Laura, never. Especially his daughter.'

'Did you know the lease was in Knoxey's name? Laura bought it but she gave it to Knoxey just after it was renewed.'

'The lease is in Laura's name, you know, not Geoff's. She'll not sell it.'

'They were going to retire next year, to South Africa.'

I couldn't take it all in. The future was unclear – what would happen to the pub, to Laura, to Peg, to May? I went back into the main bar, where I think there was loud music, and dancing, and more drinking. Escapist reckless drinking.

I was very drunk when we finally left. I hope everyone was.

Laurie Lee's poem, I remembered the rest of it now.

*And the fir tree warms to a bloom of candles,*
*the child lights his lantern,*
*stares at his tinselled toy;*
*our hearts and hearths*
*smoulder with live ashes.*

*In the blood of our grief*
*the cold earth is suckled,*
*in our agony the womb*
*convulses its seed,*
*in the last cry of anguish*
*the child's first breath is born.*

The pub remained resolutely open, resolutely impervious and continuous, the landlord representing but twenty years in two hundred and fifty. Would it all feel better if we thought like that? Laura took on the licence, officially became the pub's landlord, and Peg, May and the other staff stood by her. There was a lot of talk about what Knoxey would have wanted.

Han and I didn't surrender to their sorrow, or probe or cry. Annie was less than a month old when Geoff died, and her birth, so close to his death, shaped our grief. It was too sad to think of Laura, her empty apartment in South Africa and the years ahead, the man she was to end her life with gone. It was too sad to think of what would happen to the family and community that centred on Geoff and his pub, of the fate of Peg and May. And so we didn't, and we picked up Annie and held her.

December the twenty-fourth was a Leggers' night, when the die-hard locals always came along with a few others. But this Christmas it was closed. Christmas Eve would have been too hard.

Liz, the snug bar regular who ran the horse yard, had split up with Jeremy, Tom was temporarily girlfriendless and his lodger John had departed with his girlfriend to the Welsh Borders. Alan, too, was alone, and Spider, with no Leggers', had nowhere to go. Han and I and four-week-old Annie weren't going anywhere, so they all came to Lettem, and Norman joined us. We sat around a huge log fire and suspended the jam pot from the chimney chain that hung above it. In it we made mulled wine, steamed quickly over the fire, and in the sticky burnt residue we fried alcohol-soaked sausages. The room smelt of food and spices, warmth and England. It was hot, fuggy and mellow and we laughed, smoked rollies and told our stories. We took our little worries and regrets, and our sadness over Geoff, or our more tempered memories, and we hit them hard. Our anxieties were blown up the chimney in fumes of food and drink and they climbed away with the floating wood embers.

New Year's Eve the sky was clean and clear, without even the tiniest wisp of cloud in its endless cold blue. A thick, crisp frost tinkled on the ground as the sun came up over Bee Copse. In the fading light of the afternoon, we wrapped Annie tight and slid down the lane on the ice to the pub. Underneath the beech trees on the towpath the leaves crunched, and we kicked sticks on to the ice of the frozen canal.

We sat in the snug bar by the fire with Peg and drank a Guinness and passed Annie round like a torch. Laura came down, wheezing with bronchitis, her eyes full and tired. I had still not written to her, nor found the words to offer anything but embarrassment at my own celebration of life and that of my daughter. I think she would have understood. I hoped she did.

We didn't go to the pub that evening; we had no one to look after Annie and didn't want to impose on Laura by putting her to sleep in one of her rooms upstairs above the bar. But if I'm honest, perhaps the real reason that I stayed away was because I was uncomfortable with my happiness and scared of seeing her pain.

Instead, we accepted an invitation to dinner from an old school friend who now worked in the City and who was staying near Calne at his parents' house for New Year. As he took our coats he promptly told me 'he couldn't understand what I was doing with my life', and then introduced me to a guest.

'Ian, this is Bonky.'

Later, only after we had heard it used several more times could we believe it, and even then we struggled to use it.

'Um, er, Bonky,' Han said, 'could you pass the salt, please?'

Along with Bonky and her husband, the other guest was called Rupert but known as Rupsie. He wore suede shoes, yellow socks and mustard-coloured cord trousers and worked as an assistant to a Tory MP. Our voices bounced around what felt like an unheated dining room, and as soon as the meal was over we went into the drawing room to play 'games'. Charades.

At the end of the evening it was suggested that, as the bed we were to sleep in was so small, I might like to sleep in the attic with Rupsie. As Han and I cuddled for warmth in the even colder spare bedroom, we giggled. 'I'm not going to the bloody attic with Rupsie,' I laughed, wondering why we weren't at The Leggers'.

On New Year's Day, back at Lettem, Norman was coming for lunch, so I plucked and drew a brace of pheasants and some pigeons that had hung in the porch since the shoot the Saturday after Geoff had died.

'What do you think we should do about the shoot?' I had asked Spider after Geoff died. 'Cancel it?'

'I don't think Knoxey would have wanted that. He'd be fucking out there if one of us was dead.'

'Crack on?'

'Crack on.'

We did, but the day wasn't what it should have been, not for me and Spider. But our guns enjoyed their day and their cheer kept us moving forward.

'Good crack,' said Spider afterwards. 'Knoxey would have liked that.'

Over our New Year's roast, Norman told us of the family lunch he had been to after Christmas at a pub in Bishop's Cleeve, organised by his aunt.

'I got into a bit of trouble, actually. My nephew, he's got a degree in media studies or something,' Norman said. 'What type of a degree is that? I asked him. That's not a real thing, is it? What do you mean? said my sister-in-law. That is one of the highest paying jobs you can get, in television and the like, she said. She got quite angry, like. That can't be right, can it, "*media studies*"?' Norman gently laughed, looking for confirmation.

As we ate the pheasants, I thought of the shoot three days after Geoff died and the lunch afterwards at The Leggers' without him. Laura and Peg had already reopened, the show had to go on. I had meant to stop and have a toast to Geoff and a minute's silence but I hadn't, and I thought Spider would never forgive me for burying Geoff so quickly and wordlessly.

I tried to remember how many days it was after my father's death that I went back to school. Five? I was ten. None of the boys talked about it, their fathers hadn't died. No one was crying, no one was sad, life went on as normal. Not feeling, this must be normal.

Was it just my parents' generation and class who behaved like this, hiding their own grief, many glossing over the pain of others, at least as it concerned how they treated me as a child and my loss? Or were they just English, these studied masks we wore with death in our midst? Whom were they supposed to help?

I thought it was for the best, not dwelling on our losses or making too much of their memory, my mother told me later, a decision she said, my father would have agreed with.

Even I had hoped that our being at the pub for the shoot lunch would be the right thing too; moving on, not looking back. I, who had carried so much anger within me about the way my mother had dealt with my father's death (even though it was probably the only way she could have survived), and against some of her friends and family who had followed her lead. When Geoff died I wondered if my mother was right after all, and I was shocked at the ease with which I applied lessons in loss learnt so early in life. As an adult I had seen other ways of mourning, had disagreed so strongly with my parents' approach; but now reverted to long-ingrained reflexes. Now I could see bared clear how my mother had continued, for her sake and her children's, and felt guilty at my lack of understanding that had caused so much disagreement between my mother and me over so many years.

Alan had been strangely ill at Geoff's funeral, in agony, barely able to stand; such a transformation from the man we had just spent Christmas Eve with. He had told us a story that night of mulled memories of a childhood sweetheart whom he had lost track of, and who he had found out was dead the morning of her funeral. The day after Geoff's funeral Alan was admitted to hospital, and over the next three weeks he fought for his life. The doctors eventually found out he had a rare disease, not often diagnosed in time, that rapidly attacks the organs. Later he told me how people didn't want to talk about that either, even some friends and family. Facing the death of life's possibilities was too hard for some.

Alan survived, somehow. That's not me, I'm not going to die, he had said; I'm a survivor; dying, that's for others.

There was a story, he told me, of men hanging on to the side of an upturned lifeboat after a wreck at sea. It wasn't the young and fit that survived, but those who had the most to fight for, those with children and young families.

Perhaps that was my mother, clinging to her own upturned lifeboat, unable ever to speak of the ship that had sunk, thinking only of surviving, of coping and caring for me and my nine-month-old sister.

# CHAPTER II
# NEW YEAR

At Geoff's wake Tom and I learnt we were born on the same day of the same year. Exactly ten years later, Tom's father died, and so did mine, and that too we somehow uncovered among the day's drinking and the resolute efforts to talk of anything but death.

'What might be nice now', someone had said, 'is a nice refreshing tequila,' and that's how we went on.

Perhaps it was discovering these unusual coincidences (and that we lived in the same small village) that gave our friendship such an unusual footing. Tom's slow process of careful evaluation had come to an end, and so began a whole new dimension to our life at Lettem Cottage. One day Tom was someone Han and I saw now and again, the next he was someone much more than that.

For the Saturday of our birthdays, Spider had invited Tom and me on his beaters' day, the day when the gamekeeper invites beaters and friends as guns for the final day of the shooting season.

The first time I ever went shooting was with my older cousin and his air rifle when I was six. It was the day my parents returned to my father's sister's house from somewhere, they didn't say where, with news that made my mother cry so much my aunt suggested I go for a walk with my cousin and shoot tin cans. It was news about my brother: he wouldn't be coming home with us. Just like four years later when we would speak little of my father's death, nor did we speak then of my older brother's death from leukaemia.

He was eight. I remember that first night with my parents, lying beside their bed on a mattress in my aunt's spare bedroom, my father trying to console my desperate mother. Then nothing really, no memories, only a silence within which I lost a lot of things a six-year-old boy needed to learn.

Never having been on a proper shoot, and doubtful as to my shooting abilities, I asked Tom to give me a lesson. He agreed, but not before protesting that he wasn't the man for such a thing and suggesting the names of others.

Tom was wearing neither coat nor jumper. Weather conditions would have to be extremely cold before Tom, like Spider, wore any sort of a coat. This deep winter's day, the sun a hazy glow low in the afternoon sky over Frimley Wood, our breath thick and the ground frozen, warranted nothing but a shirt. After lunch, Douglas arrived and we all hopped over the garden wall and set up a borrowed clay trap behind the wall in the Humpty Dumps.

'Ready?' shouted Douglas, eager to get on.

'Hang on, Doug,' replied Tom. Douglas responded by sending over a pair of clays. '*Hold tight!* Doug's on it. DOUG!! HANG ON!!'

'Ready?'

'Jesus,' muttered Tom, smiling at me. 'HANG ON A MINUTE THERE!'

Norman had lent me his shotgun and was no doubt sitting somewhere unobserved, watching his hopeless neighbour embarrass himself. Tom gave instructions patiently without a hint of the showman, showing me first how to hold and mount the gun safely.

'All right, Doug,' he said, 'send a couple over when you're ready. We'll just take a look at them.'

Nothing.

'Douglas?'

Nothing.

'I'll go,' I say, and start to walk over. Whoosh. Two clays fly over me.

'Ready?' shouts Douglas.

'When I say pull, Doug.'

Whooosh!

'Ready?'

'Jesus,' Tom said, shaking his head.

'I tell you,' Douglas boomed. 'If anything ever happened to old Norman, I could get a job doing that I could, and all that. I'm pretty good at it!'

'You are, Doug, you are,' said Tom.

Tom gracefully shattered single clays and pairs into compact puffs of black powder, giving tips as he went; then he passed the shotgun to me. He had little chance and less intent of turning a novice shot into a classy gun over a few dozen clays. Instead, he concentrated on drilling into me how to neither kill anyone nor embarrass myself; hitting anything would be a bonus. He had a word, too, about what I would wear. Apparently my Parish Farm attire wasn't going to cut it, so we begged and borrowed the necessary.

'Hit anything then?' Norman grinned as we walked back over Home Paddock to the garden wall.

'Too right,' Tom said, without missing a beat. 'Finest shot in the county.'

If I said I'd hit one in five, I'd be exaggerating.

Some say that a beater's day is only proper when the person whose shoot it is and the guns who have shot regularly that season come and beat for the beaters. Roles are reversed as a thank you for the season's efforts. The regular guns even lay on and serve a lunch. Others say that tradition died without a whisper a long time ago.

It had on Spider's shoot, at least for this season; the family that owned the farm wasn't there and Spider had had to organise another group of beaters. Spider was in his full shooting tweeds, and every gun had made the effort to dress his best. I was glad Tom had insisted on the tie and had lent me some kit. I'd even borrowed a flat cap.

Of the ten guns, only Tom and I had not been beating Spider's shoot and I felt like something of a freeloader. But Tom told me it was Spider's prerogative to ask whom he liked. The other guns were John, up from the Borders for the weekend, who had beaten on Spider's shoot and other beaters, fathers and sons who had happily slogged through long, wet, cold shoots simply for the pleasure of those days and the enjoyment of this one.

A properly driven shoot differed from a Parish Farm Shoot in several important respects. The proper one was organised, there were plenty of birds to shoot and it was a good deal more earnest, certainly at the times when the guns were standing and waiting for the birds to be driven over. Banter was restricted to between drives and, unlike at Parish Farm, where misses were readily spotted and commented on by beaters and guns alike, here a more reserved etiquette existed.

Half of Spider's farm sat on high ground, with open fields and long views west towards Chedworth and the Churn Valley. The rest of the farm was deep, narrow valleys crested by high woodland; brooks and bridges, barns and steep lanes. We shot in woodland and valleys and open fields, with birds coming from every drive.

The excitement of standing alone, a gun to your left and right, silence from the woods in front and then the sound of dogs and people working through the undergrowth; *they're getting closer, get ready*. The view distracts, the smell of winter, of damp undergrowth, sometimes the patter of rain on the peak of your cap or the shoulders of your borrowed jacket. A rabbit hurtles out, 'no ground game', *don't shoot*. Startled songbirds. Then suddenly the heavy flapping of wings and the cry of the pheasants.

'Over,' shouts a beater. *Is it coming my way?* You want it to and you don't, you'll miss, you won't, this is the one, this is your moment and then a flurry of shots and the sound of breaking guns; *my GOD, there!* Up! Fire, again! *MISSED!* Reload, quick, fumble, drop a cartridge, another, close, bring up the gun, *remember what Tom said*; safety off as you mount and aim, fire, miss! *No! SHIT! How did I miss that? Fuck*; reload; *quick, FIRE! NO, shit, not again*; pheasants falling left and right, out of the corner of your eye Tom fluidly and effortlessly firing, hitting and reloading, his black Lab retrieving his birds. And then it's over and the last pheasant has flown and the last shot fired, one or two small pops, out of sight, further down the line. Your heart is racing. *Shit, how did I miss again?*

*I'm not aiming, that's what I'm not doing*, I say to myself as I walk to the next drive, my thoughts racing. *Aim. You can do it, calm down*. I'm a hopeless amateur, I shouldn't be here, I'm letting Spider down, I hope Tom doesn't see me, I'm having the time of my life, this is so much fun, this is so damn beautiful, my feet are freezing, I can't believe I'm here, what a day.

The last drive of the day, a long thin covert stretched across a wide open field. It would be beaten right to left, but the pheasants, once up, would swing towards us to the woods and the valley behind. At each drive there was a stick with a number attached, marking where you were to stand; with each drive, each gun moving two 'pegs' up the line. On my left, a young boy, fifteen or so, and to the left of him Tom and then John. I hadn't hit a single bird all day. Not one.

Up they came but none towards me. Then a magnificent cock pheasant hurtled out of the covert and charged directly towards the boy. He brought up his shotgun and fired, twice, missed. Should I, shouldn't I? Damn it, I fired, the pheasant now behind the line. And as I fired I saw Tom's shotgun in the air, tracking the same bird. It fell. It just tumbled out of the sky. My God, I'd hit one!

Hadn't I?

Did Tom get it? Shit, it was Tom. Wasn't it? No, I hit it, I'm sure I did.

Later I told him I did.

'I saw it,' he said. 'Lovely shot. Well done.'

Later that evening we held our first big party at the cottage; Han had persuaded Tom to make the birthday party she had organised for me a joint one. We invited everyone we knew locally and surprised ourselves how many that was, surprising our guests with cocktails stronger than they looked.

'I'm glad you came, Laurs, you look wonderful,' said Han.

'Thank you, darlings,' said Laura.

Norman made one of his late arrivals, spruced up and ready to go. He slipped in and was soon nattering away with the one celebrity at the party.

'That's Adam Thwaite, that is,' he told Han later.

'Yes.'

'They're famous, they are.'

'Really, what for?' We didn't know Adam well ourselves. He was engaged to an old friend of ours who had come to the party.

'Mowers. They made mowers.'

Han thought of lawnmowers.

'No, I don't think we had theirs in Australia.'

'Oh.'

Later, Han realised Norman was talking about hay mowers, and Norman had concluded that the reason Thwaite mowers weren't in Australia was because the weather was so hot they couldn't make hay. The Thwaites used to make all the mowers in the South-West. Everyone had a Thwaite mower, Norman told us. He had one himself up in the yard.

When Norman said he had to go, the party was buzzing along.

He had enjoyed the night, he said, but the calves needed feeding. Han was adamant he couldn't leave. I would go and help him, then we'd come back. In the starlight, we stumbled out of the cottage and up to the yard, where in the light of a single candle balanced on a wooden beam, Norman stood deep in shit and tipsy on Cava cocktails, putting the young calves on to the cows. From the cottage came the sound of music, and voices, carried-clear in the air of the cold January night.

At the end of the party I escorted Tom and his last guests up the lane and home, weaving and mumbling. The sky was completely cloudless, the stars brilliant and endless above us. It was a good night, a good day.

'I did shoot that pheasant, didn't I?'

'Yes, you did,' Tom smiled.

I don't know to this day if I shot that bird or not, but I'm pretty sure I didn't.

'Hello.'

'Hey, Norm.'

'You busy?'

'No.'

'Oh.'

He looked at me, considering, the rain horizontal behind him and Frankie's Tree thrashing above.

'I've got a breached calf in the yard.'

'Need a hand?'

'Could you?'

'Sure.'

The shed was shadowy and wintry. A cow stood untroubled, grazing placidly on some hay. From her rear a single calf's hoof was just visible.

'It'll drown, you see. If we don't get it out.'

'Right.' This was a bit more Nature than I needed.

Norman reached into the cow, found another hoof and pulled it out. Now there were two tiny, gooey protrusions. He fixed a piece of rope with a loop at each end to the hooves.

'If I'm here on my own and I start pulling and I can't get it out, it'll go back in you see.'

As we began to pull, our feet slipped on the shit-covered floor. We braced ourselves and tried again. We were soon sweating and straining, our efforts in doubt. Then, with no more trouble than pulling a tight cork from a bottle, it came, and in a second, this shapeless, lifeless thing plopped out to the floor. Norman ducked down just in time to half break its fall on to the hard ground. There she lay, black, moist and glistening. Norman kneeled beside her in the dirt, his arms and shirt covered in blood and mess, his long hair sweaty and fallen out of place. Gently he took his fingers and cleared the calf's mouth, and wiped her face with some straw. She wasn't breathing and he rubbed her like a baby, calm and intent.

'She's all right?' I asked anxiously, the excitement clear in my voice.

Norman rubbed the calf. And she breathed.

'Yes,' he said quietly. He pulled himself up. He looked weary.

We wanted spring to come but it was still firmly winter. The paddock was grazed to nothing, the ground mud and shit with little grass. Wet, brown stains surrounded the half-eaten, soaked feed. It was bleak, and animals and humans were sodden and glum, even Norman: too much work, complaints about Douglas, no sign of Murray, cows selling at two hundred pounds a head, calves bought in at twenty-five pounds and the difference no reward for the feed or time and effort. He even snapped, sort of, at Sneaky when she escaped; something I'd not seen before. Winter was long, and Geoff's death and Norman's weary mood and bruised optimism were only reminders.

We heard that the Mad Professor's ancient Mini Metro had been torched. The Mad Professor, as Tom called him, was the nephew of a very famous deceased English stage and screen actor. There was no evidence that he was mad, but the name seemed to fit. His car had been taken out of his garage and set fire to in the middle of the night.

His real name was Nigel, but to us he was just the man who shuffled past the cottage each day with his dog, and who composed the crossword puzzle for the parish magazine. At the pub, we heard of a proposal (apparently made by the chairman of the parish council) that a collection should be made to buy him a new car, but it was voted down, and Nigel, who also served as the newspaper delivery man for the village, now had to walk to do his rounds.

The rector's letter in the next edition of the parish magazine made no reference to the Professor's loss. There was, however, a full-page letter addressed to the parishioners of the village, from PC176 Henry Lennard, our Rural Beat Officer (Cotswolds North).

Written, it said, after much consultation with many of us in the village (the consultation group was unspecified), the letter started by saying that our village was a place of peace, beauty, tranquillity and a 'good quality of life'. However, PC Lennard went on to say, a 'small number of antisocial individuals are committing offences that erode this quality of life'. These offences were listed as un-specified serious damage to property (there was the cricket club, vandalised shortly before we arrived in the village, the lawn and now Nigel's car, that we knew of) and 'an attack on the church'. (This description of the apparent attempt to undermine the role of the church in our community – in fact the consumption of stolen Communion wine in the church belfry – made it sound more political than it possibly was.) In short, the village 'was beginning to experience the type of problems usually associated with large inner cities'.

Here the tone, language and direction of the letter changed in such a way that one suspected the author of the letter was perhaps not PC Lennard.

'Quality of life' (the third use of this expression that might mean 'high house prices') 'comes at a price, and in this instance the price is moral courage.'

Moral courage. The language was familiar: a village of moral cowards, all fully informed as to who had done what, when and how, but too scared, too amoral to speak out. Simultaneously appealing to and criticising those whose help was sought was once again the approach.

*Several members of the village have contacted me giving the names of individuals they believe to be involved with these disturbances but in order to secure a prosecution or formal warning it is necessary to commit words to paper and in extreme cases even be prepared to attend court. Rest assured, should anyone come forward with such information the ball would roll very quickly and you would see results.*

*Parents — are you aware of the location and standard of behaviour of your children? Remember that you are responsible for their actions. Do they congregate to the annoyance of others? Do they behave in a manner of which you can be proud?*

*Adults — do we bear grudges which should be forgotten? Are we as bad or worse than our children? Have we forgotten words like tolerance and citizenship? Ask yourself what you can do for the benefit of your community?*

*To the idiots perpetrating these crimes,* YOU HAVE BEEN WARNED.

Lots of people in the village suspected who the lead 'idiot' was. Norman told me the person's great-uncle had been one of the last full-time labourers on a nearby farm.

'I can't tell you his name, though. His grandad was a good bloke, he was. I used to shoot with him.'

There weren't many farm jobs for his grandson. Or houses that he could afford to live in, in the village he was born in. Maybe that was his grudge, if it was him. Maybe he was a good bloke too, just bored and angry.

Norman and I were moving sheep and the first lambs. He was moaning about the Common Market, as he still liked to call it, which, along with the government, any government, was to blame for any rural misfortune. 'It's all monoculture now. I remember looking out there,' he said, pointing to the Marsham land the other side of the valley, 'and seeing cows and sheep.'

'That's what I like about your place,' I said. 'There's cows and sheep and ...'

'Rubbish,' he laughed. The 'rubbish' had once earned him five hundred pounds. Some people from London had come down one day, in advertising or something they were, and asked if they could knock down one of his walls and park a brand-new car in his wheat field full of poppies, and then take some photos of it. Yes, he'd said.

We walked on in silence. Two buzzards circled over Valley Ground, and one drifted over towards us, scaring pigeons from the garden trees.

'They'll take a small lamb,' Norman remarked.

'You can't shoot them any more, can you?' I said knowledgeably, something Tom had told me.

'Can't you?' he replied with a toothless grin.

'Are the foxes ever a problem with the lambs?'

'I lost nearly fifteen lambs only last week.'

'I thought the hunts were supposed to put a stop to all that.'

Norman laughed dismissively.

'Tom's coming over tonight; perhaps I could ask him if he knows anyone who could try and find the culprit?' So many lambs lost in such a way seemed such a cruel waste of life. 'Would that be OK?'

'Yes,' Norman said quietly.

That night, after we'd eaten, Norman came round in his slippers. As it happened, Tom knew how to shoot foxes and had brought his rifle with him. Norman briefed Tom as to where he had seen foxes and which of his fields he had livestock in.

'Reckon you'll get any then?' he teased.

'Reckon we might,' said Tom, non-comittally.

We set out at around eleven. Tom warned me not to wear too many clothes, despite the cold; we'd be walking plenty and would soon warm up. Tom carried a large rifle with a scope and a retract-able bipod fixed to its underside. In addition, he carried a large hand-held lamp powered by a battery that he carried in a hessian bag slung over his shoulder. I took a shotgun, a handful of 'heavies' (cartridges loaded with ball bearings) and an ancient, bloodstained hessian game bag.

'You can sometimes get a young fox that will just run towards you when he hears you squeak him up, and if he's close and moving, it's yours,' Tom said to me as he handed me the shotgun.

At the garden wall, Tom flicked on the lamp and quickly moved its powerful beam across the Humpty Dumps and back before switching it off.

'Right,' he whispered. 'Walk as quietly as you can, talk as little as possible and don't smoke.' With that for instruction, we climbed over the garden wall, crossed Home Paddock and the Humpty Dumps and approached the wall overlooking Sleeves Corner.

The night was mild and still; too still for Tom, who complained that the wind wasn't loud enough to cover the sound of our move-ments. There was just enough dulled moonlight behind the clouds to make movement manageable without a light. At each wall Tom stopped, scanned the lamp around and then we carried on.

In Sleeves Corner there were sheep and lambs, and their eyes shone in the reflection of the powerful lamp. Tom flicked off the lamp almost immediately.

'Four,' he whispered, the adrenalin clear in his voice and breathing. In a brief sweep he had picked out four pairs of foxes' eyes, the animals circling the unknowing lambs like lions. 'I can't believe how many there are. Did you see them?'

'No.'

He flicked on the lamp and scanned again. This time I saw them, quick flashes of illuminated eye. They had even managed to stand with the road and houses from the village behind them, making a safe shot impossible. They were motionless, unperturbed by the light.

Tom started to make a squeaking sound, using his mouth and the back of his hand. He told me this was the sound a distressed rabbit would make when taken by a stoat. It will take the stoat some time to kill the rabbit and feed off it, even longer if it is a big rabbit and the stoat wants to carry the kill to its young. A fox, knowing a free meal is close at hand, will run to the sound, startle the stoat and feed off its kill. Young foxes, never shot at before, were particularly susceptible and could come charging in. I fingered the shotgun expectantly. But these ones were more seasoned and wouldn't come.

'We'll leave them. Get them later,' said Tom after a while, and we set off towards the Lambing Sheds. Over the wall between Pumping Station Field and Rathbury, we scanned the light. We saw a lumbering badger trudge across the field, then another, but no fox. One badger moved off behind us and disappeared, another slipped back into the woods by Rathbury House. Badgers! I'd never seen a badger.

Then we picked out a pair of eyes.

Tom passed me the lamp and sat down on the wet grass, his legs stretched out in front of him. Carefully and silently he unfolded the bipod and rested the rifle in his shoulder. He leant forward and prepared to study the distant target in the light of the beam.

'OK, now,' he whispered so quietly I could hardly hear him.

I flicked the light on and held it on the eyes.

'Off.'

I switched off. Tom was still looking through the sight.

'What is it?' I hissed, my heart pounding.

'I'm not sure. It's behind a fence.'

He tried squeaking and I put the light back on. It hadn't moved. We tried again. Still it wouldn't move. Tom kept studying the animal, but he couldn't get a good view of it.

'Shit,' he muttered.

Finally he closed up the bipod and got up. He was not one hundred per cent sure what it was. Only the very top of its head was visible. It was probably a fox, but you had to be sure, dead sure. No one wanted to shoot a cat belonging to an old lady in the village.

We crossed the canal bridge by the Lambing Sheds, moving through thick black in under the trees, obscured from the faint moon. I was getting used to walking in the dark but was glad I knew the ground. We headed through Tynings and towards the lonely barn that sat atop the hill that looked down over River Head Paddock. I could hear an owl; otherwise, the night was quiet. Tom flicked the lamp. A fox! This time I saw it too.

Tom sat down and got the rifle ready. The fox was standing still against a far fence. Tom held the lamp in his left hand, resting it against the rifle and illuminating the fox. It was so far off that at first I could only see its eyes. Finally I made out its body. There it was in another of Norman's lambing fields, a nervous ewe circling a young lamb, trying to keep the fox at bay.

BOOM!!

I was quite unprepared for the noise of the shot that came, a cannon blast that smashed across the valley and reverberated off the high trees of Rathbury Wood.

'Did it drop?' Tom asked quietly, unable to see the hit because of the glare of the muzzle flash in the sight.

'Yes. For sure.'

We got up and walked over.

There it was, quite dead, a clean shot deep into its side.

Tom examined the condition of its fur and teeth and pronounced it a dog fox; about three years old, probably, and in good health. He rolled a cigarette, passed it on to me and we stood over the animal in silence. We seemed to be marking a brief moment of respect.

'Dead before he heard the shot,' said Tom, finishing his rollie. We bagged up the dead fox in the hessian sack we had brought, and which Tom would deliver for a post-mortem as part of a government study on fox diseases. 'Let's go,' he whispered.

If foxes did need to be controlled, and it seemed clear that they did, at least in sheep country, then I could imagine no cleaner and kinder way of doing it than this. Trapping, poisoning or being chased by hounds were the alternatives. Here, though, one good man with a rifle made sense of the saying 'he didn't know what hit him'.

It was nearly 4 a.m. before we finished, seeing two more foxes and shooting one of the ones we had first seen circling the lambs when we had set out. Tom wasn't overly enthusiastic about shooting foxes, but sometimes, particularly in lambing periods, it was the only way.

We stopped and smoked a final rollie in that hour of deep night which is its stillest and coldest, and rarely seen. I could see the dark outlines of the high trees that separated the farm from the garden of Lettem House, and a downstairs light from our cottage. The moonlit hunt and the opening of my eyes to life on Parish Farm at night had had an exhilarating effect on me; it had taken me no great distance, but the journey had been to another world.

The next day, I needed to be looking for freelance work and trying to write. Instead, I embarked on the first day of my pre-spring project, an undertaking I had made to Norman on New Year's Day which now had to be fulfilled before the lambing got into its stride: clearing the Lambing Sheds.

Tom came down to see what I was about, and ended up helping out. Together we built a huge bonfire that burnt long into the night, visible from the road into the village. The blackthorn and elder cuttings, nettles and brambles were so damp that straw alone wasn't sufficient to light this monster, so we broke up dry timber we'd found in the barn and created an enormous blaze. At the day's end, we sat and smoked in the fast-closing light, admiring our handiwork. The fire chased off the March cold, its smoke and embers charging into the dusk sky. High above, buzzards floated in the wind.

'I've lived in cities all my adult life,' I remarked absent-mindedly. 'What was I doing?'

'Cities mean nothing to me,' Tom said. 'Absolutely nothing. If you put me in one, I would shrivel up and die.'

To cut down the blackthorn trees I had borrowed Dan's chainsaw and then had it serviced. The bill had come to sixty-five pounds. Tom told me I'd been ripped off. Spider wasn't so sure; labour was at thirty pounds an hour at the local agricultural engineers who had done the job. Norman was sympathetic.

'That's what's wrong with farming. Sixty-five pounds is what I get for a ton of wheat. And for that I've got to plough, prepare the land, dress the seed, plant it, fertilise it and harvest it.'

Dan, though, was pleased. I could borrow his chainsaw any time. He must have thought I had money and time to burn, doing the barns and the service. We didn't.

The truth was, I was avoiding the reality of our situation. It wasn't my barn, it wasn't my farm, and I needed to earn some money. Our huge mortgage had been obtained on the salary that had come with my old life, to be maintained on the hope of regular consultancy work and Han's job; not on her fading work and my diffident and unsuccessful efforts to find more myself. As we ate into our savings, I knew that if we couldn't make a living we would need to go back to the life we had led before, and that was something I couldn't imagine ever doing.

# CHAPTER 12

# SPRING PREDATORS

As the March gales blew through and we waited for spring, playing with Annie, writing and hanging out with Tom and Norman were my main activities, despite our looming financial crisis; I was so busy, I wondered how people had time for jobs.

Tom sensed two things in me: that I knew absolutely nothing about his world and that I wanted to learn about it. He would phone or drop by with an invitation to go shooting or to join him on some little expedition. Casually made, they were eagerly accepted.

'Tom here.'

'Hello.'

'Doing anything this morning?'

'No,' I would lie, scrapping any plans to write or look for work.

'Shot some rabbits last night up at the airfield. Want to come and do them?'

And so I'd learn how to skin and gut rabbits.

Spending time with Tom was like spending time in a library and a classroom, with the merriment of a good pub. I marvelled at how he had come to know everything he knew; how he'd become such a countryman, so practical and proficient. I had always blamed my fear of the practical on the absence of a father to show me the way, but Tom was proof positive of my own hopelessness.

It took a while for me to understand exactly what it was that Tom did for a living; as with Norman, I found it difficult to ask him direct questions, not least because they both had the ability to give an answer that was so completely incomplete it made the questioner feel a fool. How many sheep do you have? someone would ask. About the same as last year, would come the reply.

For most of his life, Tom had been a gamekeeper in various

counties in England. He now worked as a wildlife surveyor, running his own pest-control business as a sideline; mostly rabbits, corvids – birds of the crow family – and the occasional rogue fox.

The killing of rooks and crows used to be an important part of pest control in rural England. Before the days of deeper and more efficient drilling, scattered seed could be picked clean and whole fields ruined by black clouds of corvids and marauding pigeons. Even today, a large flock could cause immense damage. Equally, a struggling lambing ewe or a newborn could easily lose an eye or worse to corvids. In the old days, every year in May, shoots used to be organised to kill branchers, young rooks out of the nest but unable yet to fly and forage. Those were the days of rook pie, using the tender meat of the young birds. Some farms still had these shoots, but they were rare.

Nowadays, controlling the crow and rook population was something few farmers needed to do, except those with pheasant shoots who wanted to protect their eggs. There were exceptions: a nearby organic vegetable farm needed protection for their exposed acres of hand-planted seed, and the small local airfield was obliged by its insurers to keep large flocks of birds away. People with the skill to control corvids were rare in the new Cotswolds, and Tom was one of the last who knew how to do it.

'They're unbelievably clever, you know. They recognise this truck now. They know it's no good. If you get one of them in a trap and it escapes, that's it, you'll never get another one back in that trap, it's finished.' I had visions of rooks and crows discussing Tom. 'Bastard.'

The traps were large, rectangular cages made from the type of tall wire fencing that building contractors use to secure their sites. Once inside, the birds were free to fly around; there was food and water, refreshed daily, but they could not escape. The trap itself would be surrounded by two strands of electric fencing to keep the foxes away. Setting a good trap took several weeks as it was assembled slowly, luring the birds in; but it would be a while before he would show me what happened then.

Tom's nearest client was the airfield used by light aircraft. Although they were completely legal, Tom had his traps set as far out of sight of the main buildings as possible.

'Got to be a bit careful. Lot of townies out here now.'

If the rooks and crows were a danger to the pilots and to freshly planted seed, the magpie was an altogether more villainous bird. While rooks, jays and jackdaws were largely opportunistic killers, magpies (along with crows) were intelligent and thorough birds that would search diligently in buildings, hedges, trees, anywhere they might find a nest. They were prolific killers of young songbirds in their nests as well as voracious egg thieves. Despite being less numerous and more attractive than corvids, with their striking black-and-white plumage and long graduated tails, magpies were held by countrymen like Tom to be a far worse predator, the enemy of the English songbird. Magpies could be seen flying down a hedge, their heads down and moving side to side searching out even the best-hidden nest, and there was little they would miss. Their harsh 'tscharr-ackackack' chattering and swaggering gait did not add to their limited charm. With large numbers of magpies about, as well as domestic cats, spring was a dangerous time for any nesting bird and her brood.

Just as hitting the foxes hard marked the onset of lambing, setting the magpie traps in March marked the beginning of the new season, preparing for the songbirds that would be born and the magpies who would prey on them. Like Tom's larger crow traps, the magpie traps also had to be set well away from public footpaths. Signs saying how the trap was humane and in accordance with Royal Society for the Protection of Birds guidelines did not prevent the occasional release of a magpie and the vandalising of a trap.

'It's townies. They don't understand what the little bastards do. A pair of magpies can devastate an entire hedgerow of nests in minutes. I've seen them do it.'

Tom's evening ritual was driving or walking around the traps as he fed and watered the decoys and discovered what had been caught. Tom would reach into a trap, grab the decoy, place it carefully in a hessian sack tied with a plastic tie and lay it on the ground. If you tried to change the water and put the fresh food in without taking this precaution, the bird would normally succeed in escaping. The sacks would jump and shake on the grass, and then go still, the bird resigned to its temporary fate.

It took me time to get used to the brutality, psychological rather than physical, of keeping a magpie alive to capture and kill others. Not that I said such a thing to Tom.

The fate of the captured magpies was swift and certain. Unless he needed more decoys, he would reach in, grab the bird and pull it out. To ensure a humane and quick kill, he would first get his hands firmly round the magpie, the bird pecking at Tom's ungloved hands. Then, holding the bird still in one hand, its legs and wings tightly bound round its body, he would immediately take what was known as a 'priest' and hit the bird smartly over the head. One blow did it. His priest was a short, heavy-headed piece of wood, so called for its effectiveness in humanely killing a fish or other small animal. The dead bird would move on the ground, twitching with the last contractions of its nervous system. I could never really believe they were dead by then, but on closer inspection they always were. Tom was very efficient.

Controlling rabbits was something Tom also did for his clients, mostly on planned expeditions at night using a lamp and a silenced small-calibre rifle. (A shotgun would leave nothing to eat, and one blast would see every rabbit in hearing distance scamper for its warren.) It was at night that the rabbits would dare to stray further from their holes and out into the fields. The key was good shooting. A neat head-shot meant a quick, painless death for the animal, and besides, no butcher would want a rabbit that had been shot in the guts.

Tom would always have a rifle with him as we drove around the traps, in case he saw a rabbit or two. Driving home from the traps one night on a client's farm, we saw rabbits in a field to the left of the track we were on. The farm was immaculate – brand-new barns, carefully restored buildings, big new gleaming machinery, hedges and fences and gates all beautifully maintained. I couldn't imagine it could ever recoup what had been spent on it, but that probably wasn't the point. The contrast between this and Parish Farm was shocking and envy-generating. It was said farmers had to be inventive in order to survive, but inventiveness here was at least in part spending plenty of the one thing Norman didn't have: cash.

'Now you know how to skin one, why don't you have a go?' Tom said, passing me the rifle. It was a smaller rifle than the one he used on the foxes, with a five-bullet magazine, scope and silencer.

Leaning out of the truck window I took aim. It was dusk and three rabbits were feeding close to their warren.

'In the head, then, gut shot's no good to anyone.'

There's an awful lot of killing in Tom's life, it occurred to me. I didn't much want to kill anything. I fired.

'Very tidy. Better get it then.'

I searched up and down the hedge, but there was nothing there. I wasn't sure I had hit it but Tom was adamant. He got down on his hands and knees and started to push his arm down the rabbit holes as far as he could.

'You'd be amazed how far they can move after you've killed them. It's the nerves. The contractions can bounce them around like a tennis ball. Gravity stops them; look in the lowest place,' he instructed me.

I got down and joined him, searching in the holes, expecting to get my hand bitten by something invisible and angry. The holes were ten or twelve feet from where the rabbit was when I had shot it. *This can't be possible.*

'Here it is,' he said, unsurprised, pulling a dead rabbit out from a hole. 'Personally, I like to leave the little ones to live a bit,' Tom teased me, knowing this was the first rabbit I had killed. 'Poor thing, young life, just came outside, seeing and enjoying the joys of spring for the first time, then wallop, you come along. But each to his own.' His humour was poker-faced. 'Better not tell Han.'

Easter Day and Han and I went to church. Twelve hundred people lived in the four villages that made up the Sheepfold parishes; thirteen hundred attended a service over Christmas and so was proof of the health of the Church, the rector said. On Easter Day, the church was about four-fifths full. The rector's wife arrived late with sheep for the children to look at. One of the rector's daughters was back from London, and she read the Easter story just as she had the Christmas one, and everyone from the village listened appreciatively.

It was striking how few people there we knew, other than Norman; or how few we even recognised, given our two years in the village. Some faces we knew by sight but few others. They were mostly old, from the matchbox houses, as Norman called them.

'I used to know everyone in the village, but since the matchbox houses I don't keep up,' he said, referring to the old people's bungalows and the cul-de-sacs. 'They just come and go, don't they?'

Only the rector had visited us when we had arrived and, since then, just one person whom we had not met at the pub – a retired midwife called Deborah. She lived in Lettem Mews, one of the old converted greyhound kennels that the Simpsons had kept at Lettem House. She had dropped in because our post had been mixed up.

'I delivered a baby on your floor. And I was very friendly with the doctor's wife who lived here before that. She was a midwife too. Of course, they've ruined the community health care system now.'

It seemed fine when we had Annie, but Deborah had opinions.

'My neighbour's selling her house. It's by far the smallest. You can't really call it a house, actually. They want £215,000 for it.' At least ten times the earnings of everyone I knew who worked on the land, for probably the smallest house in the village. 'And another £5,000 for the curtains and fittings, which you wouldn't really want.'

Mr Proctor himself was moving on from Lettem House. Price rumours had now climbed from £1.5 million to £2.25 million, but it still hadn't sold.

It was said that Mr Proctor had bought Lettem House from a property developer who had bought it from Simpson for £175,000 but then sold it to Proctor just six months later. Proctor had received permission to build the mock-Georgian houses in its grounds as well as converting Lettem Mews into some smaller homes. Ambitious building developments of this type, in the heart of Cotswold villages, often came with demands from the planners to provide low-cost housing, and the development of Lettem Mews was believed by many to have been part of such an agreement. Whether it was locals or outsiders and weekenders who bought the Lettem Mews properties I don't know, but the mock-Georgian houses were built and I was told the Lettem Mews properties went for in the region of £84,000 each. At the time, it's doubtful that anyone who needed low-cost housing thought they were very low-cost, and they certainly weren't now.

'That's a lot of money for a dog shed, my mother said,' Norman once laughed.

The Larches we knew, and Miss Dibden. And the Malverns, a retired army officer and his wife, I had met once. They lived in a plain modern house bought off-plan on a plot of land sold by the then owners of one of the big houses back in 1984. This was before the matchbox houses and Glebe Field Close (the new cul-de-sac near the war memorial), and Mrs Malvern thought she had been the first outsider the village had seen.

'I had a dog, and I didn't have a phone, so taking the dog to the telephone box was a wonderful way to meet people,' Mrs Malvern said. 'Everyone was so kind. I'm so sorry no one came to see you when you moved in, but it's just impossible now since Glebe Field. People come and go all the time.'

I had met Mrs Malvern when I went to get Annie enrolled on the church electoral register, in order that she could be christened there. What do you do? Mrs Malvern had asked me.

'I'm trying to do a bit of writing actually.'

'Oh really. Any success?'

'No.'

'Well, never mind. You look a very contented young man to me. You see, people today think they should be happy every day, but happy days are rare and should be stored away and saved for rainy ones. Contentment is much more important.'

We walked home from church in the drizzle, Annie in her pram. Maggie had waited patiently outside the church for us, and back at the cottage Sukey hobbled out to meet us. We had wanted to stay after the Easter service for coffee and cakes, but Norman and Tom's mother and mine were coming for lunch. We talked a little about the first Christmas after our fathers' deaths, how both mothers had forged on for their children, Tom's mother filling the house full of guests, my own taking us to stay with friends. Tom carved a duck that he had shot, gently mocking my own efforts, which only reminded me once more of how readily he had acquired skills a father might teach a son, ones that I had not. Han asked Norman if he had stayed behind after the service.

'I did stay for a cake, yes. They're free,' he said, pausing briefly. 'One way, I s'pose, of getting people to church,' he smiled.

Tom's client list was small but extremely blue-chip. You had to 'know what you were about,' 'how to behave', as he put it, and not to be short of a bob or two if you were to retain him. There was no shortage of money in Gloucestershire, but Tom found the other commodities were increasingly rare.

'You won't fucking believe it,' Tom said one night; he was in a fury.

'What?'

'That bloody idiot over at The Court,' Tom said, talking about a City multimillionaire in a nearby village, who came mostly at weekends; a weekday widow, they called his type of wife. 'You won't believe what he did.'

'What?'

'I was going round the traps tonight, and not a single magpie caught. That's a bit funny, I thought. Next thing I hear him hurtling across the lawn, gesticulating like an idiot, all very overexcited, blabbering on about how well it's going and how thrilled he is and all this bollocks. Oh yeah, I say. Know what he'd done? He'd only been round himself and emptied my traps. He had dead magpies festooned all over a bush like Christmas fucking decorations! He said he thought he was helping!'

'Wasn't he?'

'You don't touch a man's traps, you just don't,' Tom said furiously. 'And you don't have a dog and bark yourself!'

'What did you say?'

'Say? What can you say to a tool like that? But that's it, went back there later, picked the lot up, that's it. Fuck it.'

The tycoon rang later in the week, several times. His messages were plaintive. Why aren't the traps there, what's happened, could he come round and see Tom? Tom didn't return his calls. Not only had the man interfered with a man's traps, he'd barked and he'd killed magpies that Tom's friends had been asking for as decoys. Ignorance was no excuse. The man was chopped out of Tom's ordered universe in one brutal cull.

Coming home from the traps one night, we passed a manor house where Tom used to have permission to do some rough shooting (a stroll around with a shotgun, on the lookout for something for the table).

'One of them lives in there.'

'"*Them*"?' I asked.

'Yeah, you know, them.'

This 'them' was a keen supporter of the pro-hunting campaign group, the Countryside Alliance.

'He saw me one day at a country fair at the Countryside

Alliance stand,' Tom went on absent-mindedly. 'I wasn't wearing a Countryside Alliance pin or badge or anything and he told me to sign up. I didn't tell him I was already a member and asked him why I should. "Well, let's put it like this," he said. "If you don't, you won't be shooting on my land again."'

'So did you tell him you were already a member?'

'No. I told him to get fucked.'

The big news at the pub was that May was putting in a bid for the lease. Geoff, it seemed, had left everything to his grown-up children in his will, a will written before he had been given the lease to The Leggers' by Laura. He hadn't changed the will and Geoff's children believed Laura was well-off enough in her own right without needing the pub.

Laura, for her part, put on a brave face, and kept the pub and the jobs that came with it open for as long as she could. But the children were going to sell the lease.

May dropped by, full of excitement and hope, to tell us the news. The price was £90,000 with the lease up for renewal. Of course, there would be the rent to pay to Marsham and the council rates on top of that. Various people including a local hotel-restaurant, a 'hospitality company' and an ex-aggie in his late twenties were also sniffing around or in the running, depending on whom one listened to.

May talked up her chances of getting the pub, citing direct contact with Geoff's daughter (whereas others, she said, were dealing with the solicitor), and the fact that she knew and was known by Lord Rodley, who would want her type of pub, she said. Marsham still owned the freehold, and their say in whom Geoff's children sold the lease to would be key. May had already lined up money from her bank and was planning to remortgage her house, rent it out and move herself and the family to the pub.

There were so many reasons we hoped she would succeed. She would be sure to preserve the character of the pub. She would be the resident landlord and custodian of its role as part of a wider family. She had served that pub and her customers for years. She deserved it. And it offered her and her family another opportunity: a move from the housing estate in town to the countryside, an unimaginably expensive proposition in the new Cotswolds.

May tried to temper her hopes and spoke of other options. One job she had been offered was to work at the pub in the village where she had first lived when she came to England; when she was the young au pair for a Tory MP.

Han and I feared May's ambitions for the pub might be too much, a dream that better funded and savvier bidders would do her out of. As we talked beside the last fire of the long winter, there was a silence, before May lit up a ciggie and cracked a huge laugh.

We all knew things were going to change, though how we weren't so sure.

## CHAPTER 13

# APRIL RISE

Everyone wanted to believe it would turn out well, that the pub would not be taken over by outsiders unburdened by its history or associations; that it would not be turned into a 'gastro-pub', the fate of most Cotswold locals. Drinkers would feel uncomfortable, the insides would be gutted, it would become a restaurant for people who had never been there before and now talked of 'going to the pub'. But there was no danger of that, we heard. Someone had spoken to Rodley, someone else bumped into his agent, they all said the same. Marsham liked The Leggers' as it was; they didn't want a gastro-pub.

As we waited for news and digested the implications of change, the mood at the pub turned sombre. There was a night when Dave, Tom, Spider and I were the only customers in the pub, bar a gaggle of kids from the village. 'The Village Massive', as Tom would call them, slouched by the fire, looking bored, pale and slightly angry. Just as they were coming of age to become the new generation at The Leggers', it seemed as if the pub had expired before they could fully take their place. Laura was upstairs. Dave told jokes about being single and tried to make us laugh, and Spider told stories and tried to ignore the truth: that without Knoxey the place had been weakened, was dying even. Tom and I walked home disconsolate and cold. There could always be calm nights at the pub, but this one had been particularly quiet. It had not been a great Leggers' evening.

Laura did her best to keep its spirits alive and look after the employees, but winter and uncertainty fed discontent and anxiety. She and the staff now worked for absent owners as the Estate and the heirs of the lease settled privately on their future.

'This is about people's jobs. Mum's fifty-five you know, this isn't easy for her,' Peg's daughter told Han. 'I don't think they realise that it was more than a business down there.'

For Laura, it was a time of bruised expectations and compounded grief. We discovered that Geoff and Laura had decided that after twenty-one years together, they would slip off and quietly get married in South Africa that February. Laura knew that the will was not left as Geoff had wanted it; he had even made an appointment to change it in the New Year. But there was nothing to be done.

At first the executors of Geoff's will had wanted to close the pub pending a sale. Laura told us of her reaction. 'You can't do that, I said, not in a bossy sort of way, but a sort of, well, a more gentle "that's not the right thing to do" sort of way. I can do whatever I like, that was the reply.'

Peg was equally resigned to disappointment, but it hurt; it had all been so unexpected. On her way back from the pub one afternoon, she dropped by with a book on Cotswold flora and fauna that she had salvaged from Geoff's collection as the family sorted through his affairs, and came with it as a present. She sat by the fire and sighed.

'I can understand it, I suppose. They're very close to their mother,' she said of Geoff's children, 'and to them Laura has always been the woman who took their father away. But still.' She paused and looked into her tea. 'That was a long time ago.'

It was a few days after Easter when we heard the news that the lease had been sold, bought back by the Estate, but what their intentions were remained unclear. May stopped by on her way to work as I stood in the lane with Annie. May had been crying.

'It would have been so perfect, for our future, for the kids.'

'I know, May, I know.'

I gave her a hug. She didn't know to whom it had been sold, just that it wasn't to her.

When Han came home I told her the news, and with the weather closing, I went for a walk. The vernal equinox had come and gone. Some had said it was the beginning of spring, because now the days would start to win out. But winter was not letting up. The rain was ferocious, whipped by the wind. The farm was mud and water and the yard a miserable wet mess. I found Norman wearing his ripped, mud-caked leather coat, his cap, boots and a hole-ridden woolly jumper, soaked through; his hands filthy and weather-worn.

He was fixing an inner tube on a tyre for the Leyland, and we stood and chatted about Knoxey and the pub in the shelter and chaos of the barn.

'I couldn't get the ram here this year. Not allowed to move it because of the foot-'n'-mouth. All I'm getting now are spastics and singletons,' he said, the result of five less than pedigree rams from the flock having done the tupping.

'The vicar's wife helped me last night. I couldn't get my hand inside this ewe. She's got small arms.' After an hour of trying, Norman told her they'd have to give up. '"We can't give up," she said. "Can't we get a vet?" she said.' Norman laughed. 'I can't afford a *vet*.'

We loaded two bales of hay and the inner tube into the Land Rover and, in driving rain, headed off to the Lambing Sheds. At each field I jumped out and cursed the broken, tied-up contraptions that passed for gates. They were a fiddle at any time, but in the rain the string was wet and my fingers cold. How did he drive through these gates every day and not go insane?

At the barn, the rain was coming down furiously and I helped get the inner tube into the tractor wheel, which Norman inflated with a pump run off the tractor engine.

'I suppose you fix all your own tyres too,' he said, straight-faced.

The rain was soaking us and it was cold and hostile. The farm was dead, not a place for birth. 'I remember one day you said how lucky I was to live here. I remember thinking, "I'd like to show him what it's like on a day like this."'

The tractor fixed, we chugged off to inspect the sheep with Maggie, soaked but still eager, running alongside us. We were looking for ewes about to give birth to take back to the Lambing Sheds. Norman did this four times a day, whatever the weather, alone. The day was now spectacularly evil and from the top of Tynings, lights from the village burnt dull in the grey and messy dusk.

We didn't find any ewes that needed moving and went back to the Lambing Sheds. There were some lambs too feeble to stand up, some their mothers wouldn't allow to feed, others with deformed legs. These ones bleated incessantly; they were weak and they were dying. To survive, they needed to be bottle-fed or have their mothers held in place to let them feed. This needed to be done three or four times a day. Norman didn't have the time to do them all, and the weak would die.

One cold, forsaken lamb was bleating from underneath a cart, perhaps put there to die by Norman. I rummaged around and pulled her out. It was too sad. I thought of our baby daughter.

Norman asked me to hold a ewe to let its lamb feed. Nature was unforgiving and cruel and this farm was on the brink of sinking into mud and death. Can't you shoot the ones in trouble? I asked. But Norman said he couldn't, he didn't have the right type of gun.

When we were finally done, recutting pieces of string to open the gates and tying them up again as we passed, it came out of me: *How do you live with these gates?*

Norman was always quiet and stoic, but this time his voice rose.

'When can I fix them? The only time I've got is between three and seven, and then I'm sleeping.'

Lambing, feeding the cattle, feeding the lambs, lambing. No time for gates and always late for the complaints of escaped livestock from fields whose walls and fences he simply wasn't able to maintain. He even moaned about Murray and Douglas: how one or the other of them wouldn't fix gates or work with wood or were lazy, or forgot to feed the sheep; or just went on about bikes all day.

'When my father was alive, every gate on this farm swung.'

We walked home in the rain.

'My grandfather bought my aunt's husband a farm,' Norman said as we dragged another broken gate through the mud. 'He wanted to be a farmer. Fifty-seven acres over at Colesbourne, a nice little dairy it was. But he couldn't keep it up. One day he was listening to *The Archers* and someone on it sells up. That was it. Next day he calls the auctioneer and sells his cattle. Couldn't do it, farming. He'd done it for fifteen years, but you can't do it if you're not born to it.'

We stopped at the clamp. There, sheltering from the wind, was a young calf, lying down, covered in mud and wet, crushed maize.

'Can you move her on your own, Norman?'

'Yes. After my tea.' Norman ate the food Rose brought him each evening cold for lunch the next day. For tea he ate bread and jam, or honey from the Bee Man.

'I've got to get home,' I said, abandoning him.

When the rain stopped, my mother arrived to babysit, and Tom, Han and I walked to the pub in moonlight so clear our shadows followed as long and sharp as an afternoon in August, my trousers glowing white in the light. I told Tom how I despaired at Norman's situation.

'It probably doesn't get to him,' Tom shrugged. 'He's never known anything different.' He was born to it.

Suddenly there is sun.

Spring. No rain, no wind. We could sit outside again at the table, and think of the winter gone. The warmth, the sun's glare frosted by smoky, early-morning clouds, would bring back the colour blue. Tinted blossom on the crab trees and the lime that was Frankie's Tree thickened in front of us.

Maggie came bounding over the wall, excited and alert, while Sukey dragged herself through the hedge and lay on the sparkling grass, daffodils by her head, the cats stretched out on the warming flagstones. Despite the blossoming fruit trees in front of Bee Copse obscuring the hives a little more each day, Norman restated his view that spring came in May; it would be the hawthorn that would tell us so.

Still wearing winter clothes for my run, I had to stop before I could make it home, it was too warm; this was spring. Instead, Maggie and I cut down into Frimley Wood and walked. The ground, finally drying, was busy with bluebells in gently moving breeze-blown green. I saw three foxes, close, in the wide avenues that crossed the wood. They sensed us and stood still and stared. We marked the entry of the new season into their winter woods. The deer crashed across our path and moved deeper into the trees, startled at seeing us.

When we reached the pub, I sat for a moment outside on one of the benches. On my runs, I would see Knoxey come out in the early evening before the pub opened, standing there alone in the driveway as he reflected on his good fortune. When I thought of him directly, I had the clearest of images of him, and I couldn't believe he was truly gone. I still liked to think he was just on a long walk in Frimley Wood.

Now that the weather was good enough for Douglas to sit outside again, he resumed having his lunches with us, talking of bikes and the small cast of characters that made up our lives.

'Upper-class people are snitty, you see, Ian. They look down on working-class people like us because they live in a different age, like the Victorian times, they do.'

Someone he knew worked as a cleaner in one of the big houses. She had asked if she might have something to eat at the house, to save her bringing lunch, but the answer had been no.

Having money made upper-class people mean, Douglas thought.

'Look at that old car of his,' Douglas went on, talking about the cleaner's boss. 'Held together by string it is, like old Norman's Land Rover. Mean, they are.'

I don't suppose these complaints about the people in the big houses were anything new. For me they were insights that, true or not, only added to my vague reservations.

'They've got nannies and grooms coming and going all the time, they have. They don't stay, you know,' said one girl who worked as a babysitter in a nearby village. 'They had this one girl, from New Zealand she was. She said, "Can I go hunting one day on one of the horses if you're not here?" Know what they said?'

'No?'

'That's right. No, they said. She left, too, she did; they all do.'

Then there was the London man in the county who kept a few sheep 'so he could say he was a farmer', and who was said to be constantly in dispute with his neighbours over boundaries. 'This neighbour of his built this sort of tower on his ground, like scaffolding,' Tom told me, 'so he says to my mate, "Get over there and sort it out." "What do you mean?"' said my mate. '"Go and take it down, in the night." "I'm not bloody doing that," my mate said, "you fucking go and nick it if you want to."'

The most unpleasant tale I heard was of a London lawyer who was alleged to use all the loos in his large house and deliberately leave them unflushed for the young woman who was his cleaner to discover. But I liked it when Douglas would repeat his story of being asked to do a bit of casual labour by a thirty-something man who apparently spent most of his time hunting.

'He came up to me one day; he wanted me to help him clear out some barns, and all that. You wouldn't believe it!' said Douglas.

'Not paying much?'

'No, he pays all right, four pound an hour. He wanted it done in twenty minutes, then twenty minutes to rake his lawn and one hour to put some posts in. That's four days' work that is, I told him.'

'What did he say?'

'He said, he said, that's ridiculous, he said. Well, if you're going to take that attitude, I said, then you better start looking in the *Yellow Pages* because that's the only place you're going to find anyone to sweep out your barn round here, I said.'

Norman came past the wall, driving Sneaky home. Did he want to come for lunch?

'I can't, I can't. Really, I haven't got the time. If I leave these animals, they'll die, you know.'

The sun was shining, Norman was smiling and laughing. So were we again.

The ramblers wanted to see frolicking, but it was as likely in the lambing season they'd see a dying ewe or a lost lamb. They'd be shocked that farming could involve death and would call someone on their 'portable telephones' as Norman liked to call them.

'That's what they do these days, they call the RS ... whatever it is. Or the police,' Norman told Han and me. 'I just got a call.'

There was a lost lamb by the railway, could we go and find it, he hadn't the time. We put Annie in her sling and set off down the lane.

Han found it abandoned by its mother in Railway Piece, perhaps only a few hours old. He could stand and walk, just, but was quite alone. We picked him up and carried him to the yard. Norman was standing over a calf covered in dried mud which he was trying to shear off with a pair of electric shears. Han wanted to keep the lamb at home, and Norman promised to bring down a ewe later to try and get him on to her milk.

We named the lamb Pop and laid him in a plastic recycling box bedded with straw. Pushed against the wall between the bin and the Aga with the fireguard as a fence, his eyes were closed and his body was frail and weak. If he was going to die, at least he would be warm and comfortable, not taken by a fox. That evening, Norman arrived with a grubby feeder bottle containing colostrum from a ewe he had milked. The next day I cleared out our woodshed, bedded it with straw and placed two metal sheep hurdles across the door. Pop gave up his warm bed by the Aga and awaited his adoptive mother, a ewe who had lost her lamb. Pop could smell the milk but the ewe was restless and aggressive and would not stand still. I climbed in and held her still, but Pop would not suckle. We'll hand-rear him, we said to Norman.

'That's a lot of work, you know.'

'My whole day is spent feeding a baby, one more won't hurt,' Han reassured Norman as she cradled the tiny lamb in her arms. Pop had already found his mother.

Another lamb arrived a few days later.

'You did say one more wouldn't hurt,' Norman said, standing at the back door in the rain holding a little bundle of desperation. Han took him in too. Pip we called him, and so went our spring, feeding Annie and Pip and Pop. Sun-warmed, Annie would sit in her pram in the garden as we fed Pip and Pop, Pop pushing forcefully with his head against our legs to encourage his mother's teat.

It didn't take many days of bottle-feeding before they were fit and well again. We tried to make them play in the field, but they wouldn't cooperate. They leapt back over the wall and into the garden, where they nibbled the flowers and shat on the terrace.

Instead we would take them for walks across Home Paddock, where they followed us like puppies, sniffing and prancing. They ran and jumped in the greening grass; sudden vertical four-legged springs, like clumsy gazelles.

We asked Norman if Pip and Pop could avoid their destiny, whether they could become instead the flock's rams? Norman told us they were singletons, and singletons never become rams.

With the improvement in the weather, people got out more.

'You can't come through here!' Douglas shouted, hands on hips, shaking his head solemnly at two yellow-lycra-clad joggers climbing the wall into Home Paddock and heading for the gate on to the lane. 'You better not let Norman see you.'

Douglas was standing on Norman's garden wall. The middle-aged joggers carried maps folded in plastic, with compasses round their necks. They slowed to a walk but it was too late. Out of sight, from way off, carried the voice of Norman: 'YOU CAN'T FUCKING COME THROUGH HERE, YOU BASTARDS!'

The joggers stopped now. The people with the maps were always the worst, Norman said.

'Oh, sorry, we thought there was a path across here.'

'THERE'S NO FUCKING PATH. YOU KNOW THAT! WHY DON'T YOU USE THAT FUCKING MAP YOU'VE GOT!?'

'You can't come through here,' Douglas tutted. 'You better listen to what old Norman says.'

But the joggers were so close to the lane that they thought they could get out of the field before the voice arrived. They kept moving.

'Sorry, what did he say?' said one to Douglas, pretending not to hear.

From behind the hedge, invisible to them, I shouted 'DOUGLAS, GET THE GUN, GET THE GUN!'

The joggers froze, looked at each other incredulously, then turned and ran.

The bluffing and jogging was over; now they were sprinters and hurdlers. They tore back the way they had come, leapt over the wall, hardly touching the top stones, and didn't stop until they were out of sight.

'That's not right, Ian, what you did,' Douglas said, making me feel a little guilty and rather silly. 'They were very frightened.'

Later Norman arrived, but he wasn't cross, and he didn't mention what had taken place.

Along with the ramblers, Murray reappeared after a long winter migration ('He got homesick,' Norman teased), and now that it was drier, Kennie could load Norman's muck-spreader and hurtle up and down Valley Ground in an enormous cloud of flying shit and dust. Spider cleared out the village cricket pavilion and stopped by with his tractor on his way to the tip. From the back of his trailer I rescued a wooden sun umbrella for a summer that couldn't finally be coming, could it?

Spring was a time to plan projects like painting the oil tank. And restoring the canal, at a projected cost of £100 million. The British Waterways campaign, much talked about, now took shape as its Regeneration Programme Manager, Mr Freinst, began to do the rounds of village meetings and started writing letters to the local paper. Norman and I went to hear him talk in a nearby town. Before the meeting, Norman and I had a drink in a pub. It was strange seeing Norman anywhere other than Parish Farm. When we walked into the hall with all the strange faces, Norman seemed to be shaking.

Freinst was a short man, about forty, dressed in a crisp white shirt and tie, and was based in Watford. He had a laptop that projected well-made charts and pictures. He talked engagingly for an hour about the benefits of 1.8 million people coming to look at the restored canal; about new jobs, water transfer, flood relief, sustainable heritage, enhanced recreational and environmental value and 'controlled' wildlife. He referred to small matters like the M5 motorway and a village, both of which blocked his route, as 'challenges, as we like to call them'.

'There are', he said, 'fifty-five blockages and nineteen challenges.' Norman, then, was a blockage and a challenge, the immensity of which Mr Freinst could have no real idea. If anyone had any questions, Mr Freinst would be happy to try and answer them.

'I've got one,' said a man. 'When are you lot going to realise this project is neither feasible nor wanted and push off and stop bothering us?'

We tried to get Freinst to admit that they would compulsorily purchase any land that the current owners wouldn't sell to them, but he evaded the question. A man from the blockage village, whose garden stood where Mr Freinst wanted to rebuild the canal, said that £100 million would buy his village quite a nice new school, and if the national lottery did indeed have all this money to give away, couldn't they do that instead? The anglers were more worried about what would happen if water from the Severn mixed with water from their local rivers.

After the meeting, Mr Freinst tried to enlist my help in speaking to Norman. He was trying to speak with all the landowners, he said. He said he had called and left messages, but Norman wouldn't reply. I told him I couldn't much help, and said we'd better be going.

On the way back Norman bought fish and chips, which were cold when we got home and ate them with Han.

'It'll never happen,' Norman said. 'Lord Marsham, he's the chair of the landowners' group against it, and they're the biggest landowner on the route. It'll never happen.'

I wasn't so sure. Mr Freinst had a programme to manage, a laptop, a PowerPoint presentation and a ten-year plan. Marsham owned a pub on the route that would benefit from increased trade if the canal reopened, which would mean they could charge higher rents. As for the impact on their farming, a lot of the route across their land lay deep under Frimley Wood and out of sight.

It was spring and this was just the beginning.

Towards the end of April the pub news became official. Marsham, who had bought back The Leggers's lease, had a plan: to install a 'management company', and then to market and sell a new lease. Once again, we were all reassured that the Estate wanted to keep the pub as it was.

Although Lord Rodley was said to be a fan of keeping the pub as it was, many people also had the impression that he actually had little say at all in its future. Instead, people talked of 'The Trustees' as being the real holders of the reins, an anonymous and ominous-sounding group of people who were never individually named.

It was said that a prominent ex-merchant banker, who had been acquitted in an infamously expensive fraud trial, was one of them. His exact role with the Estate was never clear, but somehow he had became so intimately linked to Marsham that his name made its way on to the contracts of people renting small cottages from the Estate, as one of the Trustees of the Earl Marsham Estate Settlement (whatever that was). The banker and his trial had prompted one MP to ask the Attorney-General what the source was of medical advice given in fraud trials. Why, he asked in the House, was the Trustee 'told by someone giving medical advice several months after his trial began that he was on the verge of a mental breakdown, yet last week he was roaring up the M4 in his Porsche to look after his two properties?' Other Trustees I eventually learnt of were highly respected City lawyers who specialised in things such as 'asset protection structures' and 'estate planning for wealthy UK families'.

For their part, Lady Rodley claimed in a letter to a society-type magazine that she and her husband were 'merely custodians of an astonishingly beautiful piece of Gloucestershire', a term laden with care, responsibility and respect. She did not say where the real decision-making power lay, nor who made the decisions that might be less careful or kind.

Lady Rodley had written to the magazine because of an article that had described her, among other things, as being 'a big unkempt woman'. This had deeply hurt her, she wrote. She denied introducing herself to their journalist by saying, 'I'm Lady Rodley, we own the place.' The article painted a picture, she said, 'of an ill-mannered, pig-headed and pompous British aristocrat with a penchant for showing off possessions'. Furthermore, she wrote, she would never have said such a thing, as it was extremely bad form to use one's title as a form of introduction.

Most hurtful to Lady Rodley was the claim made in the article that she had commented to the journalist, favourably as it happened, on the polo-playing skills of a young member of the royal family. Apparently, it was 'simply not done'. Her knowledge of etiquette seemed to surprise Norman.

'You know she's not very ...' Norman paused and looked for the right word. He looked at the ground before finally settling on 'high-born'. 'She used to work in a bookshop in Cornwall.'

'I didn't know that.'

'She used to run a gift shop in Dorset,' someone I didn't know very well said to me at The Leggers' that night. 'Acts like she owns the place now, she does.'

The Trustees, then, were responsible for what would happen on the Estate, or so we were to believe. Time and again I would hear it repeated that Lord Rodley wouldn't want the pub to change, but what could he do? Out of his hands, more's the pity; it's the Trustees, you see.

It all sounded rather reasonable. Taking the lease back in, though, would ensure that the tenancy was sold to someone they approved of and at a much higher price and rent. It was the projected rent increase that spelled change. If, as rumoured, the rent was to go up from around £13,000 a year (as they said Knoxey paid) to nearer £25,000, and with any buyer of a new lease perhaps having to pay as much as or more than the £90,000 May had been reckoning on, the new tenants wouldn't be paying off that sort of money selling beer and crisps to Spider. It didn't look good.

The final days of April felt like summer. It was time for last year's lambs to go to market and, perhaps sensing this, they escaped from the yard where Norman had gathered them and sprinted down the Humpty Dumps, heading for Valley Ground. As the lambs passed in front of the cottage, Maggie raced past them so fast she failed to hear Norman's command to stop and turn them. ''ERE MAGGIE!' Norman yelled.

We got them back, eventually, into a pen in the yard. Those that were to go to market had to have their bellies shorn and their ears tagged before leaving the farm. Maggie ran up and down at the feet of the man who'd come to pick them up, dropping a stick in front of him and hoping he'd throw it to her, but he wisely ignored her.

'It's a mug's game. Never play with a sheepdog,' he said, stating what we all knew to be true, Norman and I studiously avoiding each other's eye.

We divided the pen in two and, at Norman's instruction, I would grab a sheep and pass it to him.

'Grab it by the neck and then do the waltz,' he said, despairing of my hopeless pushing and yanking. And so I did, dancing the recalcitrant beasts on their rear legs into the steady hold of Norman. Han came up with Annie and, ever the Australian, teased Norman about his English shearing skills.

'I'm past my prime now. Shearing's not for an old man like me.'

At the pub that night, Tom and Spider made only just straight-faced demands for an update on my efforts to get a rotted gatepost out of the ground. Much to their amusement I'd been at it for days. I'd tried augurs, a sort of giant corkscrew, and (much to their hilarity) I'd even poured petrol in the hole and tried to burn the bloody thing out. Tonight they laughed at the day's efforts with a chisel and the two centimetres of wood chippings I had to show for it.

'You laugh, but it's not that easy,' I said in all seriousness.

'I could have it out in a minute,' Tom laughed.

'Thirty seconds,' said Spider.

'Bollocks,' I said, and I should know. The bottom of the post had broken clean off and sat tight in its concrete footing, immovable.

'Right then, Spider, shall we go and do it then?' Tom asked, and we were off and up the lane to the cottage, despite the hour and all the beer and me still telling them they were wrong.

'I'll get a stopwatch,' I said.

Tom and Spider didn't discuss much of a plan. They got an augur, one of those lent to me by Norman, and as Spider put his not inconsiderable weight on it, Tom turned it. It was dark in the shadow of the front-door porch and I could barely see what they were doing.

It took them one minute and thirty-eight seconds. I knew I'd never hear the end of this tale. We toasted the post in the moonlight, and later I stumbled up to bed, babbling incoherently to Han about a post and the village and friends and sheep and Norman and Maggie and how we'll never leave here, we never will, we're dug too deep.

May made everyone bolder. Pip and Pop escaped from the woodshed and the magpies tapped on the window. I'd finally written to the brothers asking them if they would fix the collapsed wall of the goat barn and even move the caravan. Malcolm passed me as I was feeding the lambs.

'We're talking about you in the family,' Malcolm said.

'Oh, you got my letter then?'

'It's the others that are the problem,' he said, referring to Norman's wider family.

I asked Norman if the brothers had said anything to him about my letter.

'No,' he said, looking at me apologetically. 'It's the women that are the problem,' he said finally. 'We'll have to do something about those women, that's what Father said. Last thing he said to me two weeks before he died when he came here for the last time.' He paused, and we stood in silence looking at the caravan. 'You could burn it I s'pose.'

The cows too, docile and weary in the winter rain, were stronger as the weather warmed. Norman asked for my help. He couldn't get Sneaky, who was in labour, to go into the yard, and she was in difficulty. She was laid out by a wall in the Humpty Dumps next to Valley Ground, a calf's leg protruding from her.

At the drystone wall, Norman climbed over first. He liked to hold down a strand of barbed wire with his left hand and then, with a neat scissor movement of his legs, was over effortlessly in a moment. I went next using my preferred technique, thumb stick as a third leg, also over in a second. Next was my friend James. James was visiting from Paris. I made the mistake of giving him my thumb-stick, which he had no idea how it would aid him in climbing a wall, stumbled over it, got caught in the wire, knocked off the top stones and fell over the wall.

'Live in Paris, do you?' Norman said finally, just at the moment when his question wouldn't be directly linked to the stumble but soon enough after for it not to be forgotten.

'Yes, I do, actually,' said James sheepishly.

We got Sneaky to her feet and drove her up to the yard. Although no one thought to tell James where we were going or what we were trying to do, he was expected nevertheless to stand in the right place at the right time. Near the steam pond, Sneaky stopped and eyed the three men blocking her various escape routes. She then charged directly at James, who raised his arms at her as she went past. It was more of a wave goodbye than a command to stop. Sneaky cantered past him down the field with her calf's leg disappearing back inside her and her amniotic fluids splashing into the air. James looked a bit queasy.

Norman and I ran round her and drove her back up, but once again she stopped at the steam pond. It was a Parish Farm stand-off. Norman, quite unflappable, just stood still. Something would happen and he'd deal with whatever it was. James looked anxiously at Norman and me, hoping, presuming, that someone would take the initiative. I was worrying about a drowning calf.

There was a long, long pause.

'Can you get your friend to go round the back of her?' said Norman eventually. 'I'm not sure he's ...' Norman didn't finish his sentence but the general idea was clear.

James, dressed in trendy trainers more suitable for a stroll around the Marais, started to edge round the muddy pond. In Parish Farm style, instructions were vague to non-existent. I told James to watch his step, that the pond was like quicksand, it could gobble him up. Poor James believed me and looked terrified but eventually made his way gingerly behind Sneaky.

'What do I do now?'

Norman didn't say anything.

'Gee her on,' I said.

'What?'

'Gee her on.'

James mumbled nervously at Sneaky.

'Like you mean it,' Norman said.

'Move, then,' James said and she started to move. With Norman and me blocking Sneaky's path back to the paddock, and with her in advanced stages of labour, we've got her this time. This time, she'll have to go into the yard.

Sneaky lined up in front of the four-foot wall, slowly turned her head to look at us, then leapt clean over it and was away down the paddock. It was a giant leap from practically a standing start, without even touching a top stone. It was so unexpected that James's mouth flopped open in wonder as he sank up to his shins in mud. There was absolute silence among us until finally we heard the soft voice of Norman.

'The cow has spoken.'

James and I stood dumbfounded.

'I tell those people who are always complaining about Sneaky getting out, you see, but they don't believe me. An animal can jump anything if it wants to. It can be this high or this high, don't matter. People don't believe me.'

'I'm not surprised they don't believe you. I don't believe it and I saw it,' said James. 'The next time I read my daughter "The Cow Jumped Over the Moon", I'm going to make it much more literal.'

For her part, Sneaky did one trot round the paddock, walked back to the gate, waited for us to open it, and walked placidly to the yard, where she gave birth to a fine little heifer.

The twentieth anniversary of Geoff and Laura taking over the pub came and went with little fanfare and no news of the pub's future. As 'custodians' of this piece of Gloucestershire, there was some disappointment that Marsham, who would assume full control of the pub at the end of May now that they had bought back the lease, had still told not told the staff of their intentions.

Geoff and Laura had planned a big anniversary party. Instead, endless water flowed down the flooded lane to an empty pub. It was the wettest May in over a decade and a gloom soaked into ground that couldn't take much more. A stolen car was set on fire in Tidcombe and an ugly patch of burnt rubber and black, rain-stained tarmac scarred the lane. Han and I worried about mortgages and money. Alan, who had found out he was seriously ill, worried more about his health and how to carry on working.

Sitting on a bench made from a plank of wood set on two upturned clay pots, I stared at Alan's chickens and the elaborate vegetable patch he had less and less energy for as he told me about his treatment and its side effects. 'Every time I think I'm getting ahead in my life, I get knocked back,' he said.

That night in the pub, Dave was laughing at how he still hadn't cracked the dinner-party circuit. 'I'm Welsh, my father was a Baptist clergyman, I'm unmarried and over forty, I live in a rented cottage and I don't send any kids to the local prep school. So basically I'm screwed.'

Dave still joked that I was part of the 'dinner-party set', probably because it looked as if I might be. Owning an expensive Cotswold cottage, together with the absence of a regular job, were clear enough indicators. (To the snug bar it all sounded rather vague and if-you-say-so when I told them I did actually do a little writing from my desk overlooking Frimley Wood.)

That we had encountered some archetypes and caricatures on the rare occasions that we had entered that dinner-party world was not surprising; such people could be found anywhere. But my reluctance to meet more of them was perhaps simply a result of already formed and not easily explained misconceptions of my own. There was something about the type of people I had grown up among that made me a little uncomfortable. There was their entirely reasonable confidence in themselves, but the more I reflected back on Geoff's funeral, my own failed responses to Laura's loss, and the memories of my father's death that returned with them, the more things became clearer.

The unexplained bias I held against so many of the type that shared the background of most of my childhood friends was slowly coloured in; for the first time I began to glimpse the possible origins of my reticence to embrace them as an adult. I wondered more and more if my sense of displacement among these people was connected with an unspoken childhood jealousy of their own undepleted families, and a more adult manifestation of a hidden anger about the fact that many people had never spoken of or even acknowledged the death of my brother and father.

Much later in life, well into my thirties, I was told I had only needed to ask about my brother and father and these people would have spoken of them to me. But by then it was too late, all memory of them buried as deep as they.

Invitations were now rarer, perhaps as a result of our reluctance to embrace the initial burst of invites when we first came to Lettem, but we did venture out now and again into that world; perhaps our initial hunkering down at Lettem had been wrong-headed. But when we went to one of these dinners the talk was still mostly about children, private schools, house prices and the planned ban on fox-hunting, which, as the date approached, came across as some sort of enormous existential crisis which they were sadly having to face.

Labour backbenchers were not to blame for the ban on hunting. It was all about the Prime Minister.

'It's fucking tough to fire people these days, you know,' said a man holding forth about his farm and his business in London. 'Everyone bloody well thinks they can sue you. It's that bloody Prime Minister of ours and litigation lawyers advertising on TV. Actually, I tell you one thing that's quite surprising: our office in Liverpool, we hardly ever get sued up there. I mean, it's *Liverpool*. Maybe they can't read or something.'

Fucking French Farmers protesting were also detested. And Bloody Brussels.

Wasn't it Brussels, I ventured, that paid all the subsidies that kept British farming afloat, and wasn't it the French protesters that were fighting to keep the subsidy system going?

This set off another storm of ranting. I excused myself and went and smoked in the bathroom, looking at more photos of school teams, framed jokey cartoons about field sports and back copies of *Country Life* and *The Shooting Times*. I wanted to go home but we still had to have 'cheese and coffee', a particularly English phrase that Han always used to make me laugh about later. 'Why isn't it "cheese and wine" or "coffee and dessert"? How did your "cheese and coffee" thing ever come about?'

When I returned to the table a man spoke to me discreetly; he didn't want the others to hear him. 'Actually it's true, you know,' he muttered uncomfortably, unable to look me in the eye. 'I used to be an agricultural consultant and I never saw the books of an English farm where there would be any living at all were it not for the subsidies. There'd be a lot fewer Land Rover Discoveries driving around, that's for sure.'

After dinner someone told me that he knew the man in our village whose lawn had been poisoned and asked me if the vandal had been caught.

'No. Still a mystery.'

'Poor chap. Did you know he made an offhand remark to some neighbour in the village about someone they both knew and this got back to the chap who did it. He thinks it was this chap who did it.'

'Really?'

'Yes. Anyway, what do you make of his new security system, very elaborate, isn't it? I must say, I do wonder if he might not have been a bit more philosophical about it all. I don't know, I like Peter, I'm told he and his wife do so much for your village and the community, but I do think there is something about him that may have invited this thing, don't you think?'

Men who when I left England in 1990 had never even been to a football game now spoke about Arsenal and Beckham as if they'd been playing the game all their lives. 'Did anyone hear Becks being interviewed? I just can't believe how stupid and inarticulate he is. Can you *believe* he's the England captain?'

'I can't believe how all these people can afford to go to the World Cup. Isn't Korea meant to be bloody expensive?'

Later, a man who had taken exception to something I had said about Brussels told me that he had a theory on men. 'Basically, you know, there are two types of chaps. Dayboys and boarders. Don't you agree?' he said. I think he was implying I was the 'dayboy' sort, which, coming from a thirty-seven-year-old man, I found a bit weird, but I was too weary to remember what that was all supposed to mean.

There must have been dinner parties and people in the Cotswolds who talked about ideas and experiences, concerns and reflections, who made gentle jokes and had reasoned discussions, but somehow we never seemed to tumble into them. Han would make light of it, saying it was like playing the lotto; we just weren't very lucky. (Next time she'd buy the ticket, she said, as we drove home later.)

As we were getting ready to leave, a woman who had moved to the Cotswolds from London with her husband told me about Cirencester. 'There are just so many nice people here, aren't there?

I was in Waitrose this morning and I kept on thinking I could hear someone I knew. I'd turn round and I wouldn't know them at all! Isn't that marvellous? You just don't get that in London, do you? – people like us, everywhere you go.'

I told her about Lidl, the cheap food store, and how the checkout had been robbed at knife-point last week, and she looked crestfallen. I wasn't quite sure why; whether it was the notion that there were people in Cirencester who needed low-cost supermarkets or the idea that there were junkies holding up stores for money to buy heroin.

Was I going to the Colnbridge Village Festival this weekend, someone asked me as they passed me my coat. 'It's absolutely *super*,' he said.

'Festival' had the promise of music and dancing, food and drinking and so we went. The residents opened their gardens to the 'general public', set up three stalls selling 'bric-a-brac' and invited the Babbury School Dancers to perform. A dozen children, wearing neither costume nor their Sunday best, held hands and danced in circles to the sound of taped music from a tiny tape machine. Carloads of elderly people and bored young families trailed from house to house, admiring the Cotswold-stone houses and looking for Liz Hurley or Kate Winslet, who it was said had bought houses in the village or one nearby.

There was a brass band in a tent behind the pub, we were told. We expected the village to have gathered for drinking and eating. Instead, the tent was being taken down and the brass band had gone home. At 5.30 in the afternoon, the festival had ended, and only a few dissolute drinkers sat around with pints of beer served in plastic cups.

The pub used to be called The King and Castle, but now it had a new designer name and 'stunning specialist paint effects by the internationally renowned interior designer and decorator Hugh Roger-Smith'. There was a chef who had come by way of the Ivy and Bibendum, and they would serve 'Pimms in the summer, cognac and damn good food'.

We cycled back to The Leggers'. Leaving our tiny world never seemed to offer much reward. But I had to admit to Han later that sometimes in life you only find what you look for.

That spring had seen Han and me talking more and more about England, its society and its future and our family's place within it; how we wanted to live and where we could afford to do that.

'Money no object, do you think we should carry on living in England?' Han asked me.

Money was the object, but I tried to answer her question anyway. Avoiding a full-time job away from Lettem, carrying on at my attempts to write and carrying on meeting our mortgage were not compatible. Something was going to have to give.

'I'm not sure,' I said. 'I'm not sure.'

'Well, we need to consider that.'

'Yes, we do.'

But then the clean smell of early summer would overwhelm any doubts about staying in England and making our future here, at least for the moment. We'd set Annie on a blanket on the lawn and sit on the wall, looking out over Parish Farm and wave to Norman. This was our England.

# CHAPTER 14

# HARES

On the last day of May the rain stopped and the air was warm and windless at seven in the morning, the first summer sound of bees and songbirds in Frankie's Tree. The cock pheasant ambled out of Bee Copse and along the wall of Home Paddock down into Railway Piece. Maggie came bounding over the garden wall, wet from the morning dew, burrs stuck to her coat, looking for last night's scraps.

Having been closed for a year because of the foot-and-mouth restrictions, the cattle market in town had reopened. Norman was worried it would close for ever, like so many English cattle markets; it would be a slowing of the pulse of the town's rural life and the beginning of long trips to sell his animals. It was a small site of an acre or so behind the leisure centre on the edge of Cirencester. The council of this 'market town' was planning to sell the land to a large financial services company and an alternative site had not been found.

Norman knew I wanted to go with him to market, and one morning he knocked at the door, said hello, and waited for me to work out why he was there.

'Are you off to market then?'

'Yes.'

'Can I come then?'

'If you still want to.'

'When are you going?'

'Soon,' he said with a smile.

'That mean now?'

His smile widened.

'Now,' I said.

We drove south into town in the old Land Rover, passing the sleeping postman parked up in the track that led to Liz's horse yard. Being with Norman off Parish Farm was a rare adventure, for both Maggie and me. She sat up between us on the front seat, wet, dirty and overexcited.

'He always does that,' said Norman, pointing out the postman, 'having a kip. Whenever he's on and I drive past this way, there he is having a sleep. Post's always late when he's on.'

And thus the great mystery of the late post, which had perplexed me for two years, was solved.

We drove along the main road at a little over thirty miles an hour and in the short distance to town Norman had collected a long tail of urgent financial services executives and their cars. At the market, Norman parked on double yellow lines, blocking an exit and, in a nod to the security demands of urban environments, took out the ignition keys and left them on the dashboard. Maggie had to stay in the Land Rover.

The market, Norman told me, had been operating in Cirencester for over two hundred and fifty years. It was run by two youngish men who used to work for the firm that ran Gloucester market before it closed. The market in Cirencester – the capital of the Cotswolds, a region whose wealth had been built on wool – used to sell sheep, but now its low metal grid of pens stood empty, with weeds coming up under them and the rust slowly spreading.

Arriving on time was important because the standing space for bidders inside the cattle sheds was small and not everyone could get a good view. The men who were there to bid were the last of the last, the few remaining small farmers in the area, the few who still farmed livestock. These were farmers more like Norman, with old clothes and trousers and overalls held up with baler-twine, ruddy cheeks, wild hair and very bad teeth. It has to be said, though, that when it came to clothes, hair and teeth, no one could compete with Norman. When Norman was losing one of his teeth he would be in dreadful pain but would never go to the dentist, nor take any painkillers. Han would give him cloves to chew on. 'I suppose I'll lose 'em all one day,' he'd say and ask me if I still had my own teeth. He assumed that a full set in an adult over thirty could only mean dentures.

The auctioneer, dressed in a white coat and tie, made his way up the shed, ringing a large hand-held bell to announce that the sale was to start. The farmers pressed up against the fence, leaning in, joking and jostling for a better position as the first lot was pushed into the ring, a tiny three-week-old heifer, nervous and confused.

'Lot num'er*one*,' the auctioneer said so quickly it was hard to understand, 'lovely'immental'eifer, born May third, from Todd Ashley down 'omeleaze Farm, lovelyeifers'ealwaysbringsus, what will I have?'

It took me a while to realise Norman was bidding on the very first calf. He was leant against the wall of the shed, one foot raised slightly and pressed back against it, his arms folded in front of him. Not an inch of his body moved, save the barely perceptible blink of his eyes and the tiniest of movements of his head as he made his bid. Unless you were looking directly at him you wouldn't have noticed what he was about.

In seconds it was over; the first calf was gone and sold to Mr Ludd for just thirty-two pounds. He went on to buy two more in quick succession.

Afterwards Norman told me was 'quite satisfied' because calves at this time of year could be very expensive. Farmers tried to get two calves on to every cow, so for every singleton born they would want to buy one more. The restocking of slaughtered foot-and-mouth herds had also driven up prices, and as the morning continued most calves went for much more, some for as much as two hundred.

'I always get in early. People still getting settled, haven't arrived, chatting with their mates. Early, got to be early.'

With his three calves bought and prices going up, we left. Norman liked to pay up and get his paperwork done before the rush. When he came out of the office he found me wanting to go and buy a calf myself.

'Can't do that. I promised Hannah I wouldn't let you.'

I persisted, sort of jokingly.

'It's a disease,' he replied.

'What is?'

'Buying cattle. It's like a disease. You get one, you've got to feed it twice a day. For ever. It's a disease.'

We had a cup of tea in the market canteen and I listened to the farmers talking about the market and how they had survived the movement restrictions of foot-and-mouth. Norman, who hardly ever left Parish Farm even without foot-and-mouth, save to visit his sheep up at his ever more scattered, ever more distant rented pastures, or to come to market, knew everyone. After the isolation of foot-and-mouth there was a lot of catching up to be done.

As for the market itself, no one denied that one of the main problems was just that there were fewer and fewer farmers to make it viable. Marsham, a farmer there told me, once had about thirty-five tenant farmers, most of them with livestock. Now Marsham had, he thought, just five tenant farmers and practically all of their land was arable, and that meant thirty fewer people coming to the market.

'That wife of his is always going on about local markets, but if you want local markets, you got to have local farmers, 'aven't you?'

Another farmer at the market told me of his thirty years as a working man in and around Cirencester. He could still remember farm workers walking down to The Three Compasses and The Marlborough Arms, open all day on market day, and the many tractor dealerships in the town which were now nursing homes or garages selling expensive four-wheel drives. Farming had changed, he said.

'And look at the bloody council!' someone swore, talking about the deal to sell the site. 'Not a country person on it these days, not one.'

'Did you see the *Gazette* this week? "Plans for the cattle market" was the headline. What plans? The only plan they got is to close it.'

'Real shame, it is! Been a market town for centuries, and it's all going.'

Driving home, I plucked up the courage to ask Norman what exactly a heifer was. I took a deep breath, because however I phrased the question, I was going to sound foolish. My question to him would sound like someone asking me what the difference is between a video and a DVD.

'A heifer is a female cow that hasn't given birth. When it does, we call it a cow.'

Oh.

There was a long pause.

'Basically it's like women,' he added with a smile. 'She's a girl, then she gets married and has a baby, then she's a cow.' We drove on in silence, until after we had turned off the main road and headed into the village. 'I don't know what I'll do if they close that place,' he said.

The next morning Norman, Han and I walked down to the pub, pushing Annie's pushchair in front of us. An event had been organised by the Waterways Trust, the unveiling of a plaque by the Lord-Lieutenant commemorating the work of the Northleach Canal Trust. It was all part of the PR efforts of British Waterways to win support for the planned canal restoration.

As the hour approached, a receiving line formed up in front of the barn, waiting for the Lord-Lieutenant, the Queen's formal representative in the county.

A car was heard coming down the drive and there was much last-minute positioning and checking of shoes and hair.

'Here he is, everyone! He's coming!'

Round the corner drove a red Royal Mail van, oblivious to proceedings. In stunned silence the receiving line watched the postman get out, drop his delivery on the porch and drive off.

'You're the wrong royal, mate,' Kiwi Alison called out, with either a surprisingly accurate understanding of the Lord-Lieutenant's role or an equally confused one. She and Han were close friends; she was a chef and caterer who also worked shifts at the pub, and was as entertained as Han was by this semi-royal event. Alison and Han would swap their Antipodean observations of Cotswold life, and I wondered if Alison would finally make England her home. Alison hunted with the foxes (they were her biggest clients) but ran with the hares down at The Leggers', first amused but steadily more amazed and then perplexed by the foxes' wealth and segregation, the slow dawning of the realisation she could never afford a house here and that one of 'them' might date her but was unlikely to ever marry her.

A few minutes later, everyone heard the sound of another vehicle charging down the track. This must be him. A large Cherokee Jeep swept past Bob on the car park in the field, ignored the request not to park in front of the pub and screeched to a halt, throwing up a shower of gravel. Out clambered Lord and Lady Rodley to join the receiving line.

Finally the Lord-Lieutenant arrived and was off to unveil the plaque. Laura had helpfully suggested putting it up inside the barn, otherwise it would probably get nicked or vandalised, like a memorial tree the Prince of Wales had planted in a nearby village; they'd replanted it three times already.

'She is actually quite big, isn't she?' said Norman, referring to Lady Rodley and her letter to the magazine we had read together. 'I only ever see her sat up in her American car.'

Han commented on the jeep, the Rodleys being the very public 'Buy British' supporters that they were.

Later in the pub, we saw Freinst huddled over a map, getting briefings from the Canal Trust people. They were pointing out stretches of the canal and discussing landowners and their positions on the restoration. They all gave Norman a very wide berth.

Freinst recognised us from the meeting we had been to and came and sat down. The reason Norman hadn't been consulted was because he was going to be consulted later; the reason Freinst hadn't invited Norman to the event was because it wasn't his event to invite people to. A man came up and asked Freinst how he'd like a motorway going through his garden and warned him that in Gloucestershire, people had time and money to fight him.

'Yes,' said Freinst ruefully, 'we're learning it isn't Essex.'

Freinst said that Lord Rodley had given him some good advice. 'We had been talking to the head of the local Country Landowners Association,' Freinst went on, 'but Lord Rodley has just told me that actually he's not the man we need to be talking to at all! Rodley says that we'd be better off starting to talk to him and his father Lord Marsham if we want to get anywhere.'

For most people the morning had been an enjoyable, innocent enough event, but for Norman it was an ominous foretaste of something dreadful. We walked back home along the canal in worried silence.

'It's not going to happen,' said Norman eventually about the restoration. 'Is it?'

'No,' I said, not very convincingly.

When Norman and the family had left the ceremony, I had asked Norman if I could get him something from the souvenir stand.

'Like what?'

'A canal mug?'

'A mug? I thought the canal mug round here was me.'

At the end of the month, Norman agreed the time had come to send Pip and Pop out into the world.

'Could you put a little spray of paint on them?' asked Han. (Norman marked the ewes and the lambs with marker spray when they were born so he'd know who was who.) 'It'd be nice to be able to spot them out there.'

By the time we came back after lunch to move them, Norman had sprayed large capital letters in blue paint on to Pip's and Pop's backs: IAN and HAN they read.

We tried leading the lambs, then pulling them, but it was only by tricking them with the promise of a proffered bottle that we got them out of the pen and across the Humpty Dumps into their new home. At the gate, they scampered through ahead of us but ran back panicked as we shut the gate behind them. They bleated and cried so much we went back in and led them to the flock, which ignored them. Pip and Pop looked so strong and well in comparison with the other lambs, thanks to their months of generous and very expensive, uneconomic bottle-feeding.

It seemed ridiculous, the connection, it was so long ago, but in the middle of a Parish Farm field I remembered my first night at prep school. I was seven. I got up in the night in this big room of beds and went and cried in the bathrooms. Of course I missed my mother and father, but I felt also a sense of something I couldn't understand. A few weeks into my first term I found graffiti on the back of a toilet door: the cross, then, underneath, the name of my brother, and the initials RIP, carved with a schoolboy's penknife. Was this my brother's writing? What did RIP mean?

'Come on, boys, time to say goodbye,' said Han. We could hear them bleating for us all the way back to the cottage.

'I'm going to miss them,' I said.

Summer was to start with a party, the Queen's Golden Jubilee, and that meant the first baling of the summer was to be done. Village parties in the countryside had always used bales for seating. But the big local farmers didn't make hay any longer, not around us at any rate, and their straw bales were huge half-tonne Hesstons or round bales, taken away by contractors last August. Norman's small bales were in demand, but the wet winter had seen the last of them eaten long ago. The new harvest wouldn't be ready until later in the summer, so Douglas and I broke up a rotting Hesston hay bale while Norman got the small baler out of its winter hibernation.

We fed the hay into the baler and managed to make up fifteen small bales, which we loaded on to the trailer with the last of the linseed bales. It was good to be baling, a foretaste of summer, and Han came up with Annie to watch the miracle of the ancient baler starting up for one more year in its long rusty life.

'It's a bit rough this stuff, isn't it?' said Norman as we loaded the linseed bales. 'It'll prick the old ladies' arses.'

By the time we had the baler working, found some baler-twine, made the bales and loaded them, most of the afternoon was done. Norman wasn't paid for them and Douglas was off home for his tea.

'Are you giving your afternoon for free, then, Douglas? For the Queen?'

Douglas laughed. As if. Douglas, who had a particular way of ignoring gender, said that he liked that Diana, Prince of Wales, he liked her.

'You know what they called him, Ian?'

'What's that?'

'The People's Princess. I don't like the Queen. She's all stuck up.'

'What about the Queen Mum, she was all right, wasn't she?'

'I dunno 'bout that.'

When the Queen Mother died, a woman wrote to the *Gazette* wondering why she had been the only person to put some daffodils down at the War Memorial. It was a shame no one liked the Queen Mother like Diana, or had she got the wrong place?

'She wasn't my mum,' Norman had said.

'I'll write a note to the Queen informing her of your valuable contribution to her party,' I told Norman as I lifted the last bale on to the trailer.

'To Lizzie,' he sniggered.

With Maggie and me sitting on top of the trailer, we drove to Tidcombe. The evening was warm but windy, and on either side of the road I looked over the hedges at the tailored Marsham wheat, swaths of ripening ears murmuring in the wind like starlings gathering to roost in winter, gentle looping collective crescents, then sudden changes of wind-blown direction.

We unloaded the bales in a large Cotswold barn with its church-like ceiling and tall double doors on either side. Norman stopped and looked up in silence at the barn. It was unusual to see one of these uplifting buildings that wasn't either falling down or turned into an executive home, let alone one still being used as a working barn. I didn't say anything, and nor did he, for what seemed an age.

'It'll probably be a house soon,' said Norman finally.

That it will.

'Come on, let's go for a pint.'

We rattled down the track to the pub, where we parked the tractor and trailer. Norman left the engine on; he could only start it if it was on a hill. He was looking especially Normanish – the hole-riddled jumper, unshaven, hair wild, hands black with oil and grime.

'Do you think they'll let me in?' he asked.

'Of course they will. It's still a country pub, isn't it?'

The pub was empty, save for Laura and May who greeted us warmly; it was still a novelty to see Norman in the pub. He ordered a cider as Maggie and Pinto chased each other around our feet, and we chatted about The Leggers' and a Chinese man and a Greek Cypriot who'd come to see it.

'Robert told me he wouldn't be right before he even came round to look at it,' Laura said about Lord Rodley. '"Just look at the name," he said.'

'A lot of these foreigners have more money than English people, don't they?' Norman remarked curiously about the Chinese man, still coming to terms with an idea that for him was still relatively new.

Some aggies came in and we got up to leave.

'We best get out of the way for some better customers,' Norman said wryly.

Laura's farewell party was planned for the Jubilee weekend, but then came the invitation to keep running the pub into the summer.

As Marsham had not yet found a tenant and Laura held the licence, it meant either getting in a temporary management company, or the Estate losing the licence and having to close the pub immediately, or her carrying on temporarily. Laura of course had said she would continue, for the jobs at stake and the locals. That she wasn't yet leaving didn't seem like a good reason to cancel a Leggers' party.

Old locals returned whom Han and I hadn't seen much of before but who once had been the heart of that pub for many years. They came for Laura and to see if Knoxey really was gone. By the time the party officially started it had already been going on for most of the day. Liam led the way with the Massive and there followed an afternoon of summer Sunday drinking out on the grass bank beside the pub. In the evening Laura was given a microwave oven and a bunch of flowers, the jukebox got turned up and The Leggers' did what The Leggers' did best. Liam's gay friend Keith, who worked for an out-of-town DIY store, snogged Jen, the ex-military police-woman turned barmaid, and someone shouted there would be no more drinks served until the house saw underwear, so Big Carrie, the warehouse worker who lived down in town with her parents, produced her bra, it was pinned above the bar, and the night went on.

It didn't seem like anything was changing, or ever would, especially when it was announced that Peg and Laura were staying on into the summer. It wasn't over yet. As Tom put on his usual selection of AC/DC, I surrendered to the evening. When somebody recklessly cried out that 'what might be nice now is a nice refreshing tequila', it seemed like a sensible idea.

Tom, glass in hand, leant towards me to speak in my ear above the thumping sound of the jukebox as the pub danced into the night.

'This is it! This is how it used to be in the old days,' he shouted happily, believing they were back.

I celebrated, but it was hard. This was going to end and I wasn't sure I wanted to see it happen. I feared something different was coming, something threatening and acquisitive.

The village Golden Jubilee party was a triumph, which was a surprise; not that the village could throw one, but because so many people seemed so indifferent towards the royals, even in Gloucestershire.

In Cirencester and Tetbury most of the shops only had some sort of flag display: a couple of plastic Union Jacks and a sign or two with special Jubilee offers. An explosion of vibrant colour and imaginative celebration it was not. Mostly one saw St George's crosses flying, like the one Dan had stuck on a rough-cut hazel pole in his garden. I think his display of patriotism had more to do with the World Cup and English Beckhams and Butts than the British 'Lizzie'.

In Cirencester there had been a much-heralded campaign to restore a rope model of the royal crest, made by the town for the Queen's coronation in 1953. But the paper had dropped the story as donations failed to come in and it transpired that the town had neither the craftsmen nor the will to do the necessary.

There were some local villages having no celebration at all, save for a ten-pound-a-ticket barbecue at the local pub, but in our village someone had taken the initiative. A nice lady from one of the big houses in the village had called by with a clipboard and a list to see if we wanted to order a mug for Annie that would commemorate the golden anniversary of the Queen's reign. There would be a village street party that summer, she told Han over the garden wall ('I can't stop'). They were going to close the road from Night Lane to Rathbury Road.

'For the Silver Jubilee, they just used the village hall, what's wrong with that?' Spider's dad had complained. The new vicar's wife had won the ladies' race, he remembered, by a long way. She was fast. 'We all wanted to know how old Mrs Stanton was, but she wouldn't say. There was plenty pretty disappointed at that,' he remembered.

I remembered that year too, the summer after my father died. Bob, my mother's gardener, brought a bottle of home-made mead he had laid down at the coronation and the grown-ups sipped and cooed. Strangely, I don't remember missing my father at all.

Seen from the village, the Golden Jubilee struck me as having little to do with the Queen and much to do with returning to and embracing a type of community social interaction that only the old could remember. There were no pictures of the Queen nor speeches made about her. Perhaps the absence of a speech illustrated that our community had no clearly or even vaguely defined leader, no squire to guide us, no church we all attended whose rector knew us all.

There was, however, a crown parade and competition, a spectacular tea served on trestle tables set up in the road outside the village hall, and lots of games: a tug-of-war, three-legged races, sack races (children only), egg-and-spoon races and 'wellie wanging'. For the 'less energetic', there were competitions inside the village hall ('Catch Phrases – Where Did You Hear It?' and 'Who's Who?') and a display of photographs of 'The Old Village'.

Then there was the prize-giving and 'a disco, eating and barbecue' (burgers and sausages in rolls, fifty pence, cornettos, seventy-five pence) followed by fireworks. The village hall social club had 'kindly agreed to be open throughout the event for the sale of drinks' (fifty pence was added per round for non-members as 'temporary membership'). There was some talk of a village photo being taken, but I never got to see it.

Norman didn't come. He was invited to the Tidcombe party, to thank him for his bales.

'No one in the village invited me, and no one came and told me about it,' he said with a smile and a shrug when he saw the flyer we had received and the Jubilee mug for Annie from the parish council. Perhaps to the people who organised such things, Norman was just the hermit who lived in the run-down cottage on the very edge of the village, who had somehow been forgotten. Or they were too frightened of him to visit.

I didn't see Nicholas Marsham and his family (Lord Rodley's younger brother; he had moved to our village from Tidcombe into Rectory Farm), although I did see another family from one of the big houses. Their children didn't know any of the kids from the village they lived in, nor did the parents seem to know anyone either. They sat on their own talking to their nanny, looking a little uncomfortable. Peter Larch was there, probably wondering if the people or person who had killed his lawn last summer were there, too. But he was not going to be beaten, and he let it be known that he was standing for election to the district council.

Annie's crown won second place in the under-fives. Prizes were selected from a table of donated gifts that included deodorant, shower gel, tinned food and sweet German wine. The highlight of the day was Liam, who arrived noisily with an entourage made up of a very overexcited Keith and the young girls from the Massive. Liam was wearing an extravagant drag outfit and wore an enormous crown decorated with dozens of glued-on and dangling tampons, extraction strings all aflutter.

The judges, perhaps unable to recognise the tampon motif as it related to the royal family, awarded him first prize. Prizes were presented by the rector, with a formal handshake and no kisses for the children. Liam gave the rector an enormous hug and tried to snog him. The rector looked very uncomfortable before surrendering.

'Oh, deary me,' he chuckled rather stiffly.

'That fuckin' Liam, he's a funny fucker,' said one of the Massive.

Han stayed, but I had to take Annie home to bed and so I walked back to Lettem. I watched the fireworks standing in the middle of Home Paddock as they exploded up above the village. Their light silhouetted the trees of Lettem House and the smoke and the sound of the disco drifted gently downwind in the warm June night.

Norman complained that he hadn't the time to do any pest control, and his efforts at keeping the pigeons off the young crops were occasional. The odd shot here and there and a dead crow hung as a warning from a hedge was the best he could do. But he lent me his shotgun, an old blunderbuss, he called it. Wandering the farm, scaring off the crows and trying to bag a rabbit or a pigeon to eat, was a daily part of life at Parish Farm. As long as Norman heard the gun go bang and could see a murder of crows or a flock of pigeons rise from his fields, he was happy. He didn't think I ever actually hit anything.

'This time I've brought you proof,' I said, reaching into a game bag Tom had lent me.

'What you got, then? Too small to run away, was it?'

I pulled out the crow and showed it to him.

'It's a littl'un, just out of the nest. Probably couldn't fly.'

'Well, how do you think I shot him? Climbed up into his nest?' I didn't tell him I shot it just as it was landing.

Grinning, Norman climbed out of the water-filled hole he had been in underneath a large stone trough, took the crow, jumped up on to the wall and tied it to the telegraph pole.

As he stood on the wall I saw a rabbit far off in the middle of the field.

'It's a hare, actually,' said Norman.

'How can you tell?'

'You never see a rabbit more than fifty feet from its hole. Only a hare would move around in open country like that. You don't shoot hares, do you?'

'No.'

Norman had asked me not to, and Tom, too, had told me it wasn't done in these parts, not if you knew what you were about. ('Not that many people do know what it's about, of course,' Tom added regretfully.)

It had been estimated that there were over five million hares in England in 1900, but by 2001 it was thought there could be as few as 800,000. The decline was not a result of hunting; in fact far fewer hares were hunted or poached than a hundred years ago.

In the twenty-first century, poaching was a dying art in the county, but it still went on. A well-stocked trout pond was always going to be a draw, but a glutted market had pretty much put a stop to pheasant poaching. Deer and hares, however, were another matter, and there were all sorts of stories about what went on at night on the Marsham ground and the other estates. On one Cotswold estate the men charged by the owner with culling the deer and stopping the poaching were said to secretly sell night-shooting rights on the side. And then there were the men with long dogs (whippets, greyhounds and lurchers) and fierce cross-breeds who would poach hares at night with lamps, for the thrill of the chase and the gore of the kill. The coursers were said to come from the Welsh valleys and Birmingham, but there were a few more local than that. Tom, who had worked as a gamekeeper for most of his life, had nothing against someone going out now and again to put a rabbit on the table, but the long-dog men who poached for the love of the kill, or the men who illegally shot or set dogs on deer for the profit of the venison, were two of his most detested species among those that inhabited his natural world.

What had done for the hares wasn't shooting or poaching, but modern monoculture farming. Hares thrived off a mixed diet, and acres and acres of the same crop meant fewer varieties of food for a shorter period of the year. The move from winter-sown to spring-sown cereals had reduced the amount of stubble-land the hares could use for winter shelter, and decreased the amount of time when cereal fields were useful to them in spring and early summer. The huge industrial machines used to harvest these fields had wide cuts and moved fast and increased the numbers of hares killed during harvest. And then there was the endless spraying of herbicides, which had achieved the pristine acres of weed-free crops that could be seen surrounding Parish Farm, but which had also removed the weeds that were an essential part of the hares' diet.

'He's not doing any harm, is he?' Norman said as he jumped down off the wall. 'They're magical, you know.'

No one knew for certain why hares were such a deep-rooted, ancient part of English folklore. Some said they were the reincarnation of witches, even witches moving during the day, which explained their intuition and flighty nature, never walking, always running. Others said the hare was the earthly form of an ancient moon goddess, and they liked to sit in the fields gazing wistfully at home.

'That's a hare, that is, sat up there on the moon, and all that,' Douglas would say of the dark shapes and patterns on a full moon.

Whether you could see the hare on the moon or not, the two were inextricably connected, and women of the generation of Mrs Bruce, Roger's old neighbour, had said that hares had a mystical link to the female cycle and the moon which governed it. Like the moon, hares were immortal and fickle, never coming out in the same place or in the same pose from one night to the next. The female hare carried its young for a month, one lunar cycle, and, like the moon, they emerged mostly at night. The hare too was said to be able to change its sex, just as the new moon waned from he to she.

'The hare, that's a special animal,' Tom would say. They were said to have brought the Easter eggs at the time of the spring worship of Estre, a Saxon god of spring, a belief that probably came from the lapwings laying their eggs in March on ground near to a hare's form.

They weren't easy to see in daylight, but they liked Parish Farm. Norman's style of farming, with its smaller fields of pasture, hedgerows and the odd messy field of weed-riddled cereal, was a refuge.

'You don't see many round 'ere these days,' Norman said as the hare eventually ran off across the field. We stood in silence for a little while before he continued.

My father put these troughs in. When he was thirty and full of [ener]gy. It was one of the first things he did when he took on the

His father had dug by hand the long trenches for the piping that came all the way across the farm from the mains water pipes on the lane.

When there was a hare in Ten Acres and a full moon in the sky, things could be remembered and things could be renewed.

If Norman mocked my shooting, Tom joked about my country clothing and equipment, or rather lack of it. As we were exactly the same age, he took pleasure in lending me clothing and gun belts that fitted him fine but which were too small for me. The time had come, Tom thought, to at least get me a decent knife.

'I've got you these,' he said casually one early summer's evening when he came round, passing me a box of disposable gloves to wear when gutting rabbits. 'And this.'

For Tom, there was only one type of knife that any self-respecting bloke should have and he handed me a new Opinel. The fake Leatherman I had bought at a garage for four pounds ninety-nine was more than he could bear.

'Careful,' he said, 'it's real sharp.'

'Well, we'll have to christen that,' I said.

'Tell you what, you go off and get some pigeons and we'll fillet them when you get back.'

Han and Murray had joined Tom by the time I returned with the pigeons. Well done, he said. Han and Tom had amused themselves watching me stealthily moving down the hedgerows, me unaware that Murray had been right behind me looking for Norman, wearing his fluorescent orange Tesco's jacket.

'I didn't think Murray coming flapping down the field behind you made your fieldcraft much use,' he laughed, and Murray grinned. Murray had turned thirty-one and was out of work and as happy as ever. He stayed for a beer, and only when he was gone did Tom tell me.

'Just one other thing, Ian,' Tom said quietly as Han was in the kitchen. 'Never hold pigeons by the feet. Just not done.'

We plucked the pigeons and he showed me how to bone the breast fillets with the knife.

'Getting a pretty good shot now, isn't he? And a fancy knife to go on his belt,' joked Tom with Norman quietly watching us.

'On the ground, was it?' Norman laughed. It was on a telephone wire but I didn't tell him that, either.

Shooting from a prepared hide using decoys to continually pull in the birds to the same place was how serious pigeon-control was carried out, and Tom, of course, was a master. As on any of his expeditions, equipment and preparation were the key, and Tom would prepare for an outing like this with studied attention to detail. He took pride that his equipment was largely home-made and had been used, unbroken and never lost, year after year.

Over summer barbecues of marinated pigeon-breast kebabs, pints in the pub, or afternoons sat in carefully camouflaged pigeon hides, Tom slowly shared his knowledge as I tried to take it all in. I'd hear about a litter of cubs over at Smith's Farm shared by two vixens, and how a barren vixen would help look after a big litter. I learnt how the dog foxes follow the vixens nose to tail when they are in oestrus, and how when they mated they could twist themselves into knots of passion for up to an hour.

I'd learnt about the colours and types of partridge I had seen on the farm, how they start to hatch in Ascot week and how the season to shoot them opened in September, a month before the pheasants. He told me why the partridges sat in coveys on the ground, crowded into a small space, with each bird facing outward.

I remember Alan complaining that my eyes weren't open; that there were partridge on Marsham ground, French and even English partridge, who particularly needed more diverse feed and cover to hold them, less monoculture. But I'm not sure if that wasn't later, when the hated government and the hated EU introduced the Environmental Stewardship Programme, the only way many of the big industrial farmers could be persuaded to encourage biodiversity and restore the quality and character of their landscape. It was this government that had introduced the old Countryside Stewardship Scheme and allocated as much as £500 million to it by the time it was replaced by the Environmental Stewardship Scheme. Thanks to the first scheme, 525,000 hectares of land were included in the programme, returning 44,500 miles of grass margins – those pieces of missing land running along the closely farmed field edges that we missed when Han and I walked so much of the Cotswolds – and creating over 17,500 miles of hedgerows and over 1,300 miles of restored drystone walls. By the end of the first year of the second scheme, over 2,700,000 hectares had come under agreement, £89 million paid out to farmers in the process. Bloody government, bloody Brussels, fucking Labour and variants thereof was all Han and I heard any farmers and local Tories say. I knew myself that the big landowners and their supporters had serious complaints about the government's position on farming, but how this government's policies differed from previous ones, or what the specifics of their complaints were, I never managed to find out.

Tom and I didn't talk politics; instead it was about how to make rook pie and how only the youngest birds will do, just out of the nest, and he'd give us recipes for rabbit. Or of how keepers snared foxes in the tractor-wheel tramlines that ran through the crops, or how poachers used to take pheasants and how gamekeepers would catch them.

Tom wasn't a show-off or a bragger. Instead he just casually decorated his conversation with anecdotes and stories of rural people and places, sights and sounds. My urban history seemed so dull in comparison, its knowledge abstract and unusable. How to select a deer to cull and how to stalk it would be something of value to me. I didn't think he would be interested in how to write a good memo or in learning my views on which was the best Parisian hotel.

Tom never asked me about my life before Lettem. I had told him only that it was something I had been pleased to leave behind me, which for him was a self-evident truth. The deepening of our friendship was signposted by my letting him see more of my life before Lettem; not by telling him all its mundane details, but by casting the odd comparison to show him how much happier I now was. For his part, he marked it by acts like giving me the Opinel or taking Han and me further into his world and allowing us to see what it meant to him. Being shown how he emptied his crow traps or where he placed his drop-boxes (traps dug into the ground to catch and hold live rabbits) were, I think, signs of a bond, sharing secret places, hidden skills and our experiences of death amidst the intimacies of killing.

There weren't many people like Tom left in the village who knew the things he did. Men younger than fifty who knew about the countryside, its animals, its plants and trees, its seasons and moods, were the exception, not the rule. His knowledge, and Alan's and Norman's, had been gathered during a rural childhood which resembled the experience of few Cotswold children today. Norman's father had always had young boys working on the farm, helping out after school, working in the summer holidays, watching and learning. No more. The kids these days weren't interested, Norman said. Their parents took them to the indoor water park in Swindon instead, and they watched hours and hours of TV and played with their computers; or sent more and more of them to boarding schools in towns and cities. Didn't they? Whatever the parents did, it was rare for us to see kids down the lanes on their bikes, or playing by the canal, or building dens in Norman's woods or camping in his barns; and we never saw them helping him bump bales in the summer.

As a boy Tom had been out every day on his bike after school: trapping and fishing, catching and collecting. 'I knew all the birds' eggs because I collected them,' Tom said, 'and the butterflies and the birds, I could tell you all their names. I was out looking at them all the time.'

One June night walking back from the drop-boxes we crossed over the railway and followed a tractor tramline in the moonlight, waist-deep in rich, weed-free Marsham wheat.

'I like to see a bit of weed or wild flowers in my wheat,' Tom said.

'Well, you know where to go then,' I laughed, nodding towards Ludd-land on the other side of the lane.

We kept walking in the moonlight until we came out by the cottage. I looked up at the moon. Do you ever take all this for granted? I asked him.

'I suppose you do eventually, but not yet, not for me.'

Back at the cottage we set up the big, hand-made, rough-cut garden chairs that we kept outside by the garden wall. Han knew Pip and Pop were out there in the dark and told us she had seen a fox in their field at dusk. She knew too what foxes were capable of doing to lambs. So we sat under Frankie's Tree in the moonlight with the lamp and Tom's rifle. We talked in half-whispers and smoked, periodically sweeping the lamp across the field. And sure enough, we soon saw one, making its way along the wall of the Humpty Dumps and into Home Paddock where Pip and Pop were grazing. Tom took a shot and missed.

'Shit,' he hissed. 'Keep the lamp on her, keep it on her, Han.' The vixen, despite the incredible noise from less than fifty feet away, froze and then darted fifteen feet. Tom hissed at her, she stopped. BANG. She was dead.

I followed the arc of the lamp and brought the vixen back to the garden wall. Tom had to reassure Han that her cubs were long gone, born late February or early March.

Han went to bed and Tom put away the rifle. We opened a bottle of wine and sat and talked about our childhoods and our different ways of dealing with them. After our fathers died, Tom showed an anger we both shared, his poor mother worried that every knock at the door would be the local keeper or the troubled village bobby. I was in town at boarding school harbouring an unacknowledged rage I didn't understand and having to resort to letting off fire extinguishers.

We talked for the first time about the limp he had and the motor-bike accident that had caused it and nearly killed him as a young man. He had never mentioned it before and I hadn't wanted to ask. The truth was it could still cause him great pain, but he never complained. He talked wistfully about when he was a full-time gamekeeper. 'God, I wish you'd known me a few years back, in my heyday. Boy, we'd have had some fun.'

Pip and Pop in Home Paddock were finally settling down to sleep, and the night was quiet and still. We talked about the things that had made us laugh, and we talked about what barn conversions did for the barn owls, how the canal being restored would change Parish Farm and about the future of the cattle market and the pub. It was late when Tom went home, moonlight coating the farm in a sheen of soothing light.

After he had left, I stayed outside and thought back on the day gone. That evening the sun had set in a cloudless sky with an orange moon hanging low in the east. The summer sun's dusk mixing with the faded glow of the moon had created a strange, windless moment of eerie light; neither day nor night, dusk nor dawn. Norman claimed the wind always dropped at the exact moment of the sun setting.

A scintillation of memory from behind the curtain of night: my brother, the way he used to make me laugh.

Tom and he are gone, and alone I sit at the wall.

I think of hares on the moon and my English past remembered.

# CHAPTER 15

# JUNE

June on the farm was shearing and sheep. The warmer weather brought flies, and the flies brought maggots. Some of the sheep were infected, their rumps raw and red, alive with crawling creatures that could only be scraped off with a knife. Pip was affected terribly and Pop was limping. For all our bottle-feeding, perhaps they had lacked something that was present in natural milk which had kept most of their contemporaries healthy. They stood alone, separated from the other sheep, listless and ignored. Perhaps lambs are like humans; when one is ill, others shy away.

Norman hadn't yet been able to dip the sheep this year. To dip, you now needed a special licence, and to get that you needed to have passed a proficiency test in using the noxious poisons that were employed. Norman had been doing it all his life, and now he had been told he was in danger and that he could no longer dip. The proficiency test cost eighty-four pounds and took a day.

'I haven't got the time!' said Norman despairingly.

Our daily feeding rituals were now replaced with daily walks to the 'sickbay', as Norman called it, in the paddock behind the yard littered with derelict cars and cast-off tractors. There we put Pip and Pop (or Han and Ian, as Norman still called them), along with two recently orphaned lambs. Poor Pop. He seemed so old and sad compared with the vigorous, confident youth we had let out of the pen not so long ago.

The afternoons in the sickbay were a reminder of the reality of livestock farming, its labour intensity and the cost of doing it 'correctly': checking the flock all the time, seeking and paying for treatment, hand-rearing lambs. It just didn't pay, Norman said. He had sold seven twelve-month-old lambs for twenty-one pounds a head.

'A mate of mine', said Tom, who had stopped by to go pigeon-shooting, 'got half a pig the other day, jointed and bagged for thirty-two pounds. How's that for a price?'

'Not very good, for the bloke that sold it,' said Norman.

As we left the sick animals in the yard, I felt relieved at not having to look their sickness in the face, at leaving them to their own survival, free of my worries for them.

I remember my mother telling me how aware she had been of receiving fewer invitations after my father died. Perhaps it was because she was a single woman; it would upset the seating plans. Perhaps it was because, even though she did as expected and kept it hidden, she carried a terrible sadness that might be contagious, reminding others of the possibilities of death. Perhaps that's just how it was, my mother added.

The best shearers Norman had ever worked with were the Kiwis, he told Alison one evening. 'Rough lot, you lot!' he said to her.

Alison was one of three daughters of a South Island sheep farmer who once had over a thousand acres. Perhaps Alison saw in Parish Farm something of what she had known once and of what would probably happen here. The reform of the New Zealand agricultural industry and the end of subsidies, held by some as a model for the future of British farming, meant that Alison's family farm, built and planned on budgets that included ongoing subsidies, was lost; her father was now a picture-framer. An entire community of small farmers she had grown up with had been devastated. Many of her family's neighbours and friends had seen their homes, land and communities go to cash-rich Cantabrians and Aucklanders with money to spend, no debts to carry and cheap land to buy. Perhaps New Zealand's farming was now healthier, more profitable and sustainable, but, just as with the coal industry in the UK, the social consequences of those reforms for Alison's community had been tragic. She spoke to Norman with a tender affection that stemmed, perhaps, from her hidden fears of what was coming his way.

'What do you mean, rough?' Alison laughed.

'I used to work with this shearer from New Zealand. He cut a vein open on this sheep's stomach, you know what he said. "If you can't fix it, cut its throat. Now get me another sheep!" He was so fast this bloke, we all had to stop shearing and just pass him sheep.'

Norman did one of his little laughs. 'You know they got a proficiency test for that too now? You got to do eight sheep in an hour. Eight sheep! Twenty is what I'd call about all right.' He could see me trying to figure it out. 'That's one sheep every three minutes if you can't do the maths,' he grinned.

I wanted to go shearing with Norman, but he put me off.

'I shouldn't bother,' he said, cap off, grinning and brushing back his long thin hair. 'It's a bit of a do-it-yourself place, this one today. Rare breeds.'

'What do you mean?'

'You got to catch 'em, sort 'em, shear 'em, all yourself. It's an old boy who's got 'em, he can't do nothing. You won't want to come, it's a fiddly little job up in the hills. It's a real Cotswold hideaway, you wouldn't know it was there. Go on, then, hop in.'

Maggie sat between us and, with Murray following on behind on his moped, we set off. I'd forgotten just how little time I spent off the farm, and how a short drive now was quite the journey.

Jack's place was at the end of a long, steep, single-track lane that led only to his house. The cottage and barns sat on the edge of a steep valley, the ground falling away sharply into a narrow valley bound by woodland. I didn't think places like this still existed in the Cotswolds, so idyllic and isolated and still owned by people like Jack. Jack had a long, thick beard and was dressed in wellies, blue jeans, a denim shirt and a sleeveless blue puffa jacket. He swore incessantly, only using one swear word, which was 'fucking': fucking sheep, fucking market, the fucking this, the fucking that, all in a thick fucking Gloucestershire accent. But he was 'gettin' on', a recent widower; Norman thought he might sell up soon.

As he and Norman talked, Murray and I were sent off to bring in the twenty-six Welsh blacks. The field with the sheep in it was on one side of the valley, and it was so steep that hardly any part of it offered level ground. In places erosion and overgrazing had left parts of it as nothing more than exposed rock and soil. As soon as he was in the field, Murray instantly started to run after the sheep. Murray gave the job of moving sheep no thought. He made no plan, and the presence of an assistant (me) was nothing more than an opportunity to shout at someone other than the sheep. Even when a sheep was right by him and I stood at the other end of a field where I could contribute nothing, Murray would still scream at me.

'IAN! GET THE FUCKERS! COME ON, IAN, GET ON, GET ON! COME ON, YOU FUCKERS!' he screamed at them.

After much more screaming and running and charging up and down hillsides, we finally got the sheep into the barn, the doors of which couldn't be shut due to the heaps of cow shit and horse manure inside. We jammed them closed with a large stone, which only just held when a ram threw himself against them.

Norman set up his kit, the centrepiece of which was an ancient Listers electric motor that he hung from a barn eave above him. Hanging down from the motor was the red power line that ran to the clippers, a piece of string hanging down to be pulled as an on-off switch. As a base to work on, Norman had brought with him a large piece of broken plywood.

Norman, despite telling Tom and me that he charged as much as one pound fifty a sheep, charged Jack seventy-five pence. For each animal, for seventy-five pence, we had to bring it in, ear-tag it, worm-drench it and clip its hooves before it was shorn by Norman. On top of that, four sheep needed their horns cut off and three needed treatment for maggots. And we were expected to tie and bag the 'bonds' of wool. All for seventy-five pence. Jack's contribution was to tell us he needed to make a 'fucking phone call' and disappear.

It was 8 p.m. before we got started. Norman was not going to break his back, and so worked at a leisurely pace of about four minutes per sheep. No one displayed any sense of urgency despite the late hour and it being clear we would be here until long after nightfall.

Murray would drag the sheep out of the crush, cursing and damning 'the fucking bastards'. I'd tag the ear and force a liquid worming treatment down its mouth before passing it to Norman to shear. As with every Parish Farm task, I was not given any instruction other than 'tag them and drench them'. Tagging I'd done before, drenching was new. Once shorn I would clip each sheep's hooves. For this I did get some instruction. 'If you cut into its foot and it bleeds, they're as good as dead.'

The rams had horns that were nearly growing into their heads, in one case grown into the scalp. Jack put on a not-very-persuasive display of not having noticed this obvious fact before.

'Oh fucking hell, that's not fucking right. I haven't got the fucking heart for this any more,' said Jack.

Jack wanted to put the ram down, but Norman told him to treat it and send it to the abattoir; he'd get a few quid probably. We cut off the horns with garden clippers after failing with a blunt hacksaw. I sprayed purple antiseptic into the vivid wound.

We worked on in the fast-falling light. Jack came back with a flask of coffee and some biscuits. So we could see, he set up a shadeless table lamp on a gatepost. Norman insisted I had a shear. He had been trying to persuade me all evening. 'We can't have you going home telling the little woman you were scared to do it.'

Taking a sheep from Norman, I put it between my legs and took the comb. This was my first time and Norman was the instructor, so the instruction ran as follows: 'Off you go, then.'

Despite having watched Norman shear about fifteen sheep by now, I still had to ask where to start. Down the front, he said, and then do the this, the that and the this, using a series of technical terms for parts of a sheep's body. Words like brisket. I knew leg, tail and head. I could even identify the loin and the shoulder. I wasn't a hundred per cent sure where chops came from but I felt hopeful. But I certainly couldn't find a sheep's brisket.

As I struggled, Norman turned his back on me to enjoy his coffee and biscuit and chat with Jack, deliberately ignoring me. Murray didn't say much either, and only Jack, worried about his sheep, kept half an eye over Norman's shoulder on what I was doing. I tried to get Norman to come and take over but he let me struggle on, chuckling. Finally he put me out of my misery and finished the poor animal off. It was gruelling work: flipping, controlling and shearing a large animal that didn't want to be flipped, controlled or shorn. Even just one.

'What's all this they say about farmers getting money for nothing then?' he grinned.

In a mist of flies and with a dull, silver-blue sky silhouetting the tops of the trees across the valley, the sound came of the evening's last train entering a tunnel. It was dark and cold, near midnight by the time we were done and packed up. Jack paid Norman thirty pounds. We'd been there, three of us, for four hours and had done his entire flock husbandry; for the whole year, most likely.

'Happy with that?' asked Jack. Norman mumbled something. 'As long as you're happy, that's what fucking matters,' said Jack.

Driving home up Jack's steep lane, Norman casually ran over a rabbit and stopped to get it for Maggie's tea. I got home at midnight and drank a cold beer sitting on the garden wall.

Tom took a day off (too fine for real work) and came over to help me hang a new gate (the old post now happily removed), armed with all sorts of tools, work benches, 'noggins' and 'slithers'. As ever, he set about the job with a terrifying confidence. I told Tom that Han and I had had a row, saying only that we were a bit worried about work and how little we both had. Han had described her drying-up work as a slow slide into a soft panic, and I borrowed her phrase. Tom asked if I thought it had been PMT and suggested chocolates or flowers. I tried to change the subject as we worked under the pink flowers of the dog rose over the front door, but I think he sensed there was more going on than I had said.

'I hope you don't mind me asking,' he said, 'and don't tell me if you don't want to, but what *do* you do for money?'

His question threw me. The truth, and the cause of the tension that had triggered our row, was that we knew we were going to have to make a decision. Either I would have to go back to the life I had once led, or we would probably have to leave Lettem Cottage. The financial crisis that had been looming was upon us. We had enough money to pay the mortgage for another couple of months, and that would be that.

But instead of telling him this, I muttered something about part-time media consultancy so that I could try and write, about how things would probably pick up soon.

Gate hung, Norman stopped by on his way home for his dinner. Tom rolled his eyes, knowing what was coming.

'Not too bad, I suppose,' Norman said as he appraised the gate, which Tom took calmly, knowing that that was as good as it was going to get from Norman. As Tom loaded his tools in the truck, Norman whispered to me that he thought the hinges were the wrong way round. Tom laughed when I told him. Taking advice from Norman on gates was just too much.

That night Han went to the pub with Tom and I stayed home with Annie. I was alone and it was late when I heard a car stop outside and toot its horn before driving off. I opened the front door. The track was dark and still, the sky star-sprinkled black, and there at my feet was a pint of bitter, delivered anonymously to my door.

I drank it standing out under the stars, thinking about my conversation with Tom that afternoon, and why I hadn't told him the whole truth. It had taken Han and me a long time to face the facts of our situation; it would take longer before we could articulate it to someone else. The someone elses were all proud lovers of their England and their county: Peg, Laura, May and Kelly, Spider, Alan, Tom and Norman, and our own family in England. But it was our uncertain feelings about making our future in England that would shape our final decision.

On the last day of June, we were still asking where summer was – proper summer, hot summer; but it wouldn't come. Clouds would quickly turn warm days cold. There was no heat in the ground. Pip and Pop got well from our daily attention, but death was always somewhere.

'I had a bit of a thing,' Norman said, walking me to his car after we'd finished baling one night. In the back was a dead lamb, one born in January that had been due to go to market. He pulled it out and dropped it on the ground. Its neck was ripped open, a mess of exposed bone and dead meat. The pressure on its stomach as it hit the ground forced out a long loud fart through the open wound on its neck.

'God, that smells!'

'Its blood was warm when I found it, right by the footpath. Someone's dog, probably. That or a fox.' It helped me understand why Norman didn't care for foxes or people walking on his land with their dogs off their leads, their owners off the footpaths. Town dogs unused to sheep could run riot when confronted with a flock, killing or savaging eight or more sheep in a matter of minutes, not hours. I told Norman about a man in yellow shorts and a short-sleeved shirt I had turned back with his dog from the Humpty Dumps.

'He had a map, I suppose?' asked Norman.

'Yes.'

Generally I heard people refer to 'ramblers' or 'walkers', although

Norman didn't make such distinctions. Organised ramblers, it seemed, were quite different from people who went for walks. People who went for a walk went for a walk, often wherever they liked, even if they had a map. Ramblers travelled in groups, belonged to clubs, carried maps and generally shut gates and stuck to footpaths. They wore brightly coloured waterproof clothing and drank tea from flasks and lived in towns, which, for one 'super' Han had spoken to in the pub didn't make ramblers genuine countryside lovers because their feelings towards it were 'organised' rather than 'real'. Norman hated ramblers and walkers because they were all busybodies who interfered with what he did on his own land and brought their dogs with them.

'I'm getting sued by one of them.'

'*What?*'

'He fell off a stile crossing into my land down by River Head. Broke his leg. My fault, he says.'

'When was this?'

'Last March. They had to get a helicopter ambulance in and take him to Cheltenham hospital. Nine thousand pounds, he wants. My insurance reckons they'll probably pay him.'

'*What?*'

It hadn't come up before, now it had. Norman didn't pass on information or tell you about events in his life in a neat, linear way. Later, even much later, he'd recount events often without any reference at all to *when* something had taken place. His measured stories had a timelessness to them that made the past feel recent, and the recent long ago, no event worthy of panic or drama; like the time Han asked Norman where Maggie was, she hadn't seen her in a day or two.

'She got hit by a car.'

'*What!* Is she all right?'

'She is now. Lay in the kitchen she did, didn't move, thought she was going to die.'

It had been dark, Norman had been checking a gate. Maggie had jumped out of his open car door, and was hit by a car that brushed so close past Norman he felt it against his legs. Norman had scooped Maggie up off the road, put her in the boot – dead, he presumed – and chased the car that did it for over an hour, through small lanes and along empty midnight main roads.

'Hold tight,' said Tom respectfully. 'What happened then, Norm? You get the bastards?'

Norman had followed the car as far as the M5, and then in an effort to shake him, the car turned back into Cheltenham. At traffic lights in town Norman finally caught up; he grabbed a tyre wrench, got out of the car and ran towards the people who had knocked down his dog but they sped off through a red light. Norman kept at it.

Finally the driver of the car drove into Cheltenham police station and ran inside. He'd rather take the police than meet Norman.

'Can't say I blame 'em,' said Tom.

Norman left it there and brought Maggie home, he didn't want to deal with the police.

'When did all this happen, Norm?' I asked.

'Last week some time. After that Jubilee thing.'

July started with one of the key annual events that determined Spider's calendar: the Cotswold Country Fair.

The others were the beginning and end of ploughing and planting, the beginning and end of the rugby season and weekends spent watching Gloucester, the beginning and end of the pheasant season, the beginning and end of spraying, the beginning and end of the village cricket club season (in his capacity as chairman and head groundsman), the Hamden Air Show, the Fairford Air Show (Spider was quietly a military aviation enthusiast) and the beginning and end of harvest.

In addition, every two years there was the rugby World Cup or a Lions tour, and every ten years or so a major conflict involving the SAS and/or B-52s from Fairford flying over his house every night on their way to bomb someone. Christmas, Easter, his birthday, other people's birthdays and bank holidays were all marked too, but these were generic, indoor and therefore of less importance.

Spider was a regular attendee at The Leggers', but I had noticed that on or near the passing of one of his key dates an especially vigorous evening of celebratory drinking at the pub could be expected. Spider would also have more than his usual difficulty with his recurring back and neck problem. This was because all these events necessitated either considerable amounts of extra lifting (pheasant feed, seed bags, fertiliser and pesticide drums, wicket rollers or pints of beer) or even more time spent in his tractor or combine harvester.

'All right, mate? Get you a pint? Cotswold Country Fair tomorrow,' he would announce portentously, stretching his stiff neck, and you knew you were in for a particularly good night.

The Cotswold Country Fair, in the first week of July, was organised 'under the personal direction of Lord Rodley' and it was very much a Lord Rodley event. The fair was billed as 'where town meets country'. This was not a country fair as in a fair for country people, where farmers, gamekeepers and the like come to source products and find jobs. Nor did I sense that many of the people there were curious urbanites from England's cities. Mostly, I think it was a place where people who already lived in the countryside, in its villages and small towns, could come and see what the Cotswold countryside, or at least Marsham's version of it, was all about. They could buy green clothing they had no need for, and admire four-wheel-drive vehicles suitable for crossing muddy fields that they were as likely to need to cross as anyone who lived in London.

Held in Marsham's parkland, the fair consisted of around a hundred shops set up in tents, and a large display arena forming the centre of the ground. In addition, there were the 'Country Pursuits Arena' and displays of rural crafts, ancient and modern agricultural machinery and the ubiquitous bouncy castles and 'food' stands.

There was no main bar. (Knoxey used to do it but said it was more trouble than it was worth, being charged a heavy whack for the concession and obliged to haul all the glasses, taps and barrels into the park.) Rather, one would wander among the stands of cider and 'home-made' booze producers, most of whom came from Wales, Devon, Dorset, Wiltshire and Worcestershire; in fact, nearly anywhere other than the Cotswolds.

The same was true of many of the cake makers, cheese manufacturers and every other type of 'country food provider' and 'rural craftsmen' – the potters, sculptors and painters. We did find a drystone waller who came from the Cotswolds, but he seemed to be the exception. The lead sponsor for the entire event was a Japanese car manufacturer.

Acclaimed highlights were the Flying Gunners Motorcycle Display Team (perilous stunts sponsored by another Japanese motor company), the Horse Whisperer (a horse trainer from Wiltshire), the falconry display, the rural crafts village (coordinated by Carl, from Wiltshire), and the Dog Whisperer (a dog trainer, also from Wiltshire). Considering that all the rural craftsmen seemed to come from anywhere but the Cotswolds (possibly because a rural craftsman in the Cotswolds struggled to afford £300,000 for a semi-detached craftsman's cottage), it was a nice touch that the rural crafts village was sponsored by a leading firm of estate agents.

Best of all was the superb display of ancient and modern agricultural machinery; from horse and plough and vintage tractors to the huge state-of-the-art prairie monsters used by Marsham on their ground. Here, it was a genuinely Cotswold affair, at least for the more recent machinery. Seeing the size of these machines and comparing the current field sizes against the late-nineteenth-century Ordnance Survey maps Alan had given me, one could get to see the Cotswolds countryside up close: tractors so big you could farm a seven-thousand-acre estate with just two full-time employees and some temporary staff for harvest, ploughing and drilling.

Spider was a demonstration tractor driver and Robert Rodley joined the Tractor Man commentator in the commentary box, which was the top floor of a double-decker bus next to the show arena. Dave, the law-lecturer-cum-public-speaker, did the commentary for most of the show, but for some reason he never did the agricultural machinery parade.

'Here comes Spider in his Massey. What a handsome machine and an even better tractor,' said the Tractor Man. 'Tell me,' turning to Lord Rodley, 'do you think fifty years from now we will be looking at Spides driving one of these modern machines with the same appreciation and nostalgia we have today for the old vintage tractors here?'

'Both,' said Rodley. 'They're both classics.'

There was a message to the event. Rodley would say things like, 'At a time when there is much debate on country matters, the Cotswold Show and Country Fair has a vital role to play in communicating the understanding, care and investment required by all of us to maintain the countryside and help it flourish in the future.'

It was not easy to square notions of understanding and care with the undoubted investment estates like Marsham needed to make in intensive farming and the repercussions for rural working people and Cotswold wildlife.

The country matter at the fair that seemed more important and which most needed to be understood by the urbanites was the right to hunt with hounds. Country matters (shooting and hunting) were given their own arena and included talks by people from the Countryside Alliance. They confidently offered pro-hunting stickers to anyone who passed by, but by no means everyone took one.

'All too often,' Rodley said to the press, 'people take for granted what they have and what this country has to offer. In the Cotswolds, we're particularly fortunate to live in a beautiful part of the country with a fine heritage, and hopefully the Cotswold Show will help people appreciate this and the vital role of the countryside.'

The other agenda of the event was clearly to make a lot of money and, with 25,000 visitors and six-pound tickets, plus the stall and concession income and the Japanese sponsorship, it no doubt did. The food concessions were remarkable. Alongside talk of defending British farming and supporting local producers, huge mobile wagons sold revolting industrial sausages and burgers at extortionate prices (five pounds for a burger and chips) to the people from the towns.

But whatever its purpose or message, the fair was also everything else it claimed to be: family-orientated, entertaining, fun and memorable.

Tom's approach was to get to the fair early, before the town crowds, investigate all the stands on the lookout for bargains, then embark on 'product sampling' in the food and drink categories. One could eat and drink pretty well for most of the day without putting hand in pocket, provided one asked earnest and knowledgeable questions. Towards the end of the day, however, the cider stalls had begun to get the measure of the situation, and cash did begin to be exchanged.

We did make some purchases. Tom got me a leather belt-holder for my Opinel and himself a sleeveless Barbour jacket. The jacket, he had said in the morning, he couldn't afford, but by the end of a day sampling most of the West Country's apple-related products, he found he could. I went off and bought a ten-pound imitation Barbour jacket. Later Tom made much of it, jokingly asking me not to make purchases of this nature in the future before consulting him. We both laughed. Like carrying a dead bird by its feet, or referring to pheasants as pheasant, it was, he would always laugh, 'a minefield out there'.

That night we all went to The Leggers'. Spider talked about last year's fair compared with this, and what they should do next year and everyone got extremely pissed. Han and I looked at each other over our drinks. We weren't sure there was going to be a next year, not for us.

# CHAPTER 16

# MEMORY

The waning moon is coming up over the Humpty Dumps and Douglas and I are standing in Valley Ground looking at her ascent. We have time to look at the moon, and we take it.

'The moon looks so big,' I say. 'Why does it look so big? I don't remember the moon being this big when I lived in cities.'

'That, Ian,' says Douglas, 'that would be your mind playing tricks on yer. When the moon's up there 'igh in the sky, it looks small, doesn't it? But that, Ian, is a trick, just a trick. It only looks small because you've got nothing to compare it with up there. You just got the whole sky, and the moon won't look very big in that.

'Down 'ere though, down 'ere it's diff'rent. Down 'ere on the 'rizon, you got stuff you can compare it with, things you know, and all that. And then the moon looks much bigger. A lot of people don't know that, Ian, you'd be surprised.'

My parents had told me that the children were going to have a special 'children's funeral' for my brother. They wanted some sort of service for me to go to, but not the one with a small coffin and them barely able to stand. They'd tried to organise something different. All the children were going to be there, and they were. It was the parents that went to the church.

We sat together in a playroom above a garage. I remember feeling sad, but everyone else was laughing and playing. After a while I told the woman who was looking after us that my mother had arranged to have a special children's funeral and that we would say some prayers for my brother.

She seemed surprised. Of course we will, she said, of course we will.

Come on, children, let's say a prayer.

When I had finished reading my prayer that my mother had given me, the woman asked if there was anyone else who would like to say something. Who'd like to sing a song? Why don't you sing a song? she asked a girl.

The girl stood up and sang: 'I'll be your long-haired lover from Liverpool'. By Jimmy Osmond.

I felt angry with her song, confused and embarrassed by my prayer.

*Perhaps nothing has happened, everything is fine, I shouldn't feel sad.*

That's the last thing I remember feeling for a long time.

Later, when my father died, no one spoke with me about him either. Emotional reticence, how people daren't show their grief in front of a child, was by then nothing new.

When I was living in Paris I came home one Christmas. A thirty-something man like me, the son of friends of my parents who I think may have been at that 'children's funeral', asked me when I was coming back to England, when I would be stopping all that Continental nonsense.

He couldn't stand 'Europe', or the Prime Minister. 'It's all an act, you know. His feelings are just for show,' he said, discussing the Prime Minister's comments at the time of some national tragedy. During the long years we had known each other we had never much spoken of the losses in my family nor any sadnesses in his own. 'It's fake,' he said of the politician's feelings, 'it's not real.'

Now I had come back again, and at Lettem, with time to remember, my memories were full. I understood now the source of my reluctance to return.

England, for all its beauty, for all its charms, history, humour and devilment, was for me a place of loss; a country inhabited by people who had been reluctant to discuss things that were important to me.

I didn't ever want to do that again, lose something important and have to suppress my feelings.

Is it possible to remember the future; is the present a moon-cast shadow of the past?

One day, Parish Farm is going to wane. Norman's cottage will be gutted and renovated and a weekender, or a retired couple who finally decide on the Cotswolds instead of the Channel Islands, will move in next door. The yard will be converted into a cluster of barn-conversion houses with Smallbone kitchens and shiny new Agas. The last sheep and cattle will be taken away on a long trip to another county, and sold at a market dumped on the edge of an industrial estate. The farm's lines will be lost, her walls taken away in trucks to clad breeze-block houses, leaving pale yellow prairie and a pair of pony paddocks for the only animals still to be seen. Fibreglass tour boats will float between the Lock House and the Lambing Sheds, and Tom will have long gone, driven off by rules and house prices not set for people like him.

It would happen in thirty years, it would happen tomorrow. The world wouldn't end but it would happen, and all the years we lived here without departing would be years of waiting for its arrival.

# CHAPTER 17

# JULY

I had walked out of England as soon as I could, the spring after I left school. I lived as a tramp, walking from Vigo to Valencia, following Laurie Lee's Spanish footsteps. At the time I didn't realise what a hurry I was in to go, nor what it was I wanted to leave behind. I came back, but then I left again and began my life 'on the Continent'.

When I came back from Paris with Han, somehow I think I always knew we wouldn't stay.

There were many reasons to go and many good arguments to stay but there was no easy way to tell Norman of our decision to leave.

To talk to Norman about emotional landscapes of memory would be too obtuse; to talk about notions of 'society' and a place to bring up our children where the choices for a family's health and education were less bitterly divided, irrelevant. To talk about Han's strong, perhaps instinctive, Australian desire to own land of her own, safe from encroachment, would be to raise anxieties about Norm's own future. To talk about our desire for a house we could afford without daily returns to offices at the end of long train journeys, and the problems of home working when sharing a tiny office in a bedroom next to a baby; of our need to continue to lead as much of our lives as possible outdoors instead of in, would be to speak of experiences and fears he had never shared.

We tried to find the moment to tell him but, like the summer, it wouldn't come. We barbecued when we could, waiting for moonlit nights that should have been warmer but never were, and the courage to step into one of the easy pauses that filled our conversations.

The first weeks of July were the hay-making weeks, but still there was rain.

By the middle of the month a summer's summer arrived, the sky a cloudless, near-Provençal blue. Summer; time to cut the hay in Lower Rathbury.

The field was a maze of mowed lines of grass: some lines straight, some semicircular, short and long. As Douglas slowed the engine to turn the tractor, the voice of his singing could just be heard through the thick afternoon air.

'I keep on telling him, just go in straight lines, but he keeps going in circles,' Norman sighed.

Maggie sprinted off, leaping over the uncut high grass woven with wild flowers and insects, chasing the scent of a fox or some animal disturbed by the mowing; now seemed a moment.

Instead I started by talking about my work and our money worries, but that's as far as I got before I mumbled and stopped; I just did not want to have to tell him. I think he may have known anyway what I was trying to say, but if he did, he didn't let on.

'What you going to do then?' he asked quietly.

'I don't know,' I lied after a pause, the truth stuck in my throat.

'I'm not really the right person to ask for advice,' he said meekly.

'You don't know how lucky you are to live here, Norm. To be your own boss.'

'That's where my boss is,' he said pointing skywards. 'When it rains, it rains, when it shines, work like hell.'

The moment was gone. We stood in silence looking out over his farm. He knew how lucky he was.

The hot days of late July were not kind to Sukey. We saw her less and less as she became unable to make it through the hedge to shit on our lawn and collapse in the shade. When we heard her moaning from the other side of the hedge, thinking that Norman and Douglas would be out I went to investigate.

There she was, lying in the high nettles of Norman's garden, the sun high and harsh above. Stood over her were Norman and Douglas, staring at her in silence.

'Poor Sukey,' said Douglas. 'It's too hot I reckon, too hot for her.'

At first Norman didn't say a word. He knew it was much worse than that. Sukey was grey and gaunt, immobile in the heat; flies all over her, a trail of urine around where she lay. She had no control over her bladder and little over her movements.

'She's fifteen,' said Norman quietly, stock-still, face set.

'Poor old Sukey, eh,' said Douglas, bending down to pat her.

Han came round and joined us, and we stood over Sukey and worried about her.

'Well, better be getting off to work, and all that,' said Douglas finally. 'You take it easy there, Sukey, you want to look after yourself you do.'

Douglas headed into the field leaving just Han and me, and Norman in his slippers, standing in his back garden. Unexpectedly, I realised this was the moment, the three of us there together without the intensity of us 'going to see him to tell him we were leaving', which by now had become our plan.

'We've got a bit of news actually, Norman,' I found myself saying and just kept going. 'We're thinking we might have to move.'

Norman didn't react, not a word, he just stared at me intensely. Han was sitting on a box by his back door, with me there in my shorts in the high two o'clock sun. I stumbled on: the money to stay here, work; how sad, how very, very sad we would be to leave.

'Leaving England wouldn't make us sad. It's here, Norman, leaving here, the farm, Lettem.'

'You,' said Han. 'Leaving you.'

Norman was silent, totally silent. At first I wanted him to say something and was then glad he hadn't. It had made it easier for us to say what we had to say. Han and I waited for him to respond, which finally he did, his voice barely audible.

'Well, I can't offer you much advice. I don't know much about your work.'

The three of us stood in silence. Sukey stirred in the nettles, and Norman bent down, picked her up and moved her into the shade.

We went back next door, Han putting her arm round me. I was sagging and she had tears in her eyes.

'Well done, Ian,' she said. 'I know that wasn't easy. I couldn't have said it.'

Norman and I were baling that afternoon and we set off to walk to Lower Rathbury where the baler was. We walked in silence and I wondered what he was thinking. The first question came as we went through the gate at the top of the Humpty Dumps.

'There must be work in Cirencester, isn't there?' he asked quietly.

The questions came regularly for the rest of the day and the evening, once every half an hour or so as each new point or consideration came to his mind as we worked on with our baling. As ever, I had to remember that each question or comment wasn't a non sequitur.

'Or Swindon,' he added half an hour later as we stopped to free a jammed bale.

What Norman couldn't fathom was the sorts of jobs we would need to find to continue to pay for our untenable mortgage, nor why I felt I couldn't go back to my old life. The idea of that train to London before Annie was even awake, running from city to city in planes and staying in hotels and returning on a Friday after she had gone to bed now seemed impossible. It was a life led indoors that had left no time for memory nor for the small details of the present.

When we had moved to Lettem I hadn't been well enough for Han and me to know what we wanted, and our decision, for all its serendipity, had been based on a salary and savings we now no longer had. Ironically, it was Lettem that had taught us how we wanted to live, but it was unsustainable in the very place that lesson had been learnt.

'So that's your decision, then?' Norman asked, as once again we stopped to pull out a broken bale from the old baler. It was hot and sweaty work: hay and insects stuck to your skin; the smells of my sun cream, the hay and diesel; the smell of our summer. Only occasionally would Norman take off his cap to run his hand through his long hair.

'Yes. If we won the lottery, we wouldn't be off,' I said, telling him about my recent eighty-five-pound win. 'Have you ever played it?'

'A couple of times, yes,' he admitted.

'What would you do if you won?'

'I'd buy out Marsham, all the ground between me and the Hamden Road from Tidcombe.'

'And assuming they won't sell it to you?'

'I'd stop working, I suppose. Get a holiday chalet.'

'What, you wouldn't stop here?'

Norman thought for a moment. 'Yes, I suppose you're right. I wouldn't know what to do if I left that house. I'd be like a fish out of water.'

'Well, if you do ever win it, you know what to do, don't you?'

'What's that, then?'

'Call me and offer me a job, get a fencing and gate contractor in, hire every drystone waller in the county and buy some new tractors.'

And so we nattered, sitting on the hay cart in the sun, the work of loading it awaiting us, no rush. We reminisced about his tractor, Jock, the oldest tractor on the place, gone after fifty years. A Fordson Diesel, it was the only tractor on Parish Farm that had ever been bought entirely first-hand, ten years after his father took on the place. Jock had recently been sold, partial payment for the rusting red tractor that Norman had replaced it with.

We talked about how his father had worked till he was eighty-nine and stayed on the farm telling everyone what to do until the day he died three years later; how one of the reasons the Lettem people sold Norman's father the farm was the newly introduced Tenant's Sons Act, as he called it, which would for the first time have given Norman's father the right to pass on the tenancy to Norman.

'That Tenant Act, that was Labour that did that. If I hadn't been here, and that law hadn't been changed, they wouldn't have sold it to him, they'd just have waited until he died. But old Simpson at Lettem House, he was a bit of a high-liver he was, whisky and smoking and the like. He thought Father would outlive him, better "cash it" before he died, you might say. He was right. Father outlived him by ten years he did.'

'My grandfather,' Norman said, 'he was a Marsham tenant for fifty years, you know, and my father got nothing, nothing. When Grandfather died, they gave the farm to a lieutenant-colonel, a friend of the Marshams he was. Now it's a riding school or something.'

Instead of talking about our going, we talked about him staying, and how he always would, even though everyone wanted him gone.

'I've lived here all my life,' he'd said on that first spring day, to the London 'niddy', as he thought of me. He'd still live here all his life whether I came, went or got chucked in the dead pit. I was just passing through, I thought. What did I know about any of this world?

We looked out over the farm as the late-afternoon sun began its descent over Frimley Wood.

'Better get on with it, then,' I said, nodding to the empty cart. 'These bales won't get moved by talking about them.'

He laughed and we hitched up the cart and headed off around the field. Loaded up, Norman drove the tractor home, taking the tall, wobbly stack slowly through the gates and over the rutted tracks back to the yard. I lay out on top of the bales, smoking a cigarette and watching the sunset as Maggie ran ahead through uncut hayfields.

Back at the yard Norman said, 'That's good, that it is, isn't it, riding home on top of the bales?' He knew, he remembered, he'd made that journey as a boy and every summer since. But there was no boy now; when he went they'd have it all and it would be as if he and Father had never been.

Out shooting rabbits on warm summer nights with Tom I had every chance to tell him what Han and I were planning, but I didn't. He'd drive the truck and direct the lamp as I shot from the window with his silenced rifle. I remember every minute, the fear of their finality searing images and scents in my mind: an owl flying in the arc of the spotter lamp in front of us as we drove down a track; climbing through thick hedges to retrieve a rabbit; knowing it was probably down a hole and finding it; missing an easy shot and Tom joking or reassuring me; spilling bullets on the floor and the sound of empty cartridges under our feet; bagging a dead fox for a research survey; rolled cigarettes and gossip about adultery in the hunting set; stories about Tom making rat traps as a boy; coming home in the dawn light spotting a badger running in the early-morning dew; a muntjac stirring in the low wisps of rising ground mist and two foxes running across a half-cut field of wheat and disappearing into the stalks.

'The best part of the day,' Tom would say about these summer dawns. 'Between four and six.'

Han chatting with Tom over a beer in the garden or walking with him to the pub, she couldn't manage it either. We'd walk slowly home up the lane, another day gone without telling him.

'Sukey's about to die,' Norman suddenly said, out of nowhere. I was round at Norman's talking about our plans. He had seemed distracted. 'She can't move.'

'Where is she?'

Norman took me outside and showed me. She was lying quite still in the weeds of the vegetable garden where Norman had carried her out to. She was sodden with piss and crap, and bluebottles had descended on her in force. She was clearly beyond hope and needed to go. She lay in the searing sun, unable to drink or move, unable or unwilling to shake off the flies.

'She'll probably die in the next day or two,' he said. He seemed unsure about what to do. 'I took the dog to the vet last time, but it cost over fifty quid, it did.'

'Maybe we should put her out of her misery.'

'I haven't got the right gun for that.'

'I could borrow one, from Tom.'

He looked at me. He wasn't right. He was trying to say something and with a look of fear he finally did.

'I don't want to do it.' He didn't want to move Sukey either, into a car, into a vet's office; she'd suffer less if she died where she slept, in the ragged grass of Norman's garden.

'No, it's all right, Norman, I'll do it.'

Han came over the garden wall and comforted Sukey as best she could.

'It's life,' said Norman. 'A cycle. An animal dies, another is born. Those cows that went to market this morning, they're dead now, you know. I see killing all the time. Maybe too much.'

I went and called Tom. Could I borrow a gun? I explained why; it's not the sort of thing one asks someone to do.

'I'll do it,' I said. If I'm honest, I knew he'd offer.

'You sure about that, Ian? It's not the sort of thing you want to get wrong.'

'It's not the sort of thing you ask someone to do. I'll do it.'

'We'll talk about that when I get there. I'll be down in a minute.'

I went back and told Norman Tom was coming down.

'Do you want to be here?'

'No,' he said, shaking his head with his exasperated laugh. As if.

'Do you want to say goodbye then?'

'No,' he smiled weakly. As if.

'I got her on the first of April, you know,' he said, before counting the months on his hand. 'Fifteen years and three months.'

He knelt down briefly, whispered something to her, stroked her, stood up and was gone.

Han was crying and offered to stay with me, but I told her no; there was no point us both being there, there was nothing she could do. She went inside and played with Annie in the back bedroom, as far away as they could be.

I met Tom at the gate as he pulled up in his truck. As he parked, Norman was heading off in the little red tractor up the lane to the yard. He shouted something but I couldn't hear it, and I put my hand to my ear. 'Tell me what I owe him,' he shouted again as he passed, his face set firm.

Tom came into the garden carrying a gun suitable for what was needed, his voice low. We went directly to Sukey and examined her.

'No, she's gone. Those fucking bastard flies, they know, you know.'

'Tom, listen, I'll do it.'

'No, Ian, honestly, let me. It's a horrible thing to get wrong. I've never got it wrong myself, but I've seen it done wrong. You'd never get over it.'

'Tom, I can't watch this.'

'No, you don't.'

I climbed over Norman's garden wall to stand in the field. As I climbed over I took one quick glimpse back. Unlike Norman, I didn't have the courage to even look at her properly, let alone say goodbye. I saw Tom kneel down, gun in hand.

'There you go, Sukey girl,' he said gently as he gave her one last stroke.

I looked away. A bang. I didn't turn.

Tom walked into the field to join me. 'Don't look,' he said. 'Better have a cigarette.' Tom quietly rolled two cigarettes. It was a beautiful summer's evening but there was relief that we had done the right thing.

Passing me a cigarette and lighting it, he said, 'She wouldn't have felt a thing. Just over, just like that.' Quietly he explained how it has to be done, lining up an imaginary cross between eyes and ears. I couldn't listen too much.

'That's only the second time I have ever done that,' he said, 'and I don't ever want to fucking have to do it again.'

Han came out holding Annie and a large whisky for Tom, which he took and drank. We climbed into our garden and sat at the table. There we talked, some of the time about what had just happened, some of the time about nothing special. He stayed for forty-five minutes as we all just digested what had happened. He wouldn't stay for a meal, things to do.

I set out to bury Sukey before Norman would return. Tom had left her in a black binbag in Norman's garden. Tom had told me to dig the grave deep, in order to prevent foxes, telling a tale of an old neighbour of his who, in floods of tears, had buried his dog too shallow in his garden. The next day he woke to find pieces of his pet scattered by foxes across his garden.

'I'd stay and help but I've got stuff I need to get done,' Tom said.

Nevertheless, he came to inspect my tools under the apple tree at the end of Norman's garden. I took a pick and a shovel with me. Tom watched me get started but it was too much for him.

'I'll tell you what, I'll just pop home and get a crowbar and a steel-handled shovel. That's no good for Cotswold digging what you've got there.'

'Tom, honestly, you've done enough, you don't have to do that.'

'No, it's all right.'

He was soon back with his tools. Tom was a firm believer in the right tool for the right job.

He took one look at my hopeless beginning and started at it, first removing a large area of sods, which he carefully set to one side. We dug down through the topsoil and the ridding to the oolitic Cotswold past that lay only a few inches beneath. Once we reached it, we took it in turns, setting about the rock like the men who had made the quarry excavations in the Humpty Dumps. We used a pick and a strong steel spade, cracking the stone with a huge, heavy crowbar, lifting it and letting it smash down on to the exposed stone below. It was demanding, heavy work and we were soon sweating profusely as we dug to the four feet Tom would finally be satisfied with.

Tom asked that I get a wheelbarrow of heavy stone from the

collapsed wall of the old goat barn. We lined the bottom of the hole and the three sides with the largest and flattest ones, placing Sukey in the middle in her bag, four heavy stones on top of her bag. We filled in the rest of the hole with the soil we had dug out as well as the remainder of the stones, tamping down the soil and rock as we filled it, and finally placed a half-sheet of corrugated iron we had found over the grave. We weighed this down with yet another load of stone, in the shape of a cross.

'Do you think Norm would appreciate a marker?' Tom asked as we stood over the grave.

'Sure.'

I found two pieces of old metal pipe, which Tom lashed together with baler-twine into a cross. The horizontal bar was a tad too long, and by now Tom's perfectionism for any task was infectious. With a hacksaw I trimmed an inch or so off, and Sukey's grave was done.

Han set some wild flowers picked from Norman's garden on the grave, before the three of us sat quietly with a beer at the table.

When Tom was gone, with the sun now down over the wood, Norman came home. He seemed fine at first but I noticed he was clutching himself in a peculiar way, so much so that I even asked if he had hurt himself.

'No,' he said self-consciously. Han went and showed him the grave and came back with him for a beer. She reassured him how quick and painless it had all been and what a proper grave we had dug. Norman seemed far away until finally he spoke.

'We had this boy once who worked on the farm. Trevor, he was called. He was training to be a veterinary nurse, he was, and when there was this sick ewe he said he could shoot it with this pistol Father used to have. I heard this shot and then this boy, all shouting and screaming. "Norman! Norman! Come quick!! She won't die." And there was this ewe running around the field, bleeding and everything.' Norman stopped at the memory. 'I had to do it then.'

We were embarrassed to learn how much money Lettem Cottage would cost its next owner, when Spider was living with his mum and dad, Tom equally unable to afford a house in the village and the chances of many of the Massive being able to bring up their future families in the village, or even others like it, looking extremely slim. The phenomenon of the UK property market was old news to the English, beyond comment; its irrational values as rational to them as dot-com valuations were to Californians in 1999. The political and moral implications for working-class rural people were a closed subject. Yes, it's bad, everyone agreed, if you directly pushed them on it, but no, there is nothing that can be done about it. Now it was our turn, and Han and I weren't doing anything about it either.

We could console ourselves with the thought that Lettem Cottage was way beyond being affordable for Spider long before we had bought it, so if it had become even less affordable while we had lived in it, it was academic; but in the end, my involvement in the market meant that I had failed, or refused, to square my beliefs with my actions.

One of the estate agents who came to the house lived in the village (or so we thought). He was the son of the woman at Rathbury; our neighbour, one might say. I knew he was the Countryside Alliance coordinator for our village and assumed he would know Norman and the farm well, even if we had never met him during all the time we had lived in the village, or even seen him, in the pub, at church or at any other village event.

Seb, as he was called, was about my age, but dressed and behaved as if he was about fifty. He exuded brisk efficiency and projected the aura of a man who wouldn't normally trouble himself with such a modest house. It quickly became apparent that the village's estate agent had little idea about Norman or Parish Farm, which bordered Rathbury, and seemed more interested in gleaning information about Norman's farm. He told me a bit about his 'little community' over at Rathbury, which he said wasn't actually part of the village. 'Yes, we bought as many of the other little houses as we could when we bought the main house' ('we', I think, was him and his mum) 'because we thought if the wrong sort of person wanted to move in, we could sort of force them out, if you see what I mean.'

Right.

After a cursory examination of the house, we went outside. I offered him a seat at the table and a coffee.

'It is a lovely little place, I suppose, but of course you have to appreciate that this village isn't the best address in the Cotswolds.'

Han and I bit our lips.

'We could probably do something, though.'

'I'll be in touch,' I said, standing up to show him out as quickly as I could.

Our plan was to regroup and save money for when we would be able to afford to return to the countryside. For work reasons, for now, we would return to a city, but we planned for being elsewhere. In a few years we wanted to be able to buy a smallholding in France. We wouldn't be in the city long, we said.

That weekend we went to Brussels, where we had lived before our years in Paris, and which we thought might be the place to move to. It was a city where we had friends and contacts, and where we were confident of getting plenty of freelance work. Equally importantly, we owned a house there (or rather a Belgian bank did), and the friends who had rented it from us and kept it afloat wanted to leave at some point; they had said that if we needed to live in the house again they would be happy to work around our plans.

'Why can't you just sell *Brussels?*' my mother would say crossly, but only because she was so sad, because she so wanted us to stay. The thought of us leaving after so long away, taking her grandchild with her, was too much for her. Scott, who had now left London with his new wife and bought a house near Tetbury, relentlessly cross-examined us on our numbers.

'Because,' I was finally forced to say, telling him the exact amounts of money involved, 'by the time we pay off what we owe, and taxes and one thing and another, the amount we could reduce our payments on Lettem won't fucking cut it unless I go back to full-time work. And for me, that means London or Paris!'

'OK,' he finally conceded. 'See your point.'

We kept quiet about the house in Brussels to most of our friends, it just seemed easier. That a Brussels town house (albeit a shabby one) was less than half the price of a small, semi-detached cottage in the Cotswolds was a fact as incredible to our Belgian friends as it would be to our friends in the village. We had retirement investments, too, we might have tapped into, but there's nothing like feeling poor in your thirties with a small baby to make you worry about being penniless when you're old; anyway, still the numbers didn't add up.

We returned with our minds made up. We would put Lettem up for sale.

# CHAPTER 18
# SUMMER'S END

Tom leant determinedly against the Aga, beer in hand, and sighed deeply. It was as if his shoulders were trying not to slide away from his resolve.

'You really are our best friend here, Tom,' Han said.

'It cuts both ways,' he said.

We stood in the kitchen in silence. 'Look, I understand,' he said. 'You've got to look out for number one. It's a bummer, but it has to be done.'

'We're not dropping off the planet.'

'Yeah, I know.' He didn't sound convinced.

After May dropped off her daughter Kelly to look after Annie (as she often did), Han, Tom and I went to the pub and afterwards back to Tom's place to talk. He understood the need to move, but the decision to go and live in a city was one he found hard to accept. He'd roll a cigarette thoughtfully and shake his head; 'sure' he'd say, but some things were beyond explanation.

We'd had a few drinks so he offered to walk us home, thrusting a thumb-stick into my hand and taking his own. We walked back to Lettem, a waning crescent moon lighting our way. Han went to bed and Tom and I sat outside in the big wooden chairs looking out over Home Paddock.

'You must have left good places. Why did you do that?' I said. I didn't normally ask Tom many direct questions. Perhaps I felt time was running out.

Tom had long been a keeper on estates throughout England. His time at each place had ended usually as a result of someone dying or retiring, be it a landowner or a head keeper.

Tom spoke of his life now and how he sometimes struggled to

live in his rented cottage.

'I could buy some council flat in Stroud or somewhere, I suppose, but I'd hate it.' He was happy in his cottage and his set-up in the village; he would do anything to keep it that way, he wasn't for moving. If he thought we were cutting and running he didn't say. 'For me, you've got everything here,' he said, feet up on the wall, looking out under the moonlight across Home Paddock. 'Money. It's all bollocks, you see, it's all bollocks. You just need a roof over your head, food on the table. I mean, you've got land. Norm lets you do everything you want to do with it, shooting, walking. What more do you need?'

I let his question stand unanswered this time. Repeating the bare facts of our financial situation wasn't going to help. As for discussing alternative futures outside England, I managed only to arrive at rejecting the place he loved and would never leave, when I meant merely to explain alternatives. Our aspirations for a bigger house and Han's desire for a little bit of bush she could call her own, which we wouldn't have to work so hard for, only came across as materialistic and lazy.

The cows in Home Paddock were lying down and I turned on my torch to see what was about, the light picking out their eyes in damp, moonlit mist.

'Just make sure you consider what's truly important to you before you do this,' he said finally.

'I will,' I promised him.

As he headed home, the click of his thumb-stick on the lane carried through the night. I stayed in the chair, listening to it click-clicking in the stillness until its sound faded. Then nothing.

I woke up in the early dawn and it was raining outside, mist and rain. Lettem already felt autumnal, as if things were coming to an end. We were going to move and Lettem Cottage was on the market.

Norman visibly brightened when Han told him she would be away for a day or two.

'Getting some work, then?' he said hopefully, as we stood chatting while Douglas brought some cattle up the lane. Norman had not accepted we were leaving.

'It's the first two days I've got since Annie was born, Norm,' Han replied. 'The work's just not there I'm afraid.'

The Bee Man stopped in his truck and joined our little summer afternoon chat. The honey had not been so good this year, he said.

'Up until a couple of weeks ago, that is. Much better now.'

'They on the lime, then, now?' asked Norman.

'Oh no, Norman, that's all gone now, that is, all gone.'

The daily and the familiar were taking on a sadness that I tried to keep at bay: the Bee Man coming round, a sunset over Frimley Wood, Annie sitting on the lawn and Han pottering in the garden, a walk to the pub with Spider, moving sheep with Norman, zeroing a rifle with Tom, my runs. In Brussels, I would be running in a park, not up the White Mile past the blackberries and the straw-dusted verges. A countdown had begun as to how many times I would do them again, and things that I had hoped would last for ever were already gone: shoot picnics in the cold November Lambing Sheds, mulled wine in the chimney pot and a New Year's Eve at the pub; March alder catkins blowing in an easterly wind, spring planting and lapwings fluttering and plunging over Valley Ground; black-thorn blossom up Tidcombe Hill, May daisies and cowslips pushing up in Home Paddock, the first yellow underwing moths of June, and bale-bumping in hot July. Soon harvest would be finished, the swifts away and the swallows not long behind them, one last harvest moon and we would be gone.

As I ran, Alan pulled up alongside me in a Marsham Estate Land Rover and moved the .22 rifle on the passenger's seat to let me ride with him. We went back to Lettem and had a drink together outside with Han, sitting at the big table. It was warm.

Alan, unable to do his heavy forestry work, told Han and me of the role he had been offered controlling grey squirrels and other pests on the Estate. We should have told him of our plans, but we couldn't. Instead, we spoke of the American grey squirrel dreys, the nests they made in the hollows of trees or in a commandeered rook's nest; of coppicing and pollarding and trees, and how chestnuts had the biggest cover of any tree and that the biggest tree in England was a sweet chestnut. He told me where it was, but, too distracted, I didn't take it in.

He was happy with his Marsham job which he had begun that July. He hadn't asked for it, he said, he'd been given a helping hand;

the forestry manager had offered him the job, but there was a fair chance that Lord Marsham or his son, who had both known Alan for many years, may also have had some hand in it, knowing how ill he was. Lord Marsham had even bumped into Alan in the Estate office.

'I hope you're not doing more than you can manage, Alan,' he had said concernedly. 'We're so lucky to have someone with us who knows the Estate so well,' he had added.

When I first met Alan he didn't much care for industrial farming and its implications for wildlife and the feel of the landscape any more than anyone else I met, but he had great respect for the Marshams and believed they only did what they had to do to survive.

'That's what they are, Ian – survivors, just like you, just like me, just like Norman, only richer and better organised. They go where the money is; who doesn't?'

Their highly automated and chemical intensive farming might not employ many people, he said, but at least it was accurate, precise and unwasteful, unlike Luddie's occasional wild foray with some spray. 'They use satellite mapping, you know; state of the art it is.'

But as for the Estate as a whole – the office, the buildings' maintenance workers, the park ground and forestry staff and other activities – he said they all added up to the Estate creating jobs and putting money in people's pockets. How many jobs exactly he didn't know, nor how many were self-employed or actually employed directly by the Estate, with all the benefits that went with such a post; namely a house.

The alternative to 'modern' farming (he hated the term 'industrial' or 'factory') was concrete, he claimed, the towns and villages steadily spreading out and covering any ground that wasn't agriculturally viable, however much spray and fertiliser was needed to make it so.

'How many times you've ever seen a town ripped up and replaced with trees and fields? Once the land's gone, it's gone. At least they're keeping their place going with some integrity: they're not doing fuckin' theme parks and having zebras running around and the like.'

On this point I knew Norman and I agreed.

As for the Estate's housing, he spoke from the security of owning his own home, even if he resented people from London and local developers always knocking on his door asking him if he would sell it, just as they tried to do with Norman.

The Marshams, he said, may have put up their rents, but they maintained a sizeable stock of housing for local people to rent, people who couldn't afford to buy. And he claimed there *were* still some people who had Estate cottages at way below market prices, but how many, who or why he didn't mention.

'And a lot of them are pretty ungrateful old sods, even for it, I can tell you. Just like you lot cycling through the park and moaning about it being closed at five. I reckon they should just close it for four weeks and teach those miserable bastards what a privilege it is they're getting to walk around his Estate for free. You don't exactly see Norman throwing open his gates, do you?'

(Han said later that it always amazed her that she had never met anyone in rural England who had ever even mentioned, let alone questioned, how and when these vast estates had been acquired.)

As to the housing, Han and I didn't agree with Alan; from what we had heard the rents were becoming increasingly expensive, no more than was fair for the market, true, and, for a lucky few, some claimed, even lower, but long-term there could be only one future: more and more of the large estates' and landowners' tenants with rural skills or low incomes (whether they were working for their landlords or not) being driven out of the rented cottages in their villages and into the towns. Eventually, unless someone inherited a house for which death duties could be afforded without selling (difficult, given house price valuations), many working-class people simply couldn't expect to afford to live in the villages around us without earning massive salaries to support the sorts of mortgages they would need to buy even a simple, tiny cottage like Lettem.

If the Marshams and other big landowners were the enlightened custodians of the countryside they claimed, could they not sacrifice some small part of their profits to create some scheme to help these people, Han argued with Alan? Even give preference to the smaller farmers who needed their tiny but essential pasture and hay paddocks, instead of renting the land with the bigger houses they owned to people who wanted to use these paddocks, not for farming, but for their horses and ponies?

Even if those farmers were like Norman, I thought, as Han

spoke: struggling, fingertip survivors with broken-down fences, too proud to ask, too shy and reticent to make their occasional mumbled thank yous audible in the land where the term 'thank you' was used so much that it could become an auditable part of the national economy; where *one* quiet thank you was *never* enough.

Lord Rodley spoke of us all being particularly fortunate to live in such a beautiful part of the country, but did he mean a cottage in one of the villages or a housing estate in one of the towns? Lady Rodley spoke of looking after the small struggling farmers, but did she include Norman?

'I'm sure she does,' Alan said, pouring another glass of lemonade. It was hot.

For my part, I proposed the only solution I could see, beyond an altruism that I myself had shown no signs of signing up for with the impending sale of our house. It was a special tax on second homes in rural areas, a high one, so that people from London and elsewhere who could afford hundreds of thousands of pounds for a holiday home in a part of the world with a desperately short supply of low-cost village housing might contribute to a special fund to construct low-cost housing. These houses would be for people with or acquiring a rural skill that all these new environmental steward-ship schemes were going to demand, and which would hopefully safeguard exactly the sort of biodiverse landscape that people from the cities hoped to witness over their garden walls.

Alan listened, and shrugged his shoulders. 'You're dreaming.'

'Probably. But I wish someone would think about it all; people would think about actual *consequences* when they buy a house with five acres and kick the local farmer off. I wish someone would fucking well rent Norm a bit more land.'

'He might try the odd please and thank you,' Alan laughed.

'I know, but Norman's Norman. I wish more people understood that, too.'

There were other friends to tell who did not want us to leave England, and we continued to look for moments where a pause might allow us time to overcome our reluctance.

'Peg, we've got a bit of news.' We were sitting outside at the table, Peg playing with Annie. It was overcast with a very slight drizzle that, in the warm expectations of an August day, we tried to ignore.

Peg's face lit up.

'No, we're not pregnant. It's bad news, I'm afraid,' Han said.

'We're moving,' I said.

'To Brussels,' blurted Han, wanting to get it all out as quickly as possible, before Peg thought we might be going to Tidcombe or somewhere.

'Oh, bugger,' she said, and she and Han cried. With all that had happened, and her future uncertain at the pub, it seemed unkind not to be giving her some good news.

Peg, being Peg, was supportive and said she understood how difficult it would be for us to move. She told us how horrible it had been leaving The Marsham Arms. 'I suppose I could have gone back to Weymouth. We still had a house there. That was before Mike sold it without telling me, but Gloucestershire was home by then,' she said wistfully. 'I suppose the longer you leave it, the more difficult it will be.'

Telling Spider was no easier. I took a deep breath walking down to the pub one night, and got it out by the time we had reached the bend. He gave me a pretend kick up the backside, put his shoulders back and said things like, 'Well, that's it, isn't it?' when I stumbled on explaining the whys and the wherefores.

Everyone at the pub that night assured us, explicitly or implicitly, that we were mad to be going, quite mad. Norman and Tom hadn't let up for a second. Tom had been over that day and we were moving some of Norman's ever-escaped cattle when Norman rolled up on his bike.

'You'll never guess what Tom's banging on about,' I said to Norman.

'I will.'

'They shouldn't go, Norm,' said Tom.

'It would be a lot simpler for everyone, Ian, if you just stopped here.'

We laughed and walked on in silence.

In the pub, I drifted back to the table.

'The big estates will rue the day they got rid of all their tenants. It made sense when they could get a hundred and twenty, a hundred and fifty pounds a ton for their wheat. Knock down the walls, get the big machines in. But now, at fifty pound a ton, the maths doesn't look quite so good.' Geoff's and Laura's friend Cameron was talking to me, but my mind was with Norman and Brussels and leaving.

I left Han at the pub and went home early; it was all too much.

'What you doing for September the twenty-second?' Norman asked me.

He had received a letter back in June from the Cotswold Hunt telling him that two trains and ten coaches were being organised to take hunt supporters to a demonstration march in London. Return tickets, heavily subsidised by the Cotswold Hunt Farmers and Supporters Club, would cost fifteen pounds. The Cotswold Hunt regional transport coordinator for the village and Tidcombe (the separate hamlet of Rathbury was not mentioned) was Seb Bleardon, the estate agent.

Marchers did not have to approve of hunting, only to agree to the rights of individuals to hunt. The 'Liberty and Livelihood' march was to demand of the government five things: the right of rural people to live their lives responsibly in the way they chose; to safeguard them from prejudiced attacks on hunting and other field sports; to respect the values and customs of rural communities; to ensure that laws directed at rural people had their consent; and finally, in a wonderfully vague statement, to address the '*real* problems of the countryside' that were destroying 'its communities, its culture and its children's future'. (Presumably it was all the government's fault, certainly not that of the free market.)

I told Norman that on the first two points, I was prepared to march. However, the Countryside Alliance's wider 'rural' political agenda had always struck me as little more than a cynical appropriation of issues and politics that had nothing to do with hunting, simply in order to broaden its appeal. Worse, I said, in my very limited experience of living in the countryside, many of the local leaders of the Countryside Alliance I had come across around our village seemed to have little to do with the village whose side they claimed to be on. I suspected most of the leaders would be hard pushed to name more than a handful of the children within our community whose futures they were apparently fighting for.

'So you're going, then?' said Norman quietly, with a smile.

'Yes, but not in a bus organised by our local "community co-ordinator". He left me with the impression that Rathbury wasn't even part of "our community". I'd rather walk.'

Norman laughed. I had told him the 'not the best address in the Cotswolds' story and Norman had told me one of his. Proctor had been struggling to sell Lettem House. A local estate agent had advised him that a bit more land would help the job along. This estate agent, who barely knew Norman save in passing, had rung Norman and left a message:

'This is Stanford David James in town,' it went. 'Mr Proctor would like to sell Lettem House with more land, and he'd like to buy the field up to the village.' (This was an eighteen-acre field called Sleeves Corner, and part of Norman's farm.) 'Please give me a call.'

Norman was incredulous at the time and just as amazed in the recounting of the tale to me. 'You don't carry on that like that, do you?' he said.

Norman, Tom and his younger sister Iona came for a barbecue of Tom's trout and vegetables from Han's and Norman's shared patch. Iona had returned from living in London and was now staying with Tom while she looked for a home near her brother and mother in the countryside where she had grown up. She wanted to find a little cottage, but many landlords preferred to rent them out as holiday homes at four hundred pounds a week or more. Iona was finding it hard to rent a cottage or find a job that would match the rents. Tom still spoke about our plans as though they might not happen.

Norman showed up when it was long dark. He brought with him a basket of broad beans picked from his overrun garden and teased Han about her deformed and twisted carrots. They joked about entering them into the approaching annual village produce show, perhaps winning a prize for Best Shared Garden.

Norman had lost Maggie, so Han, Tom and Norman competed with their wolf whistles. Norman blamed his lost teeth for the weakness of his. Finally Maggie emerged out of the darkness and into the light of the barbecue fire, before hopping the garden wall and jumping up and licking us all, covered in burrs and bits of grass.

Norman told us stories about his life at the cottage: run-ins and incidents, gossip and small moments, like the time he saw two weasels fighting one dinner time, just over the lane in Long Ground. He told us he had just passed his fiftieth birthday that summer (alone, we found out) with not a card or a present from anyone; and we talked about his old neighbours and how the rector thought we were weekenders when we first arrived.

'You've probably got me to blame for that,' Norman said. 'I told him you were white settlers,' he laughed.

There was a pause as we listened to the night.

'Does anyone like lollipops?' he asked abruptly but quietly.

'I'd say,' said Tom.

Without explanation Norman disappeared and returned with lollipops from his meat freezer. We sat and ate them under a sky of herringbone cloud beneath the half-moon.

'You can't do this in Brussels,' said Tom.

The last two weeks of summer were rainy and grey. On the weekend of the village produce show, Han sat with a friend under Frankie's Tree, partly sheltered from the light, warm rain that dripped into their watercolours as they painted the cottage. Annie sat in her stroller looking out at Norman leading his cows through the poppy-studded rape in Valley Ground.

Kiwi Alison came for lunch and we made plans for Annie's christening. Alison was going to do the food. Planning this event was the only way we found we could look to the near future with any joy at all. Earlier that week, the rector had paid his second visit to our cottage during our time at Lettem, on this occasion to discuss the service. It had been one of the last fine evenings of the summer and he had sat outside at the table, this time accepting an offer of a whisky and water. We had to start by telling him we were leaving. We explained why and he was understanding.

'You're very lucky, of course. Being broad-minded and having travelled, you can think of all sorts of European cities you might go and live in. Anyone living in England would just think of London, Leeds or Bristol.' He told us of a parishioner who was selling up and buying a huge place in the Dordogne.

We talked of how much we would miss Norman and what a good friend he had been to us.

'I'm *so* pleased,' he said. 'We think the world of Norman.' He told us how Norman came once a year to the rectory to shear their sheep with 'the disabled people'. 'He's so good with them, you know, so gentle. He has a real affinity with them.' The rector's wife was one of the few people Norman was close to in the village. If you can't talk to the rector's wife, then who can you talk to? he once told me.

We talked too of house prices and the need for low-cost housing. He told us of the people in Rittleton who had put up such stiff opposition to some low-cost housing that was being built on church land in the village. Yes, people around here had changed. Taking details of our occupations for his christening forms, he smiled at the description of Han's work: web developer.

'There are so many professions now, aren't there?' he said. 'When I look through the old registers, one only sees a handful of them. Now I don't understand anyone's job description.'

We went on to talk about his rare-breed chickens and I told him about Tom's Reeves pheasants.

'Tom?'

'Yes, you know, Tom,' I said, telling him his surname. 'He lives in the village.'

'Really?'

The rector had no idea who Tom was, nor that he lived in the village. From the rectory to Tom's house on the other side of the village, it was perhaps a fifteen-minute walk. Villages and their vicars weren't like they used to be; more fluid populations, less eager churchgoers, fewer priests for their charge.

Tom was no great churchgoer himself, Sunday worker that he was, save for Christmas, christenings and funerals, and I felt for the rector and his wife, struggling to hold on to an older way of life that the rural communities themselves were steadily wilting away from.

The apples were no good this year, Norman told me over a pint, after we had moved some cows down near the railway. It had been a poor year for fruit, and the blackberries were already mostly shrivelled and gone. We'd been too busy to pick all our apples and there were some left, beginning to rot on the tree. We must pick them before it's too late, we thought.

We received an offer for Lettem Cottage from the first people who had seen it. They were a young couple, recently married, our estate agent – not Mr Bleardon – told Han. The estate agent swore how nice they were and what wonderful neighbours they would make, and we hoped she was right. We had accepted their offer, privately subject to us meeting them.

The buyer first met us when he came to meet his mother's surveyor. (The surveyor told us he had interrupted his holiday to come to Lettem. He had been doing work for her for nearly thirty years, including the brothers' houses in Fulham. He spoke well of her, but she was not, he said, the sort of woman one says no to.)

The son arrived in a new Golf. He was in his early thirties and wore trendy wraparound shades pushed back up into his blond hair. He wore a black, expensive-looking shirt outside black jeans. He had the air of someone both prosperous and unemployed. Later he told me he'd spent the last three years participating in an expedition to canoe down the longest river in forty-three European countries, which made me think that maybe Spides needed to get into the canoeing game.

'You must be Richard,' he said to me, referring to the surveyor.

'No, I'm Ian.' He seemed a little confused. 'The owner.'

Once the buyer was done with the surveyor – most of their time spent over by the old goat barn, perhaps discussing what they could build there – he stayed for a drink.

There was no doubt he was likeable, and enthused by the house, and he responded warmly as we told him about Norman and the farm. I spoke of cows and calving, and hinted heavily how giving Norman a hand now and again would be good; looking after a lamb, perhaps. It must have sounded ridiculous. He wasn't dull or antisocial, Han had a good feeling about him, and despite 'getting the goat barn' being the thing that he most wanted to talk about, we felt that Norman could do a lot worse for a new neighbour. Nor was he a weekender.

'No, not us, no, we'll not be weekenders,' he said. 'We're 24/7 people.'

He and his wife returned the next week. It wasn't long before conversation turned to the goat barn again, and whether I might have a word with Norman about 'getting it'.

'Say again?'

'You know, perhaps you could have a word with Norman about us buying it.'

There was a pause. I didn't know what to say, I wanted to throw them out.

'Perhaps you should consider just moving in first? Building a relationship?' Han said as politely as she could, rescuing me and the situation.

'Yes, yes, of course,' he said. There was a slightly uncomfortable silence, which he decided to fill. 'Is your furniture for sale?'

# CHAPTER 19

# LETTEM DAYS

Tom stopped by the house after the bank holiday Monday, tapping on the window with his stick and wondering what I was doing inside. We sat outside making wasp traps and eating blackberries. Then the calves got out. Douglas ran down the lane after them, effing and blinding, and that got me up and about and away from wherever it was I was heading. I cycled over to Spider's farm to ride with him in his giant combine as he cut the last acres of that year's harvest.

Spider's combine was state-of-the-art and we sat inside an air-conditioned cabin, comfortable and cool, surrounded by knobs, buttons and electronic displays, listening to the radio. Spider's wheat was, like nearby Marsham's, as ordered as his machine.

'She's a top chemist, she is,' Norman had joked about the Marsham farm manager. 'She sprays everything. That wheat opposite us? Must have been sprayed half a dozen times this year,' he had said in a hard-to-decipher mixture of disdain, admiration and incredulity.

The Royal Society for the Protection of Birds would report that this type of intensive farming, which had created these pristine, wild-flowerless acres, had reduced the numbers of twenty-four common birds in the UK by up to a third in the last twenty-five years. Between 1970 and just before we arrived at Lettem, the skylark numbers had plummeted by fifty-two per cent, the yellowhammer by fifty-three per cent and the corn bunting by eighty-eight per cent. Alan would say these birds were still about on Marsham ground, just like the English partridge; my townie eyes just couldn't see them. We left it at that.

From Spider's combine we saw a woodcock flash up from the wheat and a fox sprint out from the high golden stalks, over the cut stubble and away. Sitting high above the wheat, we could see the badger and deer runs through the fields, and small circles where the deer had slept at night. We didn't see any corn buntings.

Our conversation was of the christening, farming, pesticides, the fact that Spider hadn't had a raise in three years, and the farm manager who seemed to get most of the praise for doing little of the work. The entire eight-hundred-acre farm was handled by just Spider and the manager, with some summer help for harvest. Spider spoke wistfully of when he and Huggs worked for 'The Captain' as they called him. Captain Perkin Furleigh was the last tenant farmer at Rectory Farm, now home of Nicholas Marsham. At harvest time, The Captain would offer Norman and his father the use of his grain dryer.

It was hard to picture Marsham letting Norman do that now, Norm showing up with his grubby corn at their gleaming facility, but I thought it just as likely that Norman would be too proud to ask. Spider concentrated on his work and lifted the cutting-head of the combine as he turned in the headlands before starting another swath through the wheat.

Later in the pub, he admitted to me that up in the cab he'd done some thinking.

'You've got time to think about all sorts of stuff. What could be; what should be. I've been thinking a lot about you and Han leaving. It's only just beginning to sink in, I s'pose.'

He put down his pint.

'Bloody shame, it is. If I win that lottery, I'm keeping you here,' he said, and then gave me a bear hug. 'But that's all pie in the sky, isn't it?'

'Yes,' I said. 'I suppose it is.'

I cycled home past harvested fields, the air smelling of cut wheat. Norman stopped by and drank cider with us. We talked about the canal and the plans they had for it, and how this bloke Norman knew (whose garden and workshops stood on the old route) was not to be moved.

'"They're not moving me," he says. "I'm a shearer I am, they're not moving me. I'm a shearer."'

A train passed along the railway. As a boy, Norman used to take that train every day to school, cycling to and from Hamden station.

'One day as we were coming along this girl I was sat next to said, "Look at that old farmer." "That's my dad that is," I said. "I've shared this carriage with you every day for four years," she says, "and you've never said that's your farm."'

Norman stayed to eat, and the warm night was spent drinking more cider and reminiscing. Perhaps our departure had triggered in Norman a need to tell us more. Now that he knew we were going, there wouldn't be time for our normal slow unravelling of history.

He told of his twenty years working for his father for just six pounds a week; how he spent it on a scooter, an older version of Spider's Vespa. The big night was Wednesday, at The Nelson or The Drillman's.

'Wednesdays, Young Farmers Club and a few tarts if you were lucky,' he laughed.

Norman received six pounds and full board and lodging from Father, and every Thursday or Friday the van from Jesse Smith's, the butcher in Cirencester, would deliver two joints, one for Mrs Bruce next door, one for his mum. They had roast beef every Sunday, always roast beef. Now it seemed most of Jesse Smith's customers in town were white settlers, probably the only ones who could afford it, and Norman's meals were left by Rose outside his back door, wrapped in tin-foil. Most people now bought their meat from Tesco's, while Jesse Smith made plans to create Jesse's Bistro and Jesse's Cheese Shop in the old stable yard behind their shop selling olives and 'international cheeses'.

We talked about the cattle market and whether its fate would be the same as Gloucester market's, now closed and deserted.

'We used to own that,' he said matter-of-factly about Gloucester market.

'We?'

'The freemen,' he said. Norman was one of just a hundred or so freemen of the city of Gloucester. He could sell anything in the city without a licence and he could be called on, he smiled, 'in times of national emergency'.

By now we were tipsy on the cider. It didn't take much to get Norman a bit tipsy. He wasn't a big drinker; it made him want to sleep. It was late and time to go and feed the calves.

We rounded up the cows from the rape in Valley Ground and in pitch-black steered them up to the yard and into the barns with the calves. Inside the barns there were no lights and little straw on the manure-covered floor. One or two candles stood on rusty upturned biscuit-tin lids high on the beams, but they were unlit; only for emergencies. Norman pushed and prodded the cows and calves to get them to move around so all of them could feed.

I stood in the shed and listened to the calves feeding, Norman's shadow thrown on to the slate-and-slat ceiling by a small torch, a tool I had never seen him use in all his hours in the dark. This was a task he did every day, twice a day, year after year. The barn doors were broken or held in place by string, and his work seemed so very hard and so very alone.

In bed that night I can't sleep; thinking about Norman and the farm, of winning the lottery and staying here for ever. He can't do all that alone.

'It's what he does,' Han tried to reassure me. 'Now go to sleep.'

Annie was to be christened in the village, but with the rector on holiday, Russell from Storeton was going to conduct the service. Russell was an enormously likeable man: funny, engaged, a tremendous raconteur and fabulously indiscreet. In his seventies, a little portly but not fat, he had a slightly thespian manner about him. He came for tea and we sat outside at the big table on the terrace.

He had only been ordained when he was sixty. Most of his life he'd worked as a journalist and sub-editor on publications like *House Beautiful* and the *Daily Sketch*, where he wrote the Rolf Merlin astrology column. He'd had his spell as a 'creative artist', as he self-deprecatingly called his efforts at being a writer. To subsidise his art he had worked in the subterranean Lyons ice cream cathedral in Olympia, where the workers walked around with miners' lamps for light in order to keep the temperature down. He had a literary agent in New Bond Street with smart leather furniture who, despite the fact that Russell's family were living on turnips and Oxo, as he put it, kept encouraging Russell to stick at it.

'I used to say to my wife, well, I must keep at it, he has an office in New Bond Street with smart leather furniture, he must know what he's on about.' Then he met his agent working down at the ice cream cold store, also engaged as a day labourer. '"What the effing hell are you doing here?" I said. "Some research, dear boy, research."'

We chatted on, a little gossip, some laughs, and we found our way on to the Countryside Alliance.

'Liberty and livelihood? That's a slogan stolen from the first nineteenth-century agricultural unionists, who were appallingly treated by the landowning, hunting classes. The brazen cheek of it, don't you think?' Russell didn't have much time for the CA. He hadn't spotted them when the livelihoods of entire coal-mining communities, often in rural areas, were being destroyed by Thatcher's love of market forces. The notion that it was an alliance of people who loved the countryside he found laughable. 'An alliance? With the ramblers and the twitchers and the right-to-roamers who want to walk on their land? Where are they? I'd like to see Shakespeare's lover and his lass trying to run through the green corn "with a hey, and a ho, and a hey nonino" nowadays! I wonder what sort of reception they'd get now?' Russell laughed.

I kept quiet about Norm's views on trespassers, probably best.

'It's a single-issue pressure group, nothing more, nothing less. And the PM? He doesn't have a choice. He doesn't want the bother of it all, but it has been on their manifesto for years, and if he ignores it, he'll just get a private member's bill every year for ever. It's about democracy.'

I'd clearly unleashed something Russell wanted to get off his chest. Russell thought seventy per cent of country people were actually against hunting, including most of the people in Storeton. One neighbour saw his cat killed by the hounds and was now too scared to let his dog out. Storeton was still pretty feudal, he said, with village life increasingly dominated by 'middle-class toffs coming in from their dark satanic barn conversions'.

'You know they put hounds down when they are five or six, as soon as they show any signs of slowing down? Yes, they feed them to the pack. So what all this nonsense is about their concern that they will have to put the hounds down if hunting is banned I really don't know.'

He paused, thoughtfully and regretfully. 'The only reason why I wouldn't want to see it banned is because I don't want my friends turned into criminals.'

Russell dined with the 'toffs' as he rather affectionately called them. He told me that he had once spoken up in defence of the Prime Minister, who was being slated by Lady Rodley over dinner one evening, banging on about 'that evil man'.

"'Russell,' she said, 'we don't discuss politics, sex or religion at this table.' Well, I thought, that about leaves the bloody weather. 'That reminds me', I said back to her, 'of a dinner party I was at thirty years ago. The host said the same thing when I came to the defence of Harold Wilson. Actually, what he meant to say, and what you mean', I said to her, 'is don't discuss *my* politics!'"

Russell's relationship with the 'toffs', he said good-humouredly, was about being tolerated by them; liked, even.

On he went. Rural property prices and council house sales? The most evil act of redistribution of public property since the dissolution of the monasteries. Heseltine still bragged about it, he'd heard. Rural employment? There was a woman he knew of who had employed a bloke in her village. Made him go and work on her land near Tetbury, a journey that cost him thirty pounds a week in petrol because he was too compliant. Now he worked for Tesco's in Northleach, and they gave him hard-weather gear, holiday pay, overtime and seventy-five pence above the minimum wage. He'd always worked on the land, but was now a trolley attendant and very happy, thank you.

'People knock Tesco's, but they're a very enlightened employer.' Russell much preferred Tesco's where, at the checkout, there could be 'a marchioness behind me and a countess in front of me and we all get treated exactly the same way'. When he was a child he remembered his mother being snubbed by the local shopkeeper whenever a smarter customer came into the 'so-called charming little shop'.

'Yes,' said Russell about the rector, 'Charles's always going on about the evil supermarkets and the poor farmers and "if only people would be prepared to pay more for their food". I told him: people want it cheap. It's market forces. Farmers have always voted Tory, the champions of market forces. If you want a free market, this is what you get. The only people selling at farmers' markets are toffs selling food at vastly inflated prices to other toffs. You know what Tesco's is? Tesco's is Tory capitalism at its most successful, its most dynamic and perhaps at its most rapacious. But who despises the dreadful Tesco's? The toffs shopping at Waitrose.'

He paused, reflecting.

'You know, once I was selling a watercolour to a farmer's wife in Hertfordshire. Her three cars sitting outside were plastered with "Buy British" stickers. I got her cheque safely in my pocket and then I asked her about it. "Everyone should buy British," she said. "Is that why you've got a BMW, a Renault and a jeep?" I asked. It was a case of do as I say, not as I do. Support us, but not British industry.'

The week before the christening, the early-September weather was plain wintry; summer was gone. Scott, who was going to be Annie's godfather, lent us a gazebo to put up over the terrace – there was no way all of our guests would fit into the cottage – and we had to weigh down its legs with stones to stop it from taking off in the wind. After all his years in Istanbul and elsewhere he had now come home to England and I, who had returned earlier, wanted to leave again. Later we stood under the hawthorn trees in the Humpty Dumps, waiting with our guns for flighting pigeons coming into roost. 'You can't do this in Brussels,' he said and we laughed.

Tom had given me a gift. He didn't call it a leaving gift and it was presented without any ceremony. He left it outside on the table, the letter tied to it inside a freezer bag to keep it dry from rain. It was a fine thumb-stick: straight and true, perfectly weighted and exactly the right height for me.

'As promised, and long overdue,' he wrote, 'a genuine hand-crafted "Third Leg". On no account should this be confused with cheap imitations as one often sees mass-produced at country fairs! This has character and sits well in the hand and will say a lot about the carrier. Treated with care and respect, it will carry you many miles as well as having a multitude of other uses such as a useful gate vaulter, an electric fence holder-downer, an invaluable aid when out with your gun and a very comfortable rest to lean on and point with when strolling around your estate! I could go on but the possibilities are endless.'

That evening I took it out for its first walk. It had been a day of anxieties and departure practicalities, and so I decided to walk the entire boundary of the farm, something I had never done before, taking with me the shotgun, Maggie and my third leg.

En route we stopped and talked: first with Dan in the yard doing some drystone walling by the cottage, and next with Douglas empty-ing corn from the trailer, moaning and muttering about something or other. 'This place is a bloody scrap heap!' he said, berating the bucket he was having to use.

From the yard we walked through the Humpty Dumps and out in front of Lettem House. Proctor had told me a TV presenter was moving in, in October. Proctor had written to him about his new neighbour, Norman, about the sheep, and about how if he let Norman graze them in his paddock Norman would cut the grass and take the hay; the new owner would have a job finding anyone to do such a small job around these parts otherwise, Proctor said.

By the gate into Upper Rathbury Field, we met Norman working on the combine, broken down again.

'I see you've got the finest mechanic in Gloucestershire on the job, then, Norm,' I joked, leaning on my stick. Norman grunted.

'It's a bearing problem. I rang the engineers and they told me not to use it till they've fixed it.' They hadn't come and it threatened rain. 'They do the estates first, then the big farms and then me. Last.' Norman didn't care much for agricultural engineers; the lowest of the engineering pile, he said. 'They use us to get a bit of experience and training and bugger off to do cars as soon as they can.' He bent down and patted Maggie. 'Got the gun dog, then.'

Maggie and I continued along the hedge to the far corner of Upper Rathbury Field before following the footpath that ran from the lane down to the Lambing Sheds. In Lower Rathbury Field I stopped to watch the swallows swooping as they fed. Soon they would gather on the telegraph wires in readiness for their flight south for winter, following the swifts already gone. I called out for Pip and Pop, who trotted over and pushed their heads against my legs for a bottle I no longer carried.

I wanted to shoot a rabbit, but Maggie was too busy chasing them for that. We stopped at the top of Colt House with its view of the farm, and in the fading light watched Norman still working on the immobile combine and the lights come on at Lettem Cottage.

The next night Han returned from the pub with the news, previ-ously rumoured, now made official by Laura. An ex-aggie called Jonty Something-or-Other had bought the lease to the pub as of the end of the month. He wouldn't be the full-time landlord; who that would be we didn't know.

Peg and Laura said Jonty was very nice. I'd been told he was in his twenties and owned a yachting company that rented expensive luxury boats in the Mediterranean, and now he wanted a country pub. It didn't surprise me; it seemed inevitable.

The next morning I got up and picked all the plums I could from the tree in the garden, diced them all up (save one big bowl's worth to take to a party Tom was having) and made jam. I had visions of the people buying Lettem Cottage cutting the fruit trees down and building a garage or something. It wouldn't surprise me; it was inevitable.

The weather before Annie's christening seemed set for winter, and as we prepared the house and garden we thought our party might have to be indoors. My mother arrived and happily decorated the gazebo with cuttings we picked from the hedges outside the cottage, rich with a Cotswold autumn. There were wayfaring branches, their berries turning from red to purple as they ripened in the hedges; the white beards of traveller's joy, crab apple, elderflower and its drooping berries; sprays of hazel, blackthorn heavy with sloes, rosehip and scarlet berries carefully unravelled from the hawthorn. In between rain showers I managed to mow the lawn.

But the eve of the christening the rain stopped: at Tom's party we stood in his isolated garden on what felt like a hot summer's night, drinking beer kept cool in old metal laundry tubs full of ice.

The next morning we muttered nervously about the clouds in the distance – it looked like rain – but Alison, who had arrived with the food, insisted we set up outside under the gazebo as planned. There would be no rain today, she said. Norman, who'd been up in the yard helping me get some hay bales to make a den for the children who were coming, burnt his breakfast and was running late for his bell-ringing. Han cooked him a poached egg on toast before I ran him up to church in the car. Then, contrary to every forecast, the sun came out and shone all day.

Douglas had been invited and he had said he would help guide all our guests' cars into Home Paddock, where Norman had said they could park. Douglas approached his task with great enthusiasm, racing up and down the lane on his bike, shouting and pointing. Every car that came down the lane was stopped and given the third degree by him, dressed in his biking helmet with his trousers tucked into his clips.

'Pub or chris'ning?'

'Pub?' a rather nervous-looking driver would say.

'Right then, what you want to do then is go right on down the lane, keep going, keep going, keep going, and then you'll be there. And all that.' Douglas would be off, holding up his hand to stop the next car. 'Pub or chris'ning?'

'Christening.'

'Right then, you follow me, you just follow me.' Douglas would hop on his bike and lead them into Home Paddock, where he would ensure they were parked in a neat line before zipping back out up the track and on to the lane for the next car.

Just as the first guests were arriving, we heard a tractor. It was Norman in Home Paddock with the topper, cutting a few thistles and nettles. Save for the time he cut the blackthorn bushes along a track for the shoot's 'gentry' guests, we had never seen Norman do an act of cosmetic farming, but it seemed he wanted the view to look its best. He arrived just in time for lunch, all changed and spruced. Douglas charmed everyone and then sat on the lawn to eat his lunch, helmet still on, bike brought into the garden to show the guests. He had this way of sitting on his knees, with his long legs tucked back under him, his feet splayed on the ground. It reminded me of a young foal.

After lunch we ambled up the lane to the church, led eagerly by Han's nieces down from London. Our guests stretched out in a long, leisurely string up past the yard and down to the church. In the quiet of St Michael's, we sat on the stone bench and the pews that surrounded the seven-hundred-year-old font. This was an emotional christening for a family that had known too many funerals, for my mother and Annie's Aunt Frances, and the family friends that Han and I had invited; it was a day that stood silently and happily with the past, just as it was for Laura and our friends from Lettem as we listened to the priest who had led the service at Geoff's funeral. I'd asked Russell to say a few words about my brother and father; he forgot ('*Oh, bugger,*' he said when he remembered), but it didn't matter; everyone had their own memories and thoughts. At the end of the service Russell suggested we take Annie round and introduce her to everyone individually. Annie was passed to Han's sister, and then my mother held her granddaughter in her arms and cried. Later Scott told me that Tom was in tears.

Tom and his sister gave Annie an old framed map of Gloucestershire and Alan gave a book about the canal. All of our friends from Lettem had managed to choose cards with pictures of sheep and lambs; Annie was a Cotswold baby.

In the evening, with most of the guests gone, Douglas and I moved the table to the centre of the gazebo, lit a big fire outside in the barbecue and set the table for dinner.

Alison sat at one end, warmed by the fire, Scott on her right, Alan on her left. I sat at the other end next to Han and Laura; between us were Douglas, Spider, Tom and Iona. Norman arrived to a great cheer, late as ever after feeding the cows, and after dinner May, Kelly and Bob came over. Laura told me that Norman had told her that afternoon we'd be back in two and a half years; he didn't really think we'd be gone for good.

We ate lasagne and leftover pudding and drank a lot; even Alan, who shouldn't have with all his medications for the deadly disease he was still battling. Only just in time we remembered to get Douglas to phone his mum and dad to tell them where he was and that he'd be coming home late.

When Douglas stood up, and in his usual confident booming voice said he'd better be going, we all stopped talking and turned to say goodnight to him. Standing at the end of the table lit by candles and the flames of the fire, he had everyone's attention.

'I just want to say, you all take care, now.'

Everyone started to say goodnight, but it was Tom who realised before anyone else what was about. Douglas wanted to say something more.

'Hang on, you lot, let the man speak,' Tom said.

Douglas continued, talking about me and Hannah, and lastly, as he was done, raised his Coke can.

'I just want to say that was the best party I have EVER been to in all my life. You all take care, now.'

Han, who was closest to him, stood up and gave him a big kiss and started crying.

For a moment no one knew what to say, but it was Scott who

managed to get to his feet, and despite the emotion and the wine, was able to give a speech about community, about what he had seen happen to us at Lettem Cottage and how special it was; and another toast. Next, Tom stood; he spoke with warmth and praise that Han and I struggled not to be overwhelmed by.

And then, when it seemed the speeches were over, Norman started to say some words and everyone went completely quiet. He spoke quietly but determinedly. Speaking like this in front of a group of people was so un-Normanlike that his willingness to do so was moving in itself. 'You and Han get on with the gentry and the country bumpkins like us. You're a gentleman,' he said, looking at me.

When they were finished, Han and I didn't know what to say; I could only raise my glass.

'Lettem days,' I said.

'Lettem days.'

# CHAPTER 20
# SHOT FOX

The day after Annie's christening it rained so heavily that Horse Paddock Bend flooded, as if to remind us of the weather Sunday had promised but never given. The ground was sodden and the morning saw dense, muffling fog that no sun could send off. But somehow the sun prevailed and the first fog of autumn was burnt and blown away, and we sat outside watching high cumulus glide through a warm blue sky.

The orange-brown stains of the rust fungus were turning violet on the bramble bushes, and the sloes hung fattening on the blackthorn. The mornings were soon heavy with dew, the hedges festooned with the elaborate decoration of millions of cobwebs revealed by the beads of moisture that clung to them. Norman was still trying to get that bloody combine to finish the job, raiding the old harvester that sat rusting in the yard for a spare fan belt for the equally old harvester that sat rusting in Scott's Plantation. The Marsham ground, just a few days ago cut to stubble, baled and emptied by the contractors, was already brown, ploughed, planted and sprayed. Leaves were slowly turning and tiny helicopters floated down from the lime tree. Mushrooms grew up in hidden corners of the farm and found their way unannounced to our garden table, left muddy and wet, coated in morning dew.

Yet despite these autumn signs, the rain didn't come again and it was warm and dry. Norman had an inspection coming up and the day was devoted to getting all the calves tagged and the paperwork in order.

'But that won't bother you soon, will it?' joked Norman as we talked about the inevitable rain. 'Stuck inside in the smoke and grime in Brussels.'

In the late-September summer, with all our apples, plums and blackberries gone, our last jams and chutneys made, Han began to pick the sloes. I found Han, Annie strapped to her front, filling plastic bags with sloes as the sun set over Frimley Wood.

'I know you're supposed to wait for the first frost,' she said, 'but we might be gone by then.'

The christening now over, we searched for new ways to look ahead positively, and found them in making plans for a leaving party and the thought of coming back in the winter for the shoot. We decided that the day of our party would also be the first shoot of the season.

When we had got back from our day out in London for the Countryside March, Tom and I had walked the farm to see what pheasants were about. The evening was cool but the light clean and clear, the detail of the trees and fields on the far-off hills crisp and sharp in the distance. Overhead, the ceiling climbed so high the clouds seemed somehow unrelated to earth; in the west the beginning of an autumn red sunset.

The march had been quite an event, hundreds of thousands of people from every 'walk of life'. Organising it, however, on a Sunday meant the march had had less of an impact than it deserved. Tom had gone with a minibus-load of gamekeepers and their day included them driving the wrong way round the M25 for an hour before anyone realised their mistake, their driver admitting he had never been to London before. (Tom claimed the day had resulted in his first hangover in ten years.) Scott had driven Norman and me up to London. Norman had been determined to come, saying he wanted people to know what 'real country people looked like'. We had parked in Bayswater and walked across the park where once I used to go running, and waited for hours for the march to lead off, standing in the road I had taken on my daily commute to my Docklands office; that all seemed a long time ago. It was strange being with Norman in London; stranger, too, feeling out of place in a city that had once been so familiar. Norman wanted to do the march and get home in time to feed the calves. He did not like the dim sum we ate afterwards in a Chinese restaurant in Queensway.

On our walk, Tom worked his dog, Teal. When we came to the

covert in Upper Rathbury Field, he told me to stand twenty-five feet or so from its south-east corner, near the Crab Apple Stile. As they went round the back of the covert, two pigeons flashed from the trees. I heard a shot from Tom's shotgun and saw one tumble to the ground, Teal racing to retrieve it. They entered the covert, another pigeon flew out. Gun up, fire! I'd hit it.

Just as I was reloading there he was. A dog fox trotted out of the trees, saw me and stopped. Head up and turned to me, ears forward, he looked surprised to see me there so close, preoccupied with the danger of Tom and Teal behind him.

You can't shoot him, Teal might be close behind, but no, I can hear him the other side of the covert. You can't shoot this fox, he's so magnificent and alive. You must shoot him: remember Norman's lambs; Tom will expect nothing less; you must shoot, think of the cock pheasant you saw walk in there just minutes ago.

I brought the stock up to close the barrel, mounted the shotgun, slipped the safety off and fired. He dropped instantly, falling out of sight in the grass. I reloaded, not quite believing what I had done, shaking with nerves. It had happened so fast: trot, stop, look, drop.

As I reloaded the shotgun, I thought back to the crowds of antis, screaming at us in Parliament Square. One, dressed in black and a leather jacket, pointed directly at me, his face strangely contorted.

'You're finished! *You're finished!*' he screamed.

'What's finished?' I asked him.

'Fox-hunting, stag-hunting, hare-coursing, all of it! *You're* finished and you know it and so do the lot of you!'

He was right, I think.

I looked at the dead fox and wondered what the anti would make of what I had done. That fox needed to be shot: foxes needed to be controlled, or at least on Parish Farm they did. This one had been lying up in the covert nearest to Norman's lambs, waiting for dark. His death had been instant and painless, not even time to realise his life was about to end. But hunting? Tom and others told me that they had often seen foxes playing with a hunt. (The Burns Report explicitly recognised at least the notion of 'exertion that can be regarded as falling within natural limits'.) It was rare, Tom said, that the hunt could catch a fit, seasoned fox.

Tom's view was that the foxes taken by the hunt (estimated by the Report to be less than one in ten of the fox population) were the diseased, the already injured (by shooting or hit by a car), or young, novice foxes that represented a surplus population that needed to be controlled. For those unfortunate few, it was usually a twenty-minute chase, then the end, killed by hounds – exactly how painfully no one can say, but the Report described the kill as being 'within a matter of seconds'. The Report also acknowledged that a killing in this way was 'seriously compromising the welfare' of a fox.

But during my time at Lettem everything I had read, heard or seen presented the life and welfare of foxes, including those hunted, as being better than the welfare of a supermarket chicken, an abattoir-killed cow, a town-life dog or an apartment-bound cat.

Norman had once asked if Han and I had ever noticed the way people always say how the horses enjoyed the Grand National. ('The horses look like they are having so much *fun*,' said a commentator, on cue, and Norman had chuckled.) Some people who spoke anthropomorphically of their horses and their gun dogs refuted the terror of the hunted fox; others accepted it, just as others ignored the story of the meat on their plates.

Hunting was a method of pest control known to be so inefficient that it was laughable to defend it on those grounds alone. It was an expensive sport, despite the Countryside Alliance propaganda of it being a socially inclusive 'dustmen to dukes' leisure pursuit. This was certainly not true of all hunts. Yes, there was diversity among hunt supporters ('different people value different aspects,' Lord Burns's research showed) and diversity among participants, but 'farmers and landowners are at its heart'. Nevertheless, among all the local hunts there were people who scrimped and saved to hunt; hunting was not the exclusive preserve of the landowning classes that predominantly pursued it.

'It annoys me', Tom used to say, 'that no one, *no one* is prepared to stand up and say 'I hunt because I love it!' It doesn't float my boat but I can see the pure pleasure of charging across a field with your mates, leaping over hedges. It's the social thing.'

For Tom, who knew better than anyone its failings as a method for fox control (no gamekeeper in England relied on the hunt to do the job, any more than people in England relied on the trains to get them to work on time), hunting was not only how other people had fun – as was their right – but was also an expression of nature and man's place within it. Modern farming and modern living, shopping for one's food instead of hunting for it, had removed most natural interaction between Western man and wild animal, except for the hunt. And the English fox, he thought, instinctively knew what a hunt was and that they would be hunted. It was their place in the natural order, just as it was for a beef cow to end in an abattoir. Tom would always defend the right to hunt.

During my time at Lettem, my views had gone from indifferent to protective. For all its rights and wrongs, hunting was an integral part of rural England and a ban would damage it in ways that I think few people fully understood. If you could remove hunting from the English rural landscape, it seemed to me there was nothing that could not be done to it. That so much of the damage to that landscape was being done by some people who also took part in the hunt was not the point. Most of our friends at Lettem defended hunting, not because they participated in it or especially cared for the people who did, but because they embraced it as part of a longer and deeper tradition that, intuitively, they wanted to protect. A ban was seen as the thin end of a suburban wedge that could lead to a ban on shooting and fishing. Liam, hardly the hunting and fishing type, told me his own views had changed in the nine years he'd lived in the countryside, and another friend from the snug bar, once a hunt saboteur, was now a fierce supporter.

Tom reached the edge of the covert with Teal.

'You didn't happen to see something with a long tail?' he said wryly, smiling.

I managed to point matter-of-factly to near where he stood. Tom picked up the dead animal.

'We'll just stop here a second,' he said quietly.

'You know what you want to do with that?' he asked after a moment or two. There was something in his manner towards my first fox, part pride that it was he who had brought me to this place, part closeness that I now shared something with him that was part of his life. That it had happened in my last few days at Lettem only made it more pointed.

'Take the brush?'

'No. You want to get him set up, you do.'

'Set up?'

'You know, taxidermy, set up.'

'I'm not sure what Han would think about that, a stuffed fox in the house.'

'Leave it here,' he said, placing it gently in the shade. 'Have a think about it, and we can always come and pick him up on the way back.'

We finished our walk, coming back via the fox. Tom even knew a taxidermist; the best man in England, he reckoned. We could pick up the fox, take it home and keep it in his freezer until we could drop it off with him.

I gathered up the seemingly sleeping fox. I had hit him square in his muddy-white chest, the range just right to kill him dead but not too close to damage his form. Only a nick in his ear from a piece of shot betrayed what had happened; that and the warm, sticky blood that oozed from him on to my coat as I carried him home, slung over my shoulder.

Back at the cottage, Norman was sitting outside in the dark with Han, having a beer.

'Where've you been, then?' he said. 'In the counting house?'

I tried to laugh. 'You've seen the sign I s'pose?' said Han. A 'Sold' sign had gone up outside the cottage.

'Yes.'

Just a few weeks to go now. Tom, Han and I had been in the pub the night before. Laura had told us that the new people would take over there on the fifth of November.

The last fair days of that Indian summer came on the weekend of Laura's (second) leaving party. The leaves were turning, but on the morning of the party the warm ground still retained a slight smell of summer, the air blurred with morning mist and the smoke of a bonfire drifting across from Lettem House. It was to be an exuberant, hard-dancing, hard-drinking night.

The pub was closed for the evening and the party took place in the barn. Liam and Keith put on their drag show and acted as MCs. Justin from the Get Twisted Leggers' raves did the music, wondering if this would be his last gig under the beech trees. The word was that the new tenants would be putting a stop to the raves as quickly as they would be moving Caravan Ted on, the man who lived with his dogs in a caravan behind the pub.

From raucous heckling and jeering, the packed barn fell silent, listening carefully to Laura's words.

'On a night like tonight,' she said, 'it's hard not to think of Geoff. I always thought he would be here tonight, but he chose not to be. Geoff always liked to leave a party when it was still going strong. He would have loved this evening.'

She went on to thank her 'boys and girls', but especially Peg, May, Cath and Terry. Bouquets of flowers were given, and it was done. No long speeches, no lengthy reflections, this was The Leggers'. Justin turned up the music and everyone danced.

No Leggers' night replete without it, the drama this time was to be May's Bob snogging her best friend, Cath. Tom came and told us what had happened, doing an impersonation of May. 'You've gone too fuck'n' far this time!' Cath apologised and Bob stomped off home down the canal path to begin his long walk back to town. Peg shrugged her shoulders serenely, she'd seen it all before. Laura ran around still picking up glasses; she wouldn't stop until the end. I lay outside on a table under the stars, and Tom warned me to be careful, telling me a story of a bloke who did that one rave night and, too far gone to defend himself, was mounted in plain view of about twenty people by a very fat girl from Northleach.

Later, Tom pulled Han and me out of the barn and made us form a huddle; he had something important to say.

'I know you don't want to hear it, and I know it would cause all sorts of problems, but don't do it. Don't go.'

We stood there swaying in the cold night air, holding each other; then Tom stood up straight and we went back inside and partied on.

The Indian summer ended and the first day of October was misty, wet and cold. We'd been putting on a good show for everyone, but we weren't going well. Han and I were arguing and upsetting each other as the stresses of our imminent departure intensified, its myriad practicalities and conflicting emotions overwhelming us. We had streaming colds, and I had stopped running. Subconsciously I think I knew that I couldn't go straight from running along the canal to Frimley Wood to running up Avenue Louise to the ordered park that was the Bois de la Cambre.

If we were to go, however, now was the time, with the pub changing hands, autumn setting in and us gone before the winter. We couldn't have left in spring; it would have been too difficult and the option of staying would have shown too much promise. But now nature itself seemed to support our move. Autumn toadstool stems stood hollow and brittle, and the leaves knew it was all over. The limes and sycamores had fallen first, the sycamore leaves dying and infected with spotty fungus.

I wanted it to stay wet and cold to make this leaving easier, but what came were fantastically crisp, clear mornings of empty skies, save for the high jet trails of planes carrying people who were not of this Lettem world to places that we, insanely, it seemed, were to return to.

This damn cold I couldn't shake was protecting me, closing off my senses to soften the realisation of our departure. I could see autumn now, the turning leaves, the deep brown of ploughed fields, the maturing cones on the larches and the fattening pheasants. I could see the smoky breath from my mouth and the silvery dew-dusted cobweb coatings that covered the fields, the air a shade of a degree shy of our first frost. I could see all this but I couldn't smell it.

One afternoon I felt I was about to buckle when I heard the voices of children and the sound of horses' hooves. Out in the lane, a long procession of children on ponies, holding their reins or walking alongside, trailed from the rectory to our gate. The rector and his wife and the children's parents accompanied them as dogs ran between the ponies and horses.

'It's our harvest walk,' Jill said, spotting Annie and me watching from the garden. 'We're collecting decorations for the church and then it's back to the rectory for bangers and mash. Why don't you join us?' she added enthusiastically.

I ran back inside, grabbed Annie's sling, Tom's thumb-stick and Maggie, and caught up with the tail end of the procession. The ploughed earth of Long Ground was rich and warm, and we were bathed in the yellow light of a hazy autumn sun coming down over Frimley Wood.

And so went our walk; down to The Leggers', into the woods and under the railway bridge. Maggie ran through the crowd, excited by the numbers of people and dogs and horses. Annie stared and smiled, transfixed by the children laughing and shouting and the little ponies with their constantly changing roster of riders.

We came out of the woods behind the huge Marsham drying facility and headed back to the village, all the time picking berried branches and cuttings from the hedges and the last green bracken fronds and ferns before they turned russet and crisp.

Leading her small child on a Shetland pony, a woman I had been walking with, said, 'It's such an Enid Blyton existence for kids growing up in this village, don't you think?'

When I got back, I put Annie to bed and stayed home when Han went to the pub with Tom.

*What are we doing?*

It was bad. Han tried to stir me, but she couldn't. Eventually Tom came up and found me curled up on the bed, fully-clothed, eyes closed, a pathetic figure.

'C'mon, old chum, this is no good. This isn't going to get you anywhere. Up you get, come on, we've got pheasants to feed.'

I didn't move.

'Bit of air in your face. This is no good.'

I sat up and swung my legs over the bed. 'I'm sorry, Tom. I feel terrible,' I said.

'I know.'

I pulled on my boots.

'And there aren't any fucking pheasants out there to feed anyway.'

As we walked up the lane to the yard, he did his best to be upbeat.

'I know it's a bummer, but you've got to forge on now. You've been over your decision many times, you've got to do it now and just enjoy these last few days.'

Loading up with corn in the yard we stopped and chatted with Norman. Norman was convinced, too, that there were no birds out there and joked that he had a mind to go and get a load from a local spot he knew.

'You can't do that, Norm,' said Tom, laughing, 'that's poaching!'

'It's only poaching if you shoot them there. Moving them here and *then* shooting them, that's different. That's borrowing.'

Tom was a good friend to us in that last week. His plea at Laura's party had been his best and final shot and now he resolved himself to helping us get done what we needed to do, including pulling me out of my funk. We fed pheasants, met up early in the mornings to go and empty his drop-boxes, planned the first shoot of the season and made plans with Han and me for our farewell party. Shropshire Ted was going to get a fully dressed-out deer for the party, and Archie from the village was going to spit-roast it in the garden. Tom even took me down to drop off the fox at the taxidermist.

As Tom and I drove back home up through Gloucestershire from the taxidermist, he suddenly turned off the main road past Chipping Sodbury.

'I'll show you where I used to live,' he said.

He took me to the estate where he had worked as a beat keeper. It was the best job he had ever had, a place he thought he could have been for ever. But when the head keeper retired, Tom discovered he and his successor had different ideas as to how the job should be done. It was time to go.

We drove through the pristine estate village, every house painted in estate livery, every gate, hedge and wall in immaculate condition; it was one of the most picturesque places I had seen in the Cotswolds.

'There's my house,' he said, pointing to a beautiful, large cottage beside a meandering brook. 'It's too hard to come back here,' he said. 'This is only the fourth time. I wouldn't've come; it's only because I wanted to show it to you.'

We sat and stared at the house in silence. I think he wanted to show that he knew what Han and I were going through.

Before driving home, we stopped and had a pint in his old local. The old landlord Tom had known had died and there had been a new landlord who had lasted just twelve months. Now it was run by a youngish couple, not from these parts, who told us it was a poisoned chalice taking over a pub that had long been run by a respected and loved local landlord. Nah, better to do what they'd done, let someone else take all the criticism, then take it on. The menu was elaborate and expensive. He served a poor pint. He didn't have any crisps but he did have little bowls of 'chorizo' and 'salted almonds'. Things had changed.

'Flying visits don't work,' Tom said as we drove home, 'not for a place you've really loved.' I don't think he expected us to be back and around much, and maybe this was his way of saying he'd understand that too.

Norman said that for the leaving party we could have a bonfire in the field in front of the cottages. Spider arrived unannounced with a grain trailer of stuff to burn: two enormous tractor tyres, broken-up pallets and a massive wooden cable drum. Norman brought down a huge round bale from the yard and put it in Home Paddock and together we built the bonfire round it.

When Spider left, Norman and I talked about a new grain barn and the planning permission he was applying for to build it. Unless Norman could get a new grain barn built, he could no longer sell his grain. He wanted to build it in Home Paddock next to his cottage, worried that if he built it too far away kids would break into it at night. There was a parish councillor in the village – a white settler he was, he hadn't lived there long – who was opposing it. He didn't want grain trailers coming past his house, even if with Norman's harvest that would probably only amount to a handful of trailers; past his new house in the countryside surrounded by wheat fields.

'I saw Mr Proctor the other day,' Norman said. 'We were talking about you,' he added.

'Really? What did he say?'

'That you were a bright lad. With property prices and everything I sometimes think I've got nothing to show for my life.'

'What do you mean, nothing to show? You're living in the place you want to live, in the house you want to and how you want to live. No boss, no office. That's everything. That's real freedom, Norman, and more than most people can say, even in this country.' Norman looked down and gave a snort. 'I wish we could say the same about our move.'

We walked back to the cottage together and stopped at the garden wall.

'You make sure you stop here, Norm. Don't let anyone bully you off the place.'

'That's right, that's what Mother said. "You stop here," she said. "Your brothers could 'ave done it but they didn't want to."'

'Exactly. Don't let them force you out and sell the place to Marsham, or anyone else for that matter.'

I told him if he ever did feel like jacking it in, and I hoped he never would, to make sure he got himself everything it was worth and come and buy a farm in France.

'What, go into partnership with Mr Walthew?'

'Dead right. I'm not joking, either. I'll find the farm, a small place: chickens, pigs, sheep, a few cattle, just enough for our own table. No ramblers either.'

'Really?' he said, his face lighting up at the idea of a place with no ramblers.

'Promise.'

I wake up. It's half past three in the afternoon. I've overslept and missed the shoot on the day of our leaving party. I'm in a terrible state.

I go down to the pub and am met by the new landlord. He is wearing a tie and has turned the barn into a pool hall. In the pub, he tells Peg what he wants on the menu, wine bar food, and we look at each other in mute horror.

But most strangely of all, Knoxey is there. He wanders around in the background, seen by no one but me, sad and watchful. He takes me out the back and we stand and look at Frimley Wood; how beautiful it is, Ian, how he loved it so living here.

The morning after that dream, my senses returned. For reasons I couldn't explain, four days before we were to leave, I was no longer spiralling, I felt in control. I could capture every gesture and intonation, see every detail, appreciate each second. I could see neither the past nor the future, stretching only the pleasure of the present. The departure would be another loss, but this time it would be one that nothing would prevent me from feeling, and in feeling it I would finally bury the others.

## CHAPTER 21

# LAST SIGHT

There were some pheasants out there. Not many, but it didn't matter. During the first shoot of the season and our last at Lettem Cottage, we shot two pigeons and two pheasants; a respectable Parish Farm day.

When we went downstairs at seven there was already a large pile of fresh-cut hazel beaters' sticks on the garden table; they had been cut earlier that morning, despite the rain, by Tom, and John, who had come back from the Welsh Borders for the party. Guns and beaters met in the muddy, damp yard, but by 9.30, when we headed off, it had stopped raining and the sun, once again, was with us.

We came back in time for lunch and sat in the warm sun outside, eating game casserole. Archie set up his spit-roast and serving tables, and we made the final preparations for the party and Shropshire's venison, which we had dressed in muslin cloth and hung in our woodshed.

The bonfire now stood enormous and ready in Home Paddock. Tom, Adrian, Dan and I had spent an afternoon with Norman loading a trailer full of scrap from his yard that we could burn. Secretly, I had always wanted to tidy up that yard and this was, in my final hours at Lettem, my excuse. As far as my helpers were concerned, the entire yard and the contents of every barn was scrap. Tom, at one point, even started to dismantle a shed with a collapsed roof, full of nettles and junk, before Norman spotted it and bustled over to stop him. What to most eyes was something ready to be burnt was, to Norman, master gate repairer, a perfectly decent piece of timber. Norman spent the afternoon running after us rescuing pieces of this and that, but we still managed to fill a trailer.

'It's what that lot are always going on about, isn't it? Recycling?' Norman said.

The afternoon of the party, Norman came round with an old mannequin that he'd found somewhere, and we climbed up and stood her proudly on top of the Lettem beacon. It was going to be a fine fire.

Although we were leaving England, and not just Lettem, the party was almost entirely local. We had handed out invitations at Laura's farewell party, the time and place written by Han in silver ink on the back of her business cards with our Lettem address. We invited those we had been close to and those whose presence in our lives had been more important to us than they perhaps realised. Even the rector came, dressed up in wellies and a long duffel coat.

The garden table was pushed up against the cottage wall and became the bar, music speakers placed in open windows. The party took place on the terrace and the lawn and, when the fire was lit, spilled out into Home Paddock.

The fire was a great success. It lit beautifully, the fine weather of the day having dried off the early-morning rain. By rights, it should have rained throughout the weekend, but we could stand dry outside all night. It wasn't a warm night, and those who came expecting to be inside borrowed coats or stood near the bonfire. The heat from the fire warmed us as far back as the garden wall. When the temperature had dropped, people took chairs and bales from the garden into Home Paddock and sat or stood around the fire, a trestle table carried into the field to serve as a second bar.

My father loved bonfires. I had remembered first the one that didn't light, but there were others. There was the one where I accidentally put a pitchfork through his foot while he stood back and watched it burn, and the time he burnt down the old chicken sheds that stood huge and ugly in the paddock behind the house he must have just bought. He'd have liked this bonfire, I think.

Han and I tried to talk with everyone who was there but I'm sure we failed. My memories of the night are of laughter, music and the faces of friends picked out by the shifting light of the flames; people emerging from the darkness into the light and back again. I remember Kelly and the Massive dancing; Peg's son, Lennie, and his girlfriend Nance in the kitchen busy making cocktails, and Tracey from the Massive wearing clothes so few and so short we thought she would get hypothermia, refusing Tom's efforts to get her to put more on, or was it off? I remember sitting on the garden wall with Verity, a friend from the village, and Spider, Verity one moment quite with us, the next just flopped back over the wall into the field. When they left, she tripped on a step in the dark and fell head first into the rosemary bush, Spider too pissed himself to help her. As Verity somehow pulled herself up, Spider gave me a huge hug and muttered that if she thought he was going home with that, she was very much mistaken; and then took her home.

Han finally confessed to Rose what Norman thought of her cooking and what it was he would actually eat. Norman didn't think much of pasta.

'I give him that all the time!' she screamed, laughing and horrified at the same time. 'God, why he didn't he say something, the old bugger!'

Rose had made us a leaving card made with two photos of Parish Farm taken by Dan; I hadn't known what a fine photographer he was. He said I should write a book about Parish Farm. I'd do the words, he'd do the pictures.

The terrace was full of people drinking and talking when there was an enormous explosion. A firework had come from nowhere and exploded against the wall of the house, too low and fast for anyone to see it coming. We yelped at the shock and Stevo from the Massive was running up the track and out into the lane to find the culprit, convinced we were under attack by gatecrashers. Tom egged him on. 'Go on, Stevo, get among 'em!'

Tom and Stevo found Norman in the lane, also out there looking.

'What's going on, Norm? Who did it, who did it?'

Norman just shrugged his shoulders.

Just as Stevo and Tom returned, a second barrage; this one careening across the lawn and exploding against the woodshed; a third on to the lawn.

'Watch out!' People were laughing as they ran. 'Here comes another!'

'Get down!'

It wasn't until we saw Douglas setting up more fireworks in Home Paddock that we knew who was behind it. Norman. Norman loved a good firework. Instead of launching the fireworks from bottles, he and Douglas would stick them in the ground to light them. There they would fizz dementedly with just enough force to get out of the ground but not far in the air, and the crazy, ricocheting ground-level displays would start.

'No, Doug! Put 'em in a bottle!' someone shouted, but it was too late. A firework was lit and it bounced and screamed across the field towards the big crowd standing by the fire. The crowd parted like the Red Sea and there were chairs flying, people diving and falling over, trying to balance beer bottles and wine glasses. Norman emerged from the dark, grinning ear to ear, chuckling as he went.

Later, in the metal grey of near dawn, those that were left sat in chairs round the still-blazing fire. It was down now to the densely packed straw of the round bale that had formed the core of the fire. Like a fading memory it would burn black, and then, prodded with a stick, the straw would part, air would be let in, and the fire would rage up again in a massive storm of heat and flame, sparks and embers whistling up into the starry sky above.

There were quite a few of us still there. Sitting by a fire in the middle of Home Paddock, at the end of that party, at the moment in a long evening when everyone has started to calm down, when the reminiscing and storytelling begins. And so it was that we learnt in collective awe, who it was who had weedkillered Peter Larch's lawn. They told us. Why and how. It was quite a moment.

The day after the party the movers came and emptied Lettem Cottage. The afternoon was full of last visitors and last farewells and a lot of crying. Tom took apart the garden table that we had all sat around so many times. It did seem so final now: the table in the truck, the house emptied but still, for one more Lettem night, our home.

That last evening, Tom, Iona, Spider and Norman came over. A mattress to sleep on and borrowed glasses and chairs were all that remained. We drank the champagne that Spider had given Annie for her christening and talked. We talked about the village mainly: the land, the people who owned it and the people who worked on it. On a large piece of packing paper, Spider drew a map of the fields around the village and filled in the names of ones we didn't know:

Pigeon House Ground, Twenty Acre, Peel's Piece and Number One.

Norman told us of all the little pieces of ground he and his father had once had as grazing but which now were pony paddocks, as he called them. He'd not told us before, but that summer a piece of local ground that Father and Norman had rented for sheep-grazing for over fifty years had been sold. It was snapped up by a pony lover. The day the deal was done his wife rang and left a message on Norman's answerphone. 'This is Mrs A. We'd like your sheep off our land by the end of today.'

Our conversation stopped and for a split second no one knew what to say. Then someone rescued us.

'Well, if the folk who did Larch's lawn hear about this, they'll be wanting to be getting a lot more weedkiller in,' they said, and we laughed and carried on.

The day we left it rained. Rain like we hadn't seen in months; ever, in fact. It just poured down like a tropical rainstorm and kept pouring. The sun wasn't shining on the righteous that day; there was nothing to celebrate.

Since our stuff had already gone in the lorry, Tom and Iona showed up with breakfast, brooms and brushes. There wasn't much to say. We just had to get on with it. Tom used his vacuum cleaner and soon the house smelt like his, of his dogs Flint and Teal.

It was a frantic morning to get going in time to catch our ferry and only the urgency of our departure kept us moving forward. My mother's farewells to us and especially Annie had caused her so much pain she couldn't bear to be with us. She had lost a child, a husband and another child who had nigh deserted her during ten years living abroad; never much of a son as a child, nor the man I might have been towards her as an adult, despite her love for me and mine for her. Now we were going again, taking her only grandchild too. Mum, Han and I had tried to square the circle of our reasons to leave and hers as to why we should stay, but never quite did, and all we would leave behind for now were shared failings of understanding that all of us would some day have to try and heal.

Alan called in, still ill, still fighting. We tried to find the time in the chaos to say our pieces, but we faltered and they fell, draining away in the rain. Peg stopped by with a gift, hugs and a final good-bye. Peg had been such a good friend and loved Annie like the grandchild she so badly wanted. Han and I couldn't stop and talk long with Peg; if we had we would have stopped altogether.

Iona told us that Tom had said he was going to come over in November for Annie's birthday. She was going to get him a passport; he hadn't had one in years.

It was time for Tom to go. He and Han hugged and kissed, and Tom loaded the cleaning stuff into his truck. Last load carried out, he beckoned to me from the kitchen door. I went outside and, standing in the rain, water spilling over the guttering, he said good-bye, what it meant to him us leaving. It cut both ways, as he would say. We hugged and laughed at the state we were in.

The rain was unrelenting and the lane a river of water. In the back of his truck were the two pheasants we'd shot at the weekend. 'I'll freeze them on the feather and we can eat them when you come back,' he said.

'Thanks, Tom. For everything.'

'It's not farewell.'

'No, it's not.'

'I'm going to go home now and get absolutely wasted,' he smiled and with that, he put up his window and an elder brother drove off up the lane. I stood there until he was gone.

Back inside, I wrote a note to the new owners – I hoped they'd be happy, look out for Norman – and left the piece of paper under a bottle of champagne in front of the fireplace.

A half-hour before we were to leave, Norman came round and, soaked by the rain, stood dripping on the carpet.

'This is it, then?' he asked gently.

Han began to cry.

'I don't get too emotional,' he said very quietly. 'I've seen it all before, people coming and going.' He handed us an envelope, inside it a letter that I opened and read. It was on decorated stationery, headed 'Thank you', the message written within a border of inter-woven coloured flowers and leaves.

*To Ian, Hannah and Annie. Just a note to say how sorry I am to see you go. For you have fitted in so well to this country scene, and have done so much for the good of local interests. I do wish you <u>well</u> and will no doubt see you again. I just* *hope my new neighbours are as good and straightforward as you have been. Love and Best wishes from Norman.*

I passed the letter to Han and hugged Norman.

Han read the letter and cried again. Norman took her and hugged her warmly, and they stood and held each other. As they did so, he spoke softly into her ear: 'God bless you, Hannah.'

And then he was out of the door and gone.

The whole morning had been a rush, but now we put Annie in the car and walked around the cottage, room by room, fixing memories in our minds as we said our goodbyes.

We loaded the final few things into the car, running through the rain that by now seemed unnaturally strong; violent and cruel. When Han, Annie and the cats were all in the car I made one last run down the path to lock the doors and, standing in the rain in front of the cottage, I said my final farewell.

Tears I'd fought off all morning came in heaving sobs and ran into my rain-soaked face. I returned to the car, wailing, which only set Han off again.

With the windows all steamed up and rain hammering down on the car faster than the windscreen wipers could push it away, we drove off.

As we headed up the track and on to the lane, passing the yard and turning down Rathbury Road, I could hardly see for tears and rain. I wanted to stop and look at the farm one more time but I couldn't. I drove on looking straight ahead, I dared not stop.

Lettem days. Gone.

It is that last summer before we leave Lettem.

Han and I are sitting on the garden wall under Frankie's Tree. In the distance we can see Maggie running to meet Norman as he walks slowly through the gate into the Humpty Dumps. Annie is asleep on a blanket on the lawn in the shade of the weeping cherry. High above us is a waxing half-moon.

'Could you cope if we left here?' Han asks.

'Yes.'

'How?' she asks, taking my hand.

I turn to her. My father was thirty-eight when he died. I'm thirty-six. Life renews. 'I've remembered life's possibilities.'

# ACKNOWLEDGEMENTS

Aside from my wife, to whom this book is dedicated with more thanks than space allows me to fully explain, I would like to thank first and foremost all the people who appeared in this book. I am aware that none of them asked to be written about, but when I gave many of them the manuscript to read – Norman, Tom, Laura, Peg, May, Spider among others; and not without the sorrow of memory, to my sister Frances and most especially my mother – they not only found time to read it and help me with it before publication, but moreover gave their support to my endeavour.

Special thanks must go to Norman and Tom. I hope that as an interloper I haven't let you down when I speak of your world, one that I spent so little time within and had so much more to learn about; thanks as well to Douglas and Murray and the families of Peg and May.

Thanks, too, to the people beyond that place in my country who helped me so invaluably in its preparation for publication and in the writing of this book: Carol Macarthur at PFD Ltd and the Laurie Lee Estate for their kind permission to quote from the poem 'Christmas Landscape'; Stephen Kinsella and Alice Jolly; Rob Ewens; Alan Samson and Lucinda McNeile at Weidenfeld and Nicolson; my wonderful agent David Grossman; David Elworthy, Paul Bagshawe; Vicki Shannon and most especially Luke Elworthy.

Why Luke never ended up as the editorial director of one of the world's leading publishers is beyond me, but his memoir may give some pointers.